First World War

and Army of Occupation

War Diary

France, Belgium and Germany

39 DIVISION
Divisional Troops
Royal Army Medical Corps
133 Field Ambulance
5 March 1916 - 12 December 1918

WO95/2578/2

The Naval & Military Press Ltd
www.nmarchive.com
Published in association with The National Archives

Published by

The Naval & Military Press Ltd

Unit 10 Ridgewood Industrial Park,

Uckfield, East Sussex,

TN22 5QE England

Tel: +44 (0) 1825 749494

www.naval-military-press.com

www.nmarchive.com

This diary has been reprinted in facsimile from the original. Any imperfections are inevitably reproduced and the quality may fall short of modern type and cartographic standards.

Contents

Document type	Place/Title	Date From	Date To
Heading	WO95/2578/2 133 Field Ambulance Mar 16-Dec 18		
Heading	39th Division Medical 133rd Field Ambulance Mar 1916-Dec 1918		
Miscellaneous	No 133 Fld Ambulance. March 1916 April 1916		
Heading	War Diary of 133 Field Ambulance March 1916 133 F Amb Vol 1 39th Div		
War Diary	Southampton	05/03/1916	05/03/1916
War Diary	Le Havre	06/03/1916	06/03/1916
War Diary	In The Train	07/03/1916	07/03/1916
War Diary	Estaires	08/03/1916	08/03/1916
War Diary	Sauce	09/03/1916	10/03/1916
War Diary	Estaires	11/03/1916	25/03/1916
War Diary	Calonne Sur La Lys	26/03/1916	26/03/1916
War Diary	Calonne	27/03/1916	31/03/1916
Heading	War Diary of 133 Field Ambulance From April 1st to 30th 1916 Vol II		
War Diary	Calonne	01/04/1916	15/04/1916
War Diary	Calonne	16/04/1916	18/04/1916
War Diary	Essars	19/04/1916	30/06/1916
Heading	War Diary of 133 Field Ambulance May 1916 Vol III		
War Diary	Essars	01/05/1916	31/05/1916
Heading	War Diary of 133 Field Ambulance June 1916 Vol IV		
War Diary	Essars	01/06/1916	18/06/1916
War Diary	Zelobes	19/06/1916	01/07/1916
Heading	39th Division 133rd Field Ambulance June 1916		
Heading	War Diary Of 133 Field Ambulance July 1916 Vol V		
War Diary	Zelobes	01/07/1916	06/07/1916
War Diary	Bethune	07/07/1916	31/07/1916
Heading	War Diary of 133 Field Ambulance Vol VI August 1916		
War Diary	Bethune	01/08/1916	10/08/1916
War Diary	Auchel	11/08/1916	11/08/1916
War Diary	Bailleul Aux Corneilles	12/08/1916	15/08/1916
War Diary	B Aux C	16/08/1916	19/08/1916
War Diary	Bailleul Aux Corneilles	22/08/1916	22/08/1916
War Diary	Maisnil St Pol	23/08/1916	23/08/1916
War Diary	Le Marais Sec	24/08/1916	24/08/1916
War Diary	Authie	25/08/1916	25/08/1916
War Diary	Vauchelles	26/08/1916	31/08/1916
Heading	War Diary Of 133 Field Ambulance September 1916 Vol VII		
War Diary	Vauchelles	01/09/1916	30/09/1916
War Diary	War Diary of 133 Field Ambulance October 1916 Vol VIII		
Miscellaneous	D.A.G. 3rd Echelon Base		
Miscellaneous	O.C. 133 Field Ambulance	03/10/1916	03/10/1916
War Diary	Vauchelles	01/10/1916	07/10/1916
War Diary	East Clairfaye	03/10/1916	04/10/1916
War Diary	Clairfaye	04/10/1916	31/10/1916

Heading	War Diary of 133rd Fld. Amb. From 1st November to 30th November (Volume 9)		
War Diary	Clairfaye	01/11/1916	16/11/1916
War Diary	Beauval	16/10/1916	19/11/1916
War Diary	Esquelbecq.	19/11/1916	19/11/1916
War Diary	Herzeele	20/11/1916	30/11/1916
War Diary	War Diary of 133rd Fld. Amb. From December 1st 1916 to December 31st 1916 (Volume 10)		
War Diary	Herzeele	01/12/1916	13/12/1916
War Diary	A.28.a.36	13/12/1916	31/12/1916
Heading	War Diary of 133rd Fld. Amb. From January 1st 1917 to January 31st 1917 (Volume 11)		
War Diary	A.28.a.3.6	01/01/1917	17/01/1917
War Diary	Poperinghe	18/01/1917	31/01/1917
Heading	War Diary of 133rd Fld. Amb. From February 1st 1917 to February 28th 1917		
War Diary	Poperinghe	01/02/1917	16/02/1917
War Diary	Watou	17/01/1917	21/07/1917
War Diary	Watou E.28.d.5.3	20/02/1917	22/02/1917
War Diary	Watou	23/02/1917	26/02/1917
War Diary	Tae Mill	26/02/1917	28/02/1917
Heading	War Diary of 133rd Fld. Amb. 1st March 1917. to 31st March 1917 (Volume 13)		
War Diary	Vlamertinghe	01/03/1917	31/03/1917
Heading	War Diary of 133rd Fld. Amb. From 1st April 1917 to 30th April 1917 Volume No 14		
War Diary	Vlamertinghe	01/04/1917	15/04/1917
War Diary	Poperinghe.	16/04/1917	30/04/1917
Heading	War Diary of 133rd Field Ambulance From 1st May 1917. 31st May 1917 Vol. XV		
War Diary	Poperinghe.	01/05/1917	31/05/1917
Heading	War Diary of 133rd Fld. Amb. From 1-6-17. to 30-6-17 Volume XVI		
Miscellaneous	B.E.F. Summary Of Medical War Diaries of 133rd F.A. 39th Div. 18th Corps. 5th Army.		
War Diary	133rd F.A. 39th Div. 18th Corps. 5th Army. Officer Commanding-Lt. Col. J.S. Manford		
Miscellaneous	B.E.F. Summary of Medical War Diaries of 133rd F.A. 39th Div. 18th Corps 5th Army		
Miscellaneous	133rd F.A. 39th Div. 18th Corps. 5th Army. Officer Commanding-Lt. Col. J.S. Manford.		
War Diary	Poperinghe	01/06/1917	30/06/1917
Heading	War Diaries Volume 17 From July 1st 1917 To July 31st 1917 Of 133 Field Ambulance		
Miscellaneous	B.E.F. Summary of Medical War Diaries of 133rd F.A. 39th Div. 18th Corps. 5th Army. To 2nd Army Area From 7th August. Western Front Operations-July 1917		
Miscellaneous	133rd F.A. 39th Div. 18th Corps. 5th Army. Officer Commanding-Lt. Col. J.S. Manford Western Front July 1917	01/07/1917	01/07/1917
War Diary	Gwentfarm	01/07/1917	31/07/1917
Heading	War Diary of 133rd Fld. Amb. From 1st August 1917 to 31st August 1917. Volume XVIII		
Miscellaneous	B.E.F. Summary of Medical War Diaries of 133rd F.A. Div. 18th Corps. 5th Army. To 2nd Army Area From 7th August.		

Miscellaneous			
Miscellaneous	B.E.F. 133rd F.A. 39th Div. 18th Corps. 5th Army. Officer Commanding Lt Col J.S. Manford. to 2nd Army Area From August 7th.		
Miscellaneous			
Miscellaneous	133rd F.A. 39th Div. 18th Corps. 5th Army. Officer Commanding-Lt. Col. J.S. Manford. To 2nd Army Area From August 7th	01/07/1917	01/07/1917
War Diary	Gwent Frm A 28a.3.6 Sheet 28	01/08/1917	06/08/1917
War Diary	X 26.32. Sheet 27	07/08/1917	14/08/1917
War Diary	Chippewa Camp Mba8.8 (28)	15/08/1917	17/08/1917
War Diary	Chippewa Camp	18/08/1917	25/08/1917
War Diary	Chippewa Camp. Mba88	26/08/1917	31/08/1917
Heading	War Diary 133rd Fld. Amb. From 1st Sept. 1917 To 30th Sept 1917 Volume 19		
War Diary	Chippewa Camp M6.a.8.8. Sheet 28	01/09/1917	10/09/1917
War Diary	Chippewa Camp M6a.88	11/09/1917	30/09/1917
War Diary	War Diary of 133rd Field Ambulance From October 1st 1917 to October 31st 1917 (Volume 20)		
War Diary	M21b42.sheet 28	01/09/1917	11/10/1917
War Diary	S9a58 Sheet 28	12/10/1917	12/10/1917
War Diary	59.a.5.8	12/10/1917	31/10/1917
Heading	War Diary Volume XXI November 1st 1917 To November 30th 1917		
War Diary	Haeqdoorne Dysentery Camp S9.a.5.8	01/11/1917	02/11/1917
War Diary	Chippewa M6.a.8.8	03/11/1917	12/11/1917
War Diary	Chippewa	13/11/1917	14/11/1917
War Diary	La Clytte N.7.C	15/11/1917	15/11/1917
War Diary	La Clytte N.T.C.	16/11/1917	19/11/1917
War Diary	Hospice Westoutre	20/11/1917	22/11/1917
War Diary	The Hospice Westoutre	22/11/1917	25/11/1917
War Diary	Ouderzeele J14A11	26/11/1917	28/11/1917
War Diary	Ouberzeele	29/11/1917	30/11/1917
Heading	War Diary Of 133rd Field Ambulance From December 1st 1917 To December 31st 1917 (Volume 22)		
War Diary	Ooderzeele J 14 a.11 Sheet 27	01/12/1917	09/12/1917
War Diary	Vieil Moulier (Pas de Calais)	10/12/1917	13/12/1917
War Diary	Vieil Moulier Pas de Calais	14/12/1917	29/12/1917
War Diary	Duhallow	30/12/1917	31/12/1917
Heading	War Diary of 133rd Field Ambulance R.A.M.C. From 1st January 1918 To 31st January 1918		
War Diary	Duhallow I.1.b.5.5. Sheet 28	01/01/1918	05/01/1918
War Diary	Duhallow I.1.b.8.8. Sheet 28	05/01/1918	07/01/1918
War Diary	Siege Camp B.27.a.5.5. Sheet 28	08/01/1918	22/01/1918
War Diary	School Camp L.3.a.8.4 Sheet 27	23/01/1918	27/01/1918
War Diary	Sailly Le Sec (Amiens Map)	28/01/1918	29/01/1918
War Diary	Sailly Le Sec (near Amiens)	30/01/1918	31/01/1918
Heading	133rd Field Ambulance R.A.M.C. War Diary Month Ending Feb 28th-1918 Volume 24		
War Diary	Haut Allaine	01/02/1918	01/02/1918
War Diary	Nurlu. D4.b5.3. Sheet 63	02/02/1918	28/02/1918
Heading	133rd Field Ambulance R.A.M.C. War Diary. Volume 25. March 1918		
War Diary	Nurlu D4b53 Sheet 63b	01/03/1918	09/03/1918
War Diary	Nurlu	10/03/1918	10/03/1918
War Diary	Moislans C17b80 Sheet 62c	11/03/1918	14/03/1918

War Diary	Moislans	15/03/1918	22/03/1918
War Diary	Combles	23/03/1918	23/03/1918
War Diary	Cappy	24/03/1918	25/03/1918
War Diary	Chignolles	26/03/1918	26/03/1918
War Diary	Hamel	27/03/1918	27/03/1918
War Diary	Cachy	29/03/1918	29/03/1918
War Diary	Bois de Boves Nr. Amiens	29/03/1918	30/03/1918
War Diary	Petit Cagny	31/03/1918	31/03/1918
Heading	133rd Field Ambulance R.A.M.C. War Diary. Month Ending April 30th 1918. Volume 26		
War Diary	Bovelles	01/04/1918	02/04/1918
War Diary	Avelesques	03/04/1918	03/04/1918
War Diary	Fresne-Tilloloy	04/04/1918	07/04/1918
War Diary	Hocquelus	08/04/1918	09/04/1918
War Diary	Moulle	10/04/1916	11/04/1916
War Diary	Scottish Lines 28/G23.b. Cent	12/04/1916	12/04/1916
War Diary	Manchester Camp 28/N2b.58	13/04/1916	14/04/1916
War Diary	La Clyte Camp 28/M6d.4.8	15/04/1916	15/04/1916
War Diary	Waratah Camp 28/915 C.3.8	16/04/1918	26/04/1918
War Diary			
War Diary	Remy Siding 27/1 23d28	29/04/1918	30/04/1918
Heading	War Diary of 133rd Field Ambulance Volume 27. From 1st May 1918 to 31st May 1918		
War Diary	Remy Siding 27/I 23d28	01/05/1918	05/05/1918
War Diary	Autingues Pas de Calais	06/05/1918	31/05/1918
Heading	War Diary of 133rd Field Ambulance Volume 28 From. June 1st 1918 to June 30th 1918 Vol 28		
War Diary	Autingues Pas de Calais	01/06/1918	14/06/1918
War Diary	Autingues	15/06/1918	26/06/1918
War Diary	Abbeville	27/06/1918	30/06/1918
Heading	War Diary Of 133rd Field Ambulance From 1st July 1918 To 31st July 1918 (Volume 29.)		
War Diary	Abbeville	01/07/1918	01/07/1918
War Diary	Autingues	02/07/1918	07/07/1918
War Diary	Proven	08/07/1918	08/07/1918
War Diary	Ballance Camp 27/6.d.4.2	09/07/1918	17/07/1918
War Diary	Bollezeele 27/A 22d 7.6	18/07/1918	31/07/1918
Heading	War Diary Of 133rd Field Ambulance From 1st August 1918 To 31st August 1918 Volume 30		
War Diary	Bollezeele 27/A 22d 7.6	01/08/1918	17/08/1918
War Diary	Proven 27/E6.d.42	18/08/1918	21/08/1918
War Diary	Zermezeele Area 27/1.4.6.8.77	22/08/1918	23/08/1918
War Diary	Arneke 27/a.24.a.8.5	24/08/1918	31/08/1918
Heading	War Diary of 133rd Field Ambulance R.A.M.C. From-1st Sept 1918 to-30th Sept 1918 Volume 31		
War Diary	Hillhoek 27/L20 p88	11/08/1918	05/09/1918
War Diary	Beauval	06/09/1918	07/09/1918
War Diary	Orville	08/09/1918	22/09/1918
War Diary	Driencourt 62c/ J.3.d.9.1	23/09/1918	30/09/1918
Miscellaneous	D.A.G. 3rd Echelon B.E.F, France.		
Heading	War Diary For October 1918 133rd Fd Amb Volume 32		
War Diary	Driencourt. 62c J.3.d.9.1	01/10/1918	02/10/1918
War Diary	Courcelles 62c J3.2.c.	03/10/1918	07/10/1918
War Diary	Templeux-Le Gerard	08/10/1918	08/10/1918
War Diary	Wancourt	08/10/1918	08/10/1918
War Diary	Premont	10/10/1918	15/10/1918

War Diary	Busigny	16/10/1918	16/10/1918
War Diary	Estcaufort Q31c9.5. Sheet 51B.	17/10/1918	18/10/1918
War Diary	Estcaufort	19/10/1918	20/10/1918
War Diary	Brancourt	21/10/1918	21/10/1918
War Diary	Bellicourt	23/10/1918	23/10/1918
War Diary	Marquaix	23/10/1918	23/10/1918
War Diary	Corbie	24/10/1918	31/10/1918
Heading	133rd Field Ambulance R.A.M.C. War Diary Volume 33		
War Diary	Corbie	01/11/1918	15/11/1918
Miscellaneous			
War Diary	Abbeville	29/11/1918	30/11/1918
Heading	133rd Field Ambulance R.A.M.C. War Diary For December 1st to 12th 1918		
War Diary	Abbeville	01/12/1918	12/12/1918

WO 95/2578 (2)

133 Field Ambulance

Mar '16 – Dec '18

39TH DIVISION

MEDICAL

133RD FIELD AMBULANCE

MAR 1916 - DEC 1918

March 1916
April 1916

No 133 Fld Ambulance.

Mar 16
Dec 18

March 1916. Confidential 39th Div. 133 F Amb
Vol 1

War Diary
of
133 Field Ambulance
March 1916

Vol I

Instructions regarding War Diaries and Intelligence Summaries are contained in F. S. Regs., Part II. and the Staff Manual respectively. Title pages will be prepared in manuscript.

WAR DIARY
or
INTELLIGENCE SUMMARY.
(Erase heading not required.)

Army Form C. 2118.

1.

Place	Date	Hour	Summary of Events and Information	Remarks and references to Appendices
SOUTHAMPTON	5/3/16	20	The Unit was formed on 30 Oct. 1915 at EASTBOURNE Training Centre & transferred to CROOKHAM T.C. on 4 Dec. 1915. Unit was under orders to move on 3rd March 1916 but this order was amended to 5th inst. The ambulance marched out in two trainloads & proceeded to FARNBOROUGH Station. Each trainload was entrained within 25 minutes. The trains left at 10.10 am & 12.30 pm respectively & arrived accordingly at 11.45 am & 2.15 pm at SOUTHAMPTON DOCKS. The loading on to the Ship of each party took 3/4 hour. The horses were inspected by a veterinary officer who cast one that had a lame leg & gave another to take its place.	
			The complete equipment of the unit was received so shortly before proceeding overseas that there was very limited opportunity to practise the ambulance as a fully mobilised unit.	
LE HAVRE	6/3/16	19	Crossed to FRANCE on the S.S. AUSTRALIND & were under way at 20.15, weather calm, cold & fine. Portions of Sussex Rgt., & Ammunition Column	

T2134. Wt. W708—776. 500000. 4/15. Sir J. C. & S.

Instructions regarding War Diaries and Intelligence Summaries are contained in F. S. Regs., Part II. and the Staff Manual respectively. Title pages will be prepared in manuscript.

WAR DIARY
or
INTELLIGENCE SUMMARY.
(*Erase heading not required.*)

Army Form C. 2118.

Place	Date	Hour	Summary of Events and Information	Remarks and references to Appendices
			Column crossed with us. Arrived off LE HAVRE at 6 on 6th inst. Snow came on in showers. Berthed at 11 a.m. Final portion of transport was clear of ship at 14·45 p. Snow continuous. Shortly after 15 o'clock we moved off to No. 1 Rest Camp which we reached without mishap at ~~4 p.~~ 17 o'clock. Thick coating of snow on the tents + all round so the interior was not ~~too~~ cold.	
In the train	7 3/16	17	Left camp at 7.30 + reached the Gare des Merchandise at 9.10, the roads very slushy on account of the snow. Entrained at Point 3 after drawing rations + forage. Portions of Sussex + Hampshire regts. were in the same train. Train moved off at 12.5. Provision of hot drinks + Y.M.C.A comforts were welcome.	
ESTAIRES	8 3/16	18	Train arrived at STEENBECQUE at 7.30, here it was discovered that a horse-box with seven horses had been cut off at ST OMER owing to a heated axle. The unit marched off at 10.15, the unloading was about 1½ hours owing to the train having to be moved about.	

Instructions regarding War Diaries and Intelligence Summaries are contained in F. S. Regs., Part II. and the Staff Manual respectively. Title pages will be prepared in manuscript.

WAR DIARY
or
INTELLIGENCE SUMMARY.
(Erase heading not required.)

Army Form C. 2118.

3

Place	Date	Hour	Summary of Events and Information	Remarks and references to Appendices
			Two 4-wheel + 1 2-wheel vehicles had to be left owing to the shortage of horses + long-reins. They arrived a few hours after the main party left. Reached ESTAIRE at 15.50 billets had been arranged for by orders of A.D.M.S. 39th Divn + the men were allotted to them in about 15 minutes. The D.A.D.M.S. 39th Divn met us on arrival at Detraining point + gave orders as to route, destination to the D.R.S. at the College ESTAIRE, supplies to be drawn from 8th Divn, Advanced Depot of Medical Stores at MERVILLE, also that one officer + 24 men take over Divisional Baths in the town.	
			The accommodation for the horses is bleak + scattered, only 3 being in pukka stables. The personel of B section only is billeted outside the D.R.S., they are in a loft which is adequate.	
			The Ambulance is to remain under instruction + to take over from the Detachment 103 Fd. Amb. on 6th day after our arrival.	
			The officers are billeted in private houses.	

T2134. Wt. W708—776. 500000. 4/15. Sir J. C. & S.

Instructions regarding War Diaries and Intelligence Summaries are contained in F. S. Regs., Part II. and the Staff Manual respectively. Title pages will be prepared in manuscript.

WAR DIARY
or
INTELLIGENCE SUMMARY.
(Erase heading not required.)

Army Form C. 2118.

4

Place	Date	Hour	Summary of Events and Information	Remarks and references to Appendices
Same	9/3/16	21	By orders of D.D.M.S. 34th Divn 3 officers daily are being sent to D.R.S. STEENWERCK for instruction The taking over of the baths proves to be a long business as the inventory to hand is a combined one & the articles are distributed all over the building. Orders as to water have been received as also re infectious cases.	
	10/3/16	15	D.D.M.S. (Col. Skinner) inspected; B section Tent subdivision is to go to DOULIEU for instruction at a dressing station. The inventory of baths is proceeding under Lieut COOKE of the amb. R.E. are occupying a billet there & A.S.C. are painting lorries &c. O.C. 103 Fd. Amb by authority A.D.M.S. 34 Divn will hand over all D.R.S. & Equipment to me on 14th inst. at 9 a.m.	

T2134. Wt. W708–776. 500000. 4/15. Sir J. C. & S.

Instructions regarding War Diaries and Intelligence Summaries are contained in F. S. Regs., Part II. and the Staff Manual respectively. Title pages will be prepared in manuscript.

WAR DIARY
or
INTELLIGENCE SUMMARY.
(Erase heading not required.)

Army Form C. 2118.

5

Place	Date	Hour	Summary of Events and Information	Remarks and references to Appendices
ESTAIRES	11/3/16	21.10	ADMS 39th Divn inspected + arranged with Town major for the handing over of the Baths minus the RE + ASC. The baths to be opened at latest if possible on 14th inst.	
			7 Motor Ambulances + 1 motor cycle + 17 men arrived, also the F.A.W.U.	
			The inventory of the baths was completed this morning with exception of the engine room by the F.A.W.U.	
			Lieuts GOWER + GIMLETTE + personnel of B Tent subdivision went to DOULIEU.	
			Authority for inspect wired for by order of ADMS 39 Divn for local purchase.	

T2134. Wt. W708—776. 500000. 4/15. Sir J. C. & S.

Instructions regarding War Diaries and Intelligence Summaries are contained in F. S. Regs., Part II. and the Staff Manual respectively. Title pages will be prepared in manuscript.

WAR DIARY
or
INTELLIGENCE SUMMARY.
(Erase heading not required.)

Army Form C. 2118.

Place	Date	Hour	Summary of Events and Information	Remarks and references to Appendices
Estaires	12/3/16	21.45	ADDMS here this morning about the Divisional Baths. They had already ordered 9 tons of coal which arrived this afternoon. The baths are to be in sole occupation of the ambulance. Patients may be kept in FA + DRS to total of 14 days. One heavy draught horse died today. The veterinary authorities were notified the horse was sick.	
			Visited headquarters of 103 Fd. Amb. to see officer who was lately i/c Baths to learn details of the method of running them.	
			Fine day with a good deal of sun.	
	13/3/16	20.45	A.V.C. officer came to see the horse & diagnosed pneumonia – probably contracted at LE HAVRE Rest Camp in the snow. Selling & burial arranged by this officer. Another Staff Capt. came to the baths today. 2º of Amb. painted off all vehicles today.	

T2134. Wt. W708–776. 500000. 4/15. Sir J. C. & S.

Instructions regarding War Diaries and Intelligence Summaries are contained in F. S. Regs., Part II. and the Staff Manual respectively. Title pages will be prepared in manuscript.

WAR DIARY
or
INTELLIGENCE SUMMARY.
(Erase heading not required.)

Army Form C. 2118.

7

Place	Date	Hour	Summary of Events and Information	Remarks and references to Appendices
	14/3/16	20	F.A. W.O. moved into Divisional baths today. Motor cyclist came to grief with belt trouble but passed his letters on to 134 Fd. Amb. cyclist. A.S.C. moved their lorries out of baths. Reported to ADMS that W.O. was not marine-boiler men but a unit & therefore unsuited for working baths engines.	
	15/3/16	21	Visited ADMS with O/c FAWO re engine at baths. ADMS came to inspect engine & ordered a report to be written. This was done giving above reasons & specifying No. of personnel required. Were the FAWO to perform the engine duty they could not perform their legitimate duties. ADMS saw Town Major about the R.E. occupying baths; these should be preferably in sole occupation of one unit viz 133 Fd Amb.	
	16/3/16	12.30	Town Major ordered the REWO to evacuate baths in accordance with 1st Army Routine order 171 whereby definite billets must be allotted to medical units &	

T2134. Wt. W708—776. 500000. 4/15. Sir J. C. & S.

Instructions regarding War Diaries and Intelligence Summaries are contained in F. S. Regs., Part II. and the Staff Manual respectively. Title pages will be prepared in manuscript.

WAR DIARY
or
INTELLIGENCE SUMMARY.
(Erase heading not required.)

Army Form C. 2118.

8

Place	Date	Hour	Summary of Events and Information	Remarks and references to Appendices
			+ kept for them only.	
			DDMS instructed me to apply for authority to be gazetted acting major in order to have more suitable status as O.C. Fd Amb.	
	17/3/16	21	16 Pioneer battalion were reported for duty at the baths to work the boiler. The O.C. 7 AWD appears to think he has mastered the intricacies of the boiler. The ADMS was here today chiefly about getting the baths opened by 19th. Also as to how many patients we can possibly receive; probably about 300 with a bit of a squash.	
			The Stationery boxes do not contain nearly enough forms for the working of a DRS, + FA, combined. A large indent has had to be sent in to the Base + it is slow coming. A type-writer + duplicator would be of very great assistance.	

Instructions regarding War Diaries and Intelligence Summaries are contained in F. S. Regs., Part II. and the Staff Manual respectively. Title pages will be prepared in manuscript.

WAR DIARY
or
INTELLIGENCE SUMMARY.
(Erase heading not required.)

Army Form C. 2118.

9

Place	Date	Hour	Summary of Events and Information	Remarks and references to Appendices
	18/3/16	20	Div. Baths boiler still giving trouble owing to difficulty of working out System.	
			Lecture at Med. Soc. on "Trench fever", our cases of influenza seem to be correctly diagnosis as they all have one Catarrh or another.	
			Various complaints of food deficiency by personnel & patients. All seem to end & begin with the small supply of potatoes.	
			The cases of diarrhoea all appear to be simple diarrhoea; the one diagnosed muco-colitis did pass mucus & blood but by the present state of the man the diagnosis would seem to suggest a diagnosis by 2 symptoms being present.	
	19/3/16	15.30	Divine Service held here today, also Communion.	
			Lieut H. LISTER 8th Ammun. Sub Park A.S.C. admitted with Influenza to Fd. Amb.	
			Weather perfect.	

Instructions regarding War Diaries and Intelligence Summaries are contained in F. S. Regs., Part II. and the Staff Manual respectively. Title pages will be prepared in manuscript.

WAR DIARY
or
INTELLIGENCE SUMMARY.
(*Erase heading not required.*)

Army Form C. 2118.

10

Place	Date	Hour	Summary of Events and Information	Remarks and references to Appendices
	20/3/16	22	Fine day	
	22/3/16	20	ADMS inspected hospital, during this the DDMS came + continued the inspection. In evening a wire came ordering the Bearer Division to hold itself ready to move at a moment's notice. Consequently orders were given to confine the personnel to billets &c. Divisional Baths worked today + the 133 + 134 Fd. Amb. bathed. All quite satisfactory. Wire sent to ADMS accordingly. Women engaged for laundry work. DDMS wishes all men with cuts &c to be given anti-tetanic serum. Orders – R.O. – Direct that drains, stagnant water, manure &c be cleared as much as possible!	

T2134. Wt. W708–776. 500000. 4/15. Sir J. C. & S.

Army Form C. 2118.

11

WAR DIARY
or
INTELLIGENCE SUMMARY.
(Erase heading not required.)

Instructions regarding War Diaries and Intelligence Summaries are contained in F. S. Regs., Part II. and the Staff Manual respectively. Title pages will be prepared in manuscript.

Place	Date	Hour	Summary of Events and Information	Remarks and references to Appendices
Estaires	22/3/16	20.50	Recent manure to be burnt if possible. I arranged with owners of farms where horses are billeted to have manure removed from the immediate neighbourhood of the houses. I shall have to provide horses & labour. They strongly object to having the customary pit in the yard emptied as they say the stink would be too great. Some rain all day. Arranged for the officers mess of Amb to be accommodated in a neighbouring house as ADMS wishes all the small rooms kept solely for officers on sick list. Sent in an indent for articles from Red Cross Society.	
	23/3/16	20.50	GOC & ADMS inspected. Former stated he was satisfied. Chilly day. Threatened snow early. Guns been quiet for 2 days & a night. Only 3 admissions yesterday.	

Instructions regarding War Diaries and Intelligence Summaries are contained in F. S. Regs., Part II. and the Staff Manual respectively. Title pages will be prepared in manuscript.

WAR DIARY
or
INTELLIGENCE SUMMARY.
(Erase heading not required.)

Army Form C. 2118.

12

Place	Date	Hour	Summary of Events and Information	Remarks and references to Appendices
Estaires	24	21	Reported to ADMS 39 Div: to see about returns & method of compiling. This was settled & saved much time that wd. have been spent in corresponding.	
			Received orders for amb. to be ready to move on 28th. The Pioneers at Hatts to accompany us.	
			The Ambulance taking over from us arrives tomorrow.	
			Lieut HERBERT M COTTRILL age 34 39 Div. Cyclists admitted to ARS with Myalgia.	
	25	20	ADMS 39 Div inspected - Gave orders for me to inspect ZELOBES this afternoon just before proceeding I received a wire to take over at CALONNE, on arriving there I found O.C. 134 Fd Amb had taken over. So wired for further instructions & sent an officer to ZELOBES in order to be safe either way. CALONNE was confirmed so an officer & advance	

T2134. Wt. W708—776. 500000. 4/15. Sir J. C. & S.

Instructions regarding War Diaries and Intelligence Summaries are contained in F. S. Regs., Part II. and the Staff Manual respectively. Title pages will be prepared in manuscript.

WAR DIARY
or
INTELLIGENCE SUMMARY.
(Erase heading not required.)

Army Form C. 2118.

13

Place	Date	Hour	Summary of Events and Information	Remarks and references to Appendices
			party were sent off soon after 10 p.m.	
CALONNE Sur La Lys	26	7.30	Sunday. Moved out at 9.30 arrived at starting point in good time. Rain all the time till afternoon, by which we fetched up practically dry. Men are very scattered as Divisions are marching through here day & night for 2 or 3 days. Taken over washing-house, Scabies & ordinary hospitals. Horses billeted mostly in open in very dirty ground. Arrived here at 12.15 p.m. ADMS found me at 2.15 p.m., inspected & issued instructions as to Sanitary Section proceeding on to St VENANT & FAWU also, at 9.15 received orders to say that FAWU proceeds to LESTREM forthwith; so I wired for this information to Lt. COOKE of my amb. to report by wire.	
			Have started A Section to hospital & C to Scabies. Had the wash	

T2134. Wt. W708—776. 500000. 4/15. Sir J. C. & S.

Instructions regarding War Diaries and Intelligence Summaries are contained in F. S. Regs., Part II. and the Staff Manual respectively. Title pages will be prepared in manuscript.

WAR DIARY
or
INTELLIGENCE SUMMARY.
(Erase heading not required.)

Army Form C. 2118.

14

Place	Date	Hour	Summary of Events and Information	Remarks and references to Appendices
			house boiler worked to make certain of its being ready for a battalion coming tomorrow & Tuesday. Inspected all buildings occupied by the unit between 5 & 7 pm. & rearranged certain mens' billets.	
CALONNE	27	21.50	ADMS of 24 Fd. Amb. requested me to take in any sick of 24 Fd. Amb who are passing through here. Baths worked quite satisfactorily this morning but this afternoon rain damped the hot water system with the result that the douche was not particularly hot. The boiler etc will be screened.	
			Yesterday being Sunday the mayor at ESTAIRES had his office closed so the billet forms were refused signature & stamping. Attempts were made at the Town Hall & his private residence. Lieut POWER went to investigate complaints by owners of billets & found that no complaint existed.	
			Still pouring rain & fairly strong wind. The horses may suffer.	

T2131. Wt. W708—776. 500000. 4/15. Sir J. C. & S.

Instructions regarding War Diaries and Intelligence Summaries are contained in F. S. Regs., Part II. and the Staff Manual respectively. Title pages will be prepared in manuscript.

WAR DIARY
or
INTELLIGENCE SUMMARY.
(Erase heading not required.)

Army Form C. 2118.

15

Place	Date	Hour	Summary of Events and Information	Remarks and references to Appendices
			I reported myself to O.C. 24 Fd. Amb. & offered to do anything he required.	
			A Major came here in response to my wire re supplies to inform me that the dump is at St VENANT. Today we happened to draw supplies at LA GORGUE by finding a "detail" train there & by having an indent at the same time. The Major on my suggestion wired to O.C. 134 Fd Amb as to where he should draw.	
	28	22	Strong wind - threatening of snow at 7pm. Saw DADMS at LESTREM. Two cases of measles (send NYD for confirmation) - rubella - 25 days since last possibility of contact among cases in this unit which had cases in ENGLAND.	

T2134. Wt. W708—776. 500000. 4/15. Sir J. C. & S.

Instructions regarding War Diaries and Intelligence Summaries are contained in F. S. Regs., Part II. and the Staff Manual respectively. Title pages will be prepared in manuscript.

WAR DIARY
or
INTELLIGENCE SUMMARY.
(Erase heading not required.)

Army Form C. 2118.

16

Place	Date	Hour	Summary of Events and Information	Remarks and references to Appendices
CALONNE	29/3/16	19	Attempt at snowing – Very strong wind last night – more than 20 cart-loads of manure removed from horse-stands by 1 Batt[illegible] in french-carts drawn by our horses. Very weedy looking heavy draught horse arrived – Teeth show 6 years. 4 [illegible] 18 section	
	30/3/16	21.50	Inspected Baths Laundry &c at ST VENANT for Lt Cooke of this unit; subsequently wrote a report of requirements to A.D.M.S 29th.	
			17 patients from 132 Fd Amb arrived without warning; sent 11 to CCS owing to lack of accommodation.	
			Frenchwoman reported a dead horse was in her stables left 26 inst by R.O.[illegible] this evening.	

T2134. Wt. W708—776. 500000. 4/15. Sir J. C. & S.

Instructions regarding War Diaries and Intelligence Summaries are contained in F. S. Regs., Part II. and the Staff Manual respectively. Title pages will be prepared in manuscript.

WAR DIARY
or
INTELLIGENCE SUMMARY.
(Erase heading not required.)

Army Form C. 2118.

17

Place	Date	Hour	Summary of Events and Information	Remarks and references to Appendices
CALONNE	31/3/16	22.15	ADMS 39th Div. inspected both hospitals & baths & then proceeded with Lieut Corke (O i/c Baths) to ST VENANT to arrange details of new baths.	
			Gen'l BERNARDISTON meanwhile inspected baths here.	
			Fog early; lovely sunny day afterwards.	
			This hospital ceases to be a D.R.S. A Corps Rest Station instead exists at MERVILLE.	
			Orders received to attach a motor ambulance to 59th Fd Amb while 118th Bde holds a section of the line in 79th Div' area.	
	31/3/16		R. Williams Capt OC 133 Fd Amb.	

T2134. Wt. W708—776. 500000. 4/15. Sir J. C. & S.

Instructions regarding War Diaries and Intelligence Summaries are contained in F. S. Regs., Part II. and the Staff Manual respectively. Title pages will be prepared in manuscript.

WAR DIARY
or
INTELLIGENCE SUMMARY.
(Erase heading not required.)

Army Form C. 2118.

39th Div. 133 F Amb
Vol 2

Place	Date	Hour	Summary of Events and Information	Remarks and references to Appendices
			April 1916 Confidential War Diary of 133 Field Ambulance from April 1st to 30th 1916 Vol II	

T2134. Wt W708—776. 500000. 4/15. Sir J. C. & S.

Instructions regarding War Diaries and Intelligence Summaries are contained in F. S. Regs., Part II. and the Staff Manual respectively. Title pages will be prepared in manuscript.

WAR DIARY
or
INTELLIGENCE SUMMARY.
(Erase heading not required.)

Army Form C. 2118.

18

Place	Date	Hour	Summary of Events and Information	Remarks and references to Appendices
CALONNE	1/4/16	21.15	Perfect day. Dead horse satisfactorily buried, owners of farm also satisfied.	
			Started today to send cases to Corps Rest Station, this hospital having ceased to be a D.R.S.	
			The sole motorcycle in charge broke down yesterday. O.C. Salvo sent another to take its place while under repair. Today a motor car went wrong, the reverse refusing to act.	
	2/4/16	20	Lovely day again. Capt. Chaplain conducted Divine Service at 2pm. Capt B.O. ROBINSON 12/Sussex admitted + evac'd to 32 CCS with neuralgia	
	3/4/16	21	Received orders to attach A section for instruction from 4–11 inst to 58 Fd. Amb., sending them complete except 9 men. To move off at 10 am. No transport but 2 days ration. 27 Scabies to be sent to MALASSISE.	
	4/4/16	6.15	A section marched off at 10am. Sent rations, 2nd blanket etc in a G.S. wagon which is to return today.	

T2134. Wt. W708—776. 500000. 4/15. Sir J. C. & S.

Instructions regarding War Diaries and Intelligence Summaries are contained in F. S. Regs., Part II. and the Staff Manual respectively. Title pages will be prepared in manuscript.

WAR DIARY
or
INTELLIGENCE SUMMARY.
(Erase heading not required.)

Army Form C. 2118.

19

Place	Date	Hour	Summary of Events and Information	Remarks and references to Appendices
CALONNE	4/4/16	22.15	Went to ESTAIRES; A section officers — Lieuts J. C. L. LINDEMANN + G. W. CARLETON + bearers go to A.D.Station this evening. Tent section employed in hospital. The section is under instruction of 58 Fd. Amb.	
			Detailed instructions as to treatment of contacts of smallpox arrived in ref. to the contacts coming here tomorrow.	
			Obtained the services of the billeting french interpreter to speak to the Mayor re grazing ground, with result that the latter at once disclosed the fields rented by Govt. He politely gave no information thus before.	
	5/4/16	20	Cold day. ADMS + DADMS(?) passed through.	
	6/4/16	21	DDMS inspected both hospitals. DADMS also here at same time. Former said that the Scabies men on discharge to duty may take ammunition with them. Cold day again. Received orders for myself to join A Section.	

T2134. Wt. W708—776. 500000. 4/15. Sir J. C. & S.

Instructions regarding War Diaries and Intelligence Summaries are contained in F. S. Regs., Part II. and the Staff Manual respectively. Title pages will be prepared in manuscript.

WAR DIARY
or
INTELLIGENCE SUMMARY.
(Erase heading not required.)

Army Form C. 2118.

Place	Date	Hour	Summary of Events and Information	Remarks and references to Appendices
CALONNE	7/4/16 ~~7th~~	7.55	Wires about 21 + 22 o'clock, one from M.O. i/c 184 Fab by ST VENANT for ambulance motor for urgent case. Lt Cooke went & found a man with pneumonia & sent him straight to CCS. Another from 120 (?) R/Sussex for heart case, this was brought here. It would be as well to take all such cases to CCS direct.	
		10	O.C this unit left to join A Section. Cold dull day. (17) 1 NCO and ~~three~~ two men arrived with authority to take Horse drawn Fresh but returned to Doulieu without it as they did not bring suitable harness.	
	8/4/16	21	Beautiful clear day. A Section watercart went to I.O.M. AOD for conversion. Thresh removed today.	
	9/4/16	20	Fine clear day. Two motor cycles collected from 39th Div Supply Colm Merville completing establishment.	

T2134. Wt. W708–776. 500000. 4/15. Sir J. C. & S.

Instructions regarding War Diaries and Intelligence Summaries are contained in F. S. Regs., Part II. and the Staff Manual respectively. Title pages will be prepared in manuscript.

WAR DIARY
or
INTELLIGENCE SUMMARY.
(Erase heading not required.)

Army Form C. 2118.

21

Place	Date	Hour	Summary of Events and Information	Remarks and references to Appendices
Calonne	10/4/16	19	Fine clear day. Ptes Meighan, Spall & Fry returned to duty. Baths used very little for past few days. A case of suspected scarlet fever (1st Herts) sent to CCS. St Venant	
	11/4/16	20	A section returned to CALONNE less 2 men sick. Pte Bulleymint in isolation on account of nursing a case of Cerebrospinal Meningitis. Put into a tent. The case was one in 58 Fd Amb.. Wet day.	
			A section while attached to 58 Fd Amb for instruction had nursing sub divⁿ employed in hospital & the bearer sub divⁿ at 2 A.D. Stations.	
			Wet day. 1 NCO + 12 men detailed for duty at Laundry ST VENANT under Lieut Cooke i/c.	
			On 10 inst. Lt. W. ANDREW A.+S. High. admitted & evac^d to 32 CCS with influenza.	
	12/4/16	23	ADMS 19 Div. called to enquire re accommodation here as he expects to take over shortly. Capt. W. P. RHODES C.F. 39th Div. admitted & evac^d to 32 CCS ~~[illegible]~~ with influenza.	

T2134. Wt. W708—776. 500000. 4/15. Sir J. C. & S.

Instructions regarding War Diaries and Intelligence Summaries are contained in F. S. Regs., Part II. and the Staff Manual respectively. Title pages will be prepared in manuscript.

WAR DIARY
or
INTELLIGENCE SUMMARY.
(Erase heading not required.)

Army Form C. 2118.

22

Place	Date	Hour	Summary of Events and Information	Remarks and references to Appendices
CALONNE	13/4/16	15	Ordered to put up badges of rank of a major.	
			Lt. L.C. PHARAZYN 11/Sussex admitted & evac to 32 CCS with influenza. MO i/c 11/Sussex sent a confidential memo to effect that this officer is unfit. Note passed on to OC 32 CCS	
	14/4/16	9.45	Received wire from ADMS 39 Div. that this amb. will take over from 129 Fd Amb about 19th inst. & to visit this place with an officer & to learn two motor drivers to learn routes.	
			O.C. 67 ASC MT sent round this morning for a M.O. to see a woman delivered of a child as the French Dr at MERVILLE refused to answer the call when applied to last night by a messenger with a pass signed by above O.C..	
			Lieut T.J. TAUNTON name of the amb. has measles. Sent to No 7 Gen' St OMER	

T2134. Wt. W708–776. 500000. 4/15. Sir J. C. & S.

Instructions regarding War Diaries and Intelligence Summaries are contained in F. S. Regs., Part II. and the Staff Manual respectively. Title pages will be prepared in manuscript.

WAR DIARY
or
INTELLIGENCE SUMMARY.
(Erase heading not required.)

Army Form C. 2118.

23

Place	Date	Hour	Summary of Events and Information	Remarks and references to Appendices
CALONNE	14/4/16	21	Under instructions from ADMS 39th Divn Lieut LINDEMAN + I went to 129 Fd Amb near ESSARS to have knowledge of the arrangements when we take over on 19th inst.. Also left 2 ASCMT drivers there to become cognisant of the routes.	
			Still a strong rather chilly wind + some rain.	
			Orders from ADMS 39 Div. 133 Fd Amb take over from 129 Fd Amb at WHITE HOUSE Nr ESSARS on 19th. advance party to go on 18th. Hand over here to 107 Fd Amb, I take over also ADS at LONE FARM. Also supply personal at Batts ESSARS, GORRE, LES QUESNOY to proceed on 15 inst..	
	15/4/16	22	Orders by ADMS 39 Div.	
			39 Div relieves 38 Divn in GIVENCHY + FESTHUBERT regions ~~both~~ completed by 20 April.	
			116 Inf Bde. goes to LOCON area on 14 inst + to trenches GIVENCHY section	

Instructions regarding War Diaries and Intelligence Summaries are contained in F. S. Regs., Part II. and the Staff Manual respectively. Title pages will be prepared in manuscript.

WAR DIARY
or
INTELLIGENCE SUMMARY.
(Erase heading not required.)

Army Form C. 2118.

24

Place	Date	Hour	Summary of Events and Information	Remarks and references to Appendices
			on 15 inst.	
			118 Inf Bde to FESTHUBERT section trenches 16th + night 16/17	
			117 " " to LOCON area on 16th + in Div. reserve.	
			Movements. Lieut R.C. COORE takes over Div. Baths + Laundry at LOCON + baths at ESSARS, LE QUESNOY, GORRE + LE TOURET on 15th April.	
			17th 82 San. Sect. to MESPLAUX	
			18th 132 Fd Amb to BOIS de PACAUT; + 2 officers + 20 men at ROBECQ	
			134 " " to MESPLAUX + ADS at MARAIS	
			19th 133 " " hand over CALONNE to 107 Fd Amb + take over WHITE HOUSE + ADS at LONE FARM from 129 Fd Amb.	
			133 will send ADS party – 2 officers + ~~52~~ 30 OR to LONE FARM plus 12 men for 3 aid posts on 17th to report to OC 129 Fd Amb	

T2134. Wt. W708—776. 500000. 4/15. Sir J. C. & S.

Instructions regarding War Diaries and Intelligence Summaries are contained in F. S. Regs., Part II. and the Staff Manual respectively. Title pages will be prepared in manuscript.

WAR DIARY
or
INTELLIGENCE SUMMARY.
(Erase heading not required.)

Army Form C. 2118.

25

Place	Date	Hour	Summary of Events and Information	Remarks and references to Appendices
			Clearing of Sick: of right sector (GIVENCHY section) cleared by 133 Fd Amb. of left " (FESTHUBERT ") " " 134 " " of Div. Reserve area " " 132 " " .	
			Div Hdqtrs close at LESTREM at 10 am 17th inst & open at LOCON at same hour.	
			39 Div. Code Signs received.	
CALONNE	16/4/16	20	Showery. ADMS 39th Div. conveys to Lieut R.C. COOKE through me his appreciation of the promptness with which he carried out his instructions regarding handing over of Armstrong huts, & the zealous manner in the performance of his duties while i/c of the ESTAIRES & St VENANT baths. Signed by CR MILLAR major DADMS 39 Div. d/ 16.4.16.	

T2134. Wt. W708—776. 500000. 4/15. Sir J. C. & S.

Instructions regarding War Diaries and Intelligence Summaries are contained in F. S. Regs., Part II. and the Staff Manual respectively. Title pages will be prepared in manuscript.

WAR DIARY
or
INTELLIGENCE SUMMARY.
(Erase heading not required.)

Army Form C. 2118.

Place	Date	Hour	Summary of Events and Information	Remarks and references to Appendices
CALONNE	16/4/16	21	Capt. RIVERS Commanding 39 Div! Supply Column kindly criticised freely the motor ambulances in my charge on my request. In this way I learnt exactly what he expected to find when the cars go for overhaul. He also gave me a copy of the report to be filled in by his inspecting officer for my guidance. He expressed himself as pleased with the cars.	
			I went to French Mission re the grazing field I am using. Full assistance was given. Strongly advised not to pay cash myself but to do so through the rent-officer. An interpreter will meet me at 2pm 17 inst. at CALONNE, when the owner has said he will attend.	
	17/4/16	11.30	A section viz Lieuts J.C.L. LINDEMAN & G.W. CARLETON + 42 O.R. have proceeded to WHITEHOUSE to take over A.D.S. at LONE FARM. Paraded in the rain.	
	18/4/16	11.30	Advance party under Lieut GIMLETTE proceeded to WHITE HOUSE. Received orders yesterday to hold a section ready to go to BOIS DU PACAUT on 22nd inst.	

T2134. Wt. W708—776. 500000. 4/15. Sir J. C. & S.

Instructions regarding War Diaries and Intelligence Summaries are contained in F. S. Regs., Part II. and the Staff Manual respectively. Title pages will be prepared in manuscript.

WAR DIARY
or
INTELLIGENCE SUMMARY.
(Erase heading not required.)

Army Form C. 2118.

Place	Date	Hour	Summary of Events and Information	Remarks and references to Appendices
CALONNE	18/4/16	11.30	56 Bde HdQtrs in the village. Many troops marching thro' this morning. Have sent 2 motor-ambs. & cyclist to Lieut. Lindeman at LOVE FARM to remain there.	
ESSARS	19/4/16	20	Main party of ambulance moved off at 10 am. Halted for dinner at 11.30 for 50 minutes. Arrived here about 1.30 pm. ~~[illegible]~~ Transferred scabies patients remaining to 32 Fd amb & brought Fd. amb. patients here, except ~~in both instances~~ patients of 19th Divn - respectively 15 & 7. Patients taken over here were 29 & one officer Lt. H.Y. Williams 15/R.W.F. with ac. Conjunctivitis.	
			There are sufficient billets in barns &c for B & C Section & also ASC HT & MT. Billets are limited for Sgts. For officers - 8 - there are sufficient but not good, for instance the landlady passes through the room to get to hers. General cleanliness good. Rain as usual when on move. ADMS 39 Div. came to see arrangements & accommodation.	

T2134. Wt. W708—776. 500000. 4/15. Sir J. C. & S.

Instructions regarding War Diaries and Intelligence Summaries are contained in F. S. Regs., Part II. and the Staff Manual respectively. Title pages will be prepared in manuscript.

WAR DIARY
or
INTELLIGENCE SUMMARY.
(Erase heading not required.)

Army Form C. 2118.

28

Place	Date	Hour	Summary of Events and Information	Remarks and references to Appendices
ESSARS	20/4/16	21.15	In my billet I yesterday had trouble in obtaining sitting room opening out of bedroom as an office, I obtained an interpreter who likewise failed & same with another when ADMS sent. ADMS sent another today & he has put in a requisition & now she says she is willing. Showery & windy again.	
			Today 2 wagon cartloads of horse-dung were removed to a field to be turned into ground. Obtained a load of slag to enlarge horse-stands.	
			Tailor, bootmaker & carpenter at work.	
			Capt C. G. Evill 12/Sussex admitted for Shock Mental. Slept most of day. Very quiet.	
	21/4/16	21.45	2/Lieut T. A. St John 11/Sussex for Gleet, sent to 33 CCS.	
			Saw Capt. Evill seems always to hide himself under the bed-clothes, answers all correct when questioned but seems annoyed at being worried.	
			Rain off & on & heavy this evening. Much firing going on. Prepared a stable for 8 cases, put a canvas door over door-way.	
			DADMS inspected.	

T2134. Wt. W708–776. 500000. 4/15. Sir J. C. & S.

Instructions regarding War Diaries and Intelligence Summaries are contained in F. S. Regs., Part II. and the Staff Manual respectively. Title pages will be prepared in manuscript.

WAR DIARY
or
INTELLIGENCE SUMMARY.
(Erase heading not required.)

Army Form C. 2118.

29

Place	Date	Hour	Summary of Events and Information	Remarks and references to Appendices
ESSARS	22/11/16	23.45	Rain all day. Visited A.D.S. + 3 aid posts. The ~~aid~~ ADS post has a good cellar + is adapted for protection against gas. No 3 aid post has a tube in the room + would require skilled labour. The dug outs at aid posts could be protected probably without skilled labour. The aid posts are in a ruined village close to German lines. The only satisfactory route to ADS is via LE PREOL via bridge at BETHUNE, the other road is too narrow. Diaries to be kept by M.O.'s of units + notified M.O.'s at aid posts thro' O/c ADS.	
	23/11/16	21.30	C of E Chaplain here. Lt T. J. TAUNTON returned to duty after having German measles. I visited 134 Fd. Amb. + went round it. Met there the ADMS 39 Div. Fine day. Four bell tents up, one rolled in mud + others daubed with green paint. Capt. EVILL evacuated today. No improvement. 2/Lt. W.E.C. SPENCER 12/Sussex admitted + sent to No 7 Gen Hosp. MALASSISES as chicken pox. Lt. H.G KIRK HQ. 13/Glosters admitted with influenza.	

T2134. Wt. W708—776. 500000. 4/15. Sir J. C. & S.

Instructions regarding War Diaries and Intelligence Summaries are contained in F. S. Regs., Part II. and the Staff Manual respectively. Title pages will be prepared in manuscript.

WAR DIARY
or
INTELLIGENCE SUMMARY.
(Erase heading not required.)

Army Form C. 2118.

30

Place	Date	Hour	Summary of Events and Information	Remarks and references to Appendices
ESSARS	24/4/16	9.45	Lt A. C. TAYLER 13/Sussex admitted last night 2 a.m. with G.S.W. thigh, arm & hand, sent to No 32 C.C.S.	
			Capt. J. C. MACKENZIE 286 Coy A.S.C. admitted with Diarrhoea. He was brought to hospital by military police. He was seen by 2 M.O.'s who found he had a temperature & diarrhoea. They reported that the M.P. said the officer was ill. I saw him & he spoke quite rationally, he was annoyed quietly at the police having arrested him as being drunk. I told him to go to the officers ward & that he would be treated. He was not drunk; he had had alcohol. The M.O.'s report that they are of opinion he was not drunk.	
			Perfect day. Put up operation tent, as well as the 4 bell-tents with a view of having accommodation in the event of a rush.	
	25/4/16	11.55	Capt P. CONRAD 14/Hants admitted with Shock. I went to regiment & other units round GORRE + A.D.S today; to see M.O.'s i/c	

T2134. Wt. W708—776. 500000. 4/15. Sir J. C. & S.

Instructions regarding War Diaries and Intelligence Summaries are contained in F. S. Regs., Part II. and the Staff Manual respectively. Title pages will be prepared in manuscript.

WAR DIARY
or
INTELLIGENCE SUMMARY.
(Erase heading not required.)

Army Form C. 2118.

31

Place	Date	Hour	Summary of Events and Information	Remarks and references to Appendices
			to explain system of evacuation. Units round GORRE by ambulance to be sent there on message being given to my despatch rider who will report daily. Units near ADS by ADS. The battery units overlapping 134 Fd Amb will send Emergency cases to the 134 Fd Amb, all others by me. Summer day.	
ESSARS	26/4/16	21.20	Hot day. Saw remainder of units & sites of GIVENCHY Section. Obtained vermoral solution from 134 Fd Amb.	
	27/4/16	22.25	The powders obtained both react the same to acid. I sent an orderly to enquire (in writing) & went myself later on. Then applied to ASC for Sod. Carb. as both sacks gave off a smell like SO_2 on adding acid. Gas attack last night somewhere; knives & buttons darkened & a smell in air. Lt L.R. PICKETT 133 Fd Amb. admitted with Tonsillitis. Col. Firth DDMS inspected today. Quite hot & only slight breeze.	

T2134. Wt. W708—776. 500000. 4/15. Sir J. C. & S.

Instructions regarding War Diaries and Intelligence Summaries are contained in F. S. Regs., Part II. and the Staff Manual respectively. Title pages will be prepared in manuscript.

WAR DIARY
or
INTELLIGENCE SUMMARY.
(Erase heading not required.)

Army Form C. 2118.

32

Place	Date	Hour	Summary of Events and Information	Remarks and references to Appendices
ESSARS	28/4/16	21	At 20.45 Gas alarm was heard & wire came. All warned.	
			2/Lt. J. MERCER 12/Sussex admitted with Strain Right Rectus Muscle.	
		22	Had men paraded in road with helmets on top of head ready to pull down.	
			At 21.45 Dismissed parade. Warned RMP to sound going home all on hearing 3 blasts of whistle which will be sounded by M.P. stationed at Bridge about 150x off.	
			All patients had helmets ready. Wind I imagine to be about 10 m.p.h..	
			Received a wire GAS No 133 Field Ambulance at 20.45.	
			This afternoon I visited the A.D.S. & took out Hypo & Soda Carb. powder & also a tank from horse-amb..	
			Farrier's Cart broken by turning over, horse broke away from driver. last night	
	29/4/16	11.15	Lt C.A.G. BURGESS 11/Sussex admitted with GSW Left hip & buttock to	
			Gen! BARNARDISTON inspected hospital, expressed himself satisfied. Spoke to several patients & went to all the wards.	
			Summer like Day.	

T2134. Wt. W708—776. 500000. 4/15. Sir J. C. & S.

Army Form C. 2118.

33

WAR DIARY
or
INTELLIGENCE SUMMARY.
(Erase heading not required.)

Instructions regarding War Diaries and Intelligence Summaries are contained in F. S. Regs., Part II. and the Staff Manual respectively. Title pages will be prepared in manuscript.

Place	Date	Hour	Summary of Events and Information	Remarks and references to Appendices
ESSARS	30/11/16	23	Capt J. A. TREDENNICK of Seaforths attd. R/Sussex GSW. Shoulder admitted. Perfect day. 3 incinerators at work. 2 for human excreta & another for the & some horse manure but most of this is being spread on fields by my own men. Chaplain here for Divine Service.	

M Williams
Major
OC. 133 Fd. Amb.

1/5/16

T2131. Wt. W708–776. 500000. 4/15. Sir J. C. & S.

39th Div.

133 F amb

Instructions regarding War Diaries and Intelligence Summaries are contained in F. S. Regs., Part II. and the Staff Manual respectively. Title pages will be prepared in manuscript.

WAR DIARY
or
INTELLIGENCE SUMMARY.
(Erase heading not required.)

Army Form C. 2118.

Vol 3

Place	Date	Hour	Summary of Events and Information	Remarks and references to Appendices
		May. 1916.	Confidential	
			War Diary	
			of	
			133 Field Ambulance	
			April 1916	
			Vol III.	

T2134. Wt. W708—776. 500000. 4/15. Sir J. C. & S.

Instructions regarding War Diaries and Intelligence Summaries are contained in F. S. Regs., Part II. and the Staff Manual respectively. Title pages will be prepared in manuscript.

WAR DIARY
or
INTELLIGENCE SUMMARY.
(Erase heading not required.)

Army Form C. 2118.

34

Place	Date	Hour	Summary of Events and Information	Remarks and references to Appendices
ESSARS	1 5/16	22	Perfect day. Lt. Col. Parsons O.C. 39 Div. Train inspected horses & all animals which he remarked on as looking as well as when they were handed over to unit. Lieut TAUNTON & 2 N.C.O.s went as advance party to LOCRE FARM. Lieut PICKETT back to duty.	
	2 5/16	21.30	Lieut YORKE F of Cheshires admitted with G.S.W. knee & left buttock. ADMS 39th Div. inspected. Very little rain.	
	3 5/16	22.35	Lieut. Picket & 40 O.R. relieved A section at A.D.S. G.O.C. 118th Bde came to inspect at 1.15 pm while I was lunching there. Gas alarm at 21.40, paraded everyone, dismissed all at 22.15. Ordered that men will fall in in their lofts in future.	
	4 5/16	20	Saw Rents officer re claims for Pasturage at LALONNE, one claimant has already had his field hired by British Govt.. Claims to be settled by Rents office.	

T2134. Wt. W708—776. 500000. 4/15. Sir J. C. & S.

Instructions regarding War Diaries and Intelligence Summaries are contained in F. S. Regs., Part II. and the Staff Manual respectively. Title pages will be prepared in manuscript.

WAR DIARY
or
INTELLIGENCE SUMMARY.
(Erase heading not required.)

Army Form C. 2118.

35

Place	Date	Hour	Summary of Events and Information	Remarks and references to Appendices
ESSARS	5/5/16	21	Hot day, windy this evening. Saw Medical Comforts barges at BETHUNE.	
	6/5/16	23	Met Major MILLAR DADMS & Major HORVEY BOURNE OC 139 Fd Amb & we discussed the question of advance & retirement. Could decide nothing as we did not know the General Idea.	
			2/Lt. HOLMES VR of Cheshire adm. with Impetigo Contagiosa.	
	7/5/16	24	Wet day. Capt Chaplain here. Went to ADS.	
			2/Lt. B. CLARKE 17/Sherwoods adm. with orchitis	
			" " E OSBOURNE 1/4 Blackwatch " " GSW face, R & L thigh.	
			Capt Delgado relieved Capt Cock MO i/c 1/Cambs today at 5 pm.	
	8/5/16	22	Capt. Cock G name att. 1/Cambs. adm. with Whitlow.	
			Showery day. Much cooler.	
			T/4 057303 a/Sgt. BRADLEY A.E, ASC attached to unit had his tibia fractured by his horses falling on him after backing into a ditch. Sgt Bradley was i/c of party exercising horses. He was not to blame.	
			~~[illegible]~~ 2/Lt. W.J. DEAN 254 Tun. Coy RE adm. with G.S.W. Chest.	

T2131. Wt. W708—776. 500000. 4/15. Sir J. C. & S.

Instructions regarding War Diaries and Intelligence Summaries are contained in F. S. Regs., Part II. and the Staff Manual respectively. Title pages will be prepared in manuscript.

WAR DIARY
or
INTELLIGENCE SUMMARY.
(Erase heading not required.)

Army Form C. 2118.

36

Place	Date	Hour	Summary of Events and Information	Remarks and references to Appendices
ESSARS	9/5/16	20	Wet day. 2/Lt. A.E. OGLE 1/Herts adm^d with GSW Rt. leg.	
	10/5/16	17	Lieut GIMLETTE of unit is taking over aid post + 1/Herts Rgt temporarily. M. JIQUEL, French interpreter, posted to unit. Visited detachments of my unit at baths. Lt. TAUNTON O/C A.D.S. reports that yesterday afternoon there was much shelling round the A.D.S. + near WESTMINSTER Road Bridge. Fine day with good deal of wind. 2/Lt. F.H. ROGERS adm^d with GSW Head - 255 Tun Coy RE	
	11/5/16	20	Saw ADMS 39 Div. does not wish officers to go to BETHUNE with any frequency + men should be satisfied with one visit there per week.	
	12/5/16	21	Some Showers. Lt G.S. DAVIDSON 39 Squadron RF adm^d with Influenza. Lt T. ROBERTS 17 Notts & Derby attd 117(2) Trench Mortar Bt with GSW Scalp. 2/Lt. GUY GILBEY 1/Herts with Impetigo.	
	13/5/16	22	Hot day. Lt. HERMAN 1/Cambs adm^d with Tonsillitis	

Instructions regarding War Diaries and Intelligence Summaries are contained in F. S. Regs., Part II. and the Staff Manual respectively. Title pages will be prepared in manuscript.

WAR DIARY
or
INTELLIGENCE SUMMARY.
(Erase heading not required.)

Army Form C. 2118.

37

Place	Date	Hour	Summary of Events and Information	Remarks and references to Appendices
ESSARS	14 5/16	22.35	Visited ADS in morning. DADMS came after lunch & wished to go to ADS so I went as well. We inspected ADS & the 3 Regtl. Aid Posts.	
			Showery day.	
	15 5/16	22	Showery again. Strong as possible parade for kit inspection of unit.	
			Lt. K.O. SIEDLE 174 Bde RFA admitted with Inflamn. Elbow joint.	
			Senior NCO & Sgt Dispenser of B section went to ADS to learn routine.	
	16 5/16	21	ADMS 39 Div. inspected unit as strong as possible at 5.30 pm. Also saw 2 officers & 1 O.R.. Lieut GOWER went to ADS to take over.	
			Lt. G. TURNER 254 Tun Coy RE admitted in nervous state. Diagnosed Neurasthenia.	
	17		Had had some grenades bursting over his dug-out. 2/Lt. A.D. AIKMAN 254 Tun. Coy RE admd with Influenza.	
	17 5/16		Lt. W.S. ROBERTSON 1/4 B. Watch admd. with "Incipient Pneumonia."	
			Hot day. Still air.	

T2134. Wt. W708—776. 500000. 4/15. Sir J. C. & S.

Instructions regarding War Diaries and Intelligence Summaries are contained in F. S. Regs., Part II. and the Staff Manual respectively. Title pages will be prepared in manuscript.

WAR DIARY
or
INTELLIGENCE SUMMARY.
(Erase heading not required.)

Army Form C. 2118.

38

Place	Date	Hour	Summary of Events and Information	Remarks and references to Appendices
ESSARS	18 5/16	22	2/Lt. WESTACOTT. E. G, admitted & died at A.D.S. with G.S.W. fracture & dislocation elbow - rt & shoulder.	
			D.M.S. inspected ambulance & A.D.S. accompanied by Sanitary Officer & ADMS 39th Div.	
			Hot day.	
	19 5/16	21	Quite hot. 2/Lt. CLAYTON C 17/Sherwoods admitted with sprained ankle.	
	20	21	Fine	
	21	22	Claims Commission Officer interviewed a farmer re damage to crops by horse getting loose - claimed 50 francs agreed to 25 francs.	
			Gas alarm - apparently lachrymatory - our eyes irritated. Dismissed parade & held a practice fire alarm. Mme FUVET DELRUE admitted with G.S.W. head & fingers.	
	22	21.30	DDMS here re sick rate. Saw harness & was satisfied as to its state. Lt. GIMLETTE ordered by name by ADMS to L.M.O. i/c 12/Sussex. An officer & report	

T2134. Wt. W708-776. 500000. 4/15. Sir J. C. & S.

Instructions regarding War Diaries and Intelligence Summaries are contained in F. S. Regs., Part II. and the Staff Manual respectively. Title pages will be prepared in manuscript.

WAR DIARY
or
INTELLIGENCE SUMMARY.
(Erase heading not required.)

Army Form C. 2118.

39

Place	Date	Hour	Summary of Events and Information	Remarks and references to Appendices
ESSARS			house.	
			Establishment of ASC HT reduced by 1 Sgt 1 HD 1 mule & 1 rider & MT by 1 Cpl. & 1 motor cycle.	
			2Lt Young RA 184 Bde RFA adm with orchitis.	
			2Lt ED SMYTHE 17/KRR " " GSW leg (L) fractured	
	23	2130	Visited ADS with Interpreter ZIQUEL. Latrine & kitchen are in new sites.	
			Capt DELGADO taken over MO i/c 184 Bde RFA from Lt. J. MacARTHUR who is attached to this unit for duty. Lieut RC COOKE rejoins unit, Lieut GIMLETTE posted to 12/Sussex as MO i/c..	
			1 HD horse gone to MVS with Colic	
			2/Lt AR Phillips adm with gonorrhea – 254 Tun Coy RE	
	24/5/16	22	Capt G.D. ROBERTSON posted to unit & joined.	
			2/Lt HCR BUTCHER 174 Bde RFA – Scabies, 2/Lt Cooke A 17 Sherwoods Neurasthenia	
	25/5/16	21	Some showers. Reported a farmer, for obstructing the cleaning of his forum, to Mayor, who has taken action (26) & the man is doing it by his own labour,	

T2134. Wt. W708–776. 500000. 4/15. Sir J. C. & S.

Instructions regarding War Diaries and Intelligence Summaries are contained in F. S. Regs., Part II. and the Staff Manual respectively. Title pages will be prepared in manuscript.

WAR DIARY
or
INTELLIGENCE SUMMARY.
(Erase heading not required.)

Army Form C. 2118.

40

Place	Date	Hour	Summary of Events and Information	Remarks and references to Appendices
ESSARS	26 5/16	23	Lt R R TATTERSALL 1/1 RB GSW Face, forearm comp^d fracture leg (R) Showery & distinctly cooler.	
	27 5/16	22	ADMS & OC 132 Fd Amb here re site for 132 Fd Amb. Capt. ROBERTSON detached to take temporary command of 139 Fd. Amb. while the OC is on sick list. 2/Lt AD PARKIN 1/1 Sherwoods ad^d GSW buttock.	
	28 5/16	21.30	Capt. J.S. CASSY 12/ Sussex adm^d ICT Face. Parade Church Service. A plentiful supply of dressings etc must be allowed to R.M.O's by sanction of ADMS 39 Div.	
	29 5/16	21	Fine again. Lt. CARLETON with sec sick of 117 Bde Machine Gun Coy. No 1 WESTMINSTER Bridge R^d Aid Post is vacated & HERTS REDOUBT becomes No 1 aid Post.	

T2131. Wt. W708—776. 500000. 4/15. Sir J. C. & S.

Instructions regarding War Diaries and Intelligence Summaries are contained in F. S. Regs., Part II. and the Staff Manual respectively. Title pages will be prepared in manuscript.

WAR DIARY
or
INTELLIGENCE SUMMARY.
(Erase heading not required.)

Army Form C. 2118.

41

Place	Date	Hour	Summary of Events and Information	Remarks and references to Appendices
ESSARS	30/5/16	22	2/Lt MARCHINGTON C L 1/HERTS adm^d with Perihepatitis result probably of old operation for abscess. Some rain. Cool. Much firing going on this evening. Sick of 117 Bde M. G. Coy now seen by MO of 39 Div^l RE. The Canteen run by this ambulance is much appreciated judging by the Sales. Goods are sold at BEF rates but the profit is far more by buying direct from ENGLAND.	
	31/5/16	22	By my request CRE sent an officer to inspect roof of barn used as a ward he ordered ¼ of roof (forming a floor) to be cut out as it was liable to fall at any moment on account of dry rot. The sanction of owner was not asked by RE officer as he stated it was a necessity. 2/Lt COMER, F 1/Cambs adm with Scabies.	

W Williams
Major
O.C. 133 Fd Amb.

T2134. Wt. W708—776. 500000. 4/15. Sir J. C. & S.

133 F amb

Army Form C. 2118.

Vol 4

June

Instructions regarding War Diaries and Intelligence Summaries are contained in F. S. Regs., Part II. and the Staff Manual respectively. Title pages will be prepared in manuscript.

WAR DIARY
or
INTELLIGENCE SUMMARY.
(Erase heading not required.)

Place	Date	Hour	Summary of Events and Information	Remarks and references to Appendices
			Confidential War Diary 133 Field Ambulance June 1916	

Vol IV

T2134. Wt. W708—776. 500000. 4/15. Sir J. C. & S.

Instructions regarding War Diaries and Intelligence Summaries are contained in F. S. Regs., Part II. and the Staff Manual respectively. Title pages will be prepared in manuscript.

WAR DIARY
or
INTELLIGENCE SUMMARY.
(Erase heading not required.)

Army Form C. 2118.

42

Place	Date	Hour	Summary of Events and Information	Remarks and references to Appendices
ESSARS	1 6/16	22	Fine day. ¼ of roof taken down by units' carpenters as advised by RE officer sent by C.R.E.	
	2 6/16	21	Fine day. Orders received from ADMS re Evacuation in event of a "push". 2/Lt. E.L. TURNBULL 17/KRR adm^d with GS (RG) wound foot (right).	
	3 6/16	17.30	Inspected A.D.S. & No 1 SOUTHMOOR Aid Post. Also details at Le QUESNOY & GORRE Baths. A window has been placed in cellar of A.D.S. which greatly assists light & ventilation. Capt Robertson RAMC rejoined from detached duties.	
	4 6/16	23	ADMS here. Only made enquiries re patients did not dismount. I was at ADMS' office at the time. All wheels have straw on now.	
	5 6/16	14.30	O/c ADS reports 24 cases, as result of bombing by us at 10.30 pm, arrived at ADS. Horse (HD) sent to M.V.S. with ? colic. Diagnosed due to eating slag. This will be obviated by putting earth over the slag where hay is falls.	

T2134. Wt. W708—776. 500000. 4/15. Sir J. C. & S.

Instructions regarding War Diaries and Intelligence Summaries are contained in F. S. Regs., Part II. and the Staff Manual respectively. Title pages will be prepared in manuscript.

WAR DIARY
or
INTELLIGENCE SUMMARY.
(*Erase heading not required.*)

Army Form C. 2118.

Place	Date	Hour	Summary of Events and Information	Remarks and references to Appendices
ESSARS	5/6/16		2/Lt R.C. DAVIES 1/Sherwoods adm with GSW chest & shoulder.	
	6/6/16	20	Wet day. Water cart requires 3 measures lime instead of one, probably due to wet weather.	
	7/6/16	21	2/Lt RV WALKER 6/Connaught Rangers att^d 25 Squadron RFC adm. GSW Face A flattened out french nail found in sack of corn. No distinguishing mark on bag. Sent to ADMS 38 Div for forwarding. Orders by ADMS to use economy in dressings &c, all officers informed. Complaint from owner of pipes used by me to repair a drain at Rue du College ESTAIRES. San. Sect. Sgt. was told by french Town Surveyor there was no objection to his using them. Amb. left there on 25 March, complaint sent in on 15th April.	
	8/6/16	20:30	Saw ADMS re contacts in an Armstrong Hut of Scarlet Fever case. Considered advisable to isolate the occupants in the hut for 10 days. DADMS XI Corps visited unit to address officer Quest. Referred to methods of	

T2134. Wt. W708—776. 500000. 4/15. Sir J. C. & S.

Instructions regarding War Diaries and Intelligence Summaries are contained in F. S. Regs., Part II. and the Staff Manual respectively. Title pages will be prepared in manuscript.

WAR DIARY
or
INTELLIGENCE SUMMARY.
(Erase heading not required.)

Army Form C. 2118.

Place	Date	Hour	Summary of Events and Information	Remarks and references to Appendices
			instructing officers in Fd Amb detail. Peace methods to be used as far as possible.	
			that Corps Commander wishes Transport & wagon lines to be kept smart.	
			Lt. TAUNTON returned from detached duty.	
			Horse arrived for Interpreter.	
ESSARS	9/6/16	20.15	Lt. CARLETON posted to 132 Fd Amb.	
			Lt. TAUNTON relieves Capt. FERGUSON MO ½ 11/Hants proceeding on leave.	
			Capt ROBERTSON & Lieut GOWER + 12 O.R. detailed for gas course.	
	10/6/16	18	LIEUT PICKETT posted to 17/KRRC as MO ½.	
			Lt. TAUNTON rejoined as Capt Ferguson's leave is cancelled.	
			Capt R B WATT 4/5 R.H. adm^d GSW (grenade) axilla & forearm L, Rt leg fractured, multiple wounds both legs.	
	11/6/16	11.15	Lieut HOLDEN Claims officer saw proprietor of main dressing station re section of roof removed by ? by direction of RE. Proprietor has no objection provided either that new floor is put in or money paid. He says he will claim	

T2131. Wt. W708—776. 500000. 4/15. Sir J. C. & S.

Instructions regarding War Diaries and Intelligence Summaries are contained in F. S. Regs., Part II. and the Staff Manual respectively. Title pages will be prepared in manuscript.

WAR DIARY
or
INTELLIGENCE SUMMARY.
(Erase heading not required.)

Army Form C. 2118.

Place	Date	Hour	Summary of Events and Information	Remarks and references to Appendices
	11/6/16		for use of garden occupied by tents & huts, as they keep him from using the ground. Told to send in claim through usual channels.	
			Another circular re removing manure etc & keeping billet surroundings sweet. M.O.'s to report failure of OC units to carry out their orders. Immediate compliance i.e. within 48 hours will avoid Corps Commander being notified.	
			2/Lt O T EDWARDS 254 Tun Coy RE adm with Inflam. Knee joint.	
ESSARS			Visited A.D.S. Two windows have been opened up in cellar by cutting through the sand-bags; also side-bags in front of Entrance have been removed. The cemetery is full so that the burial ground is now at GORRE. At present bodies are removed there in the A.D.S. wheeled stretcher carriers. This is being reported to A.D.M.S. Wet cold day. The men find it cold without their blankets.	
	12/6/16	21:30	A.D.M.S. came to see a patient who should have been evacuated to Base but went back to his regiment. Wet bleak day. Capt H. JONES 13/Glosters adm Pneumonia	

Instructions regarding War Diaries and Intelligence Summaries are contained in F. S. Regs., Part II. and the Staff Manual respectively. Title pages will be prepared in manuscript.

WAR DIARY
or
INTELLIGENCE SUMMARY.
(Erase heading not required.)

Army Form C. 2118.

45

Place	Date	Hour	Summary of Events and Information	Remarks and references to Appendices
ESSARS	13/6/16	20	Capt Robertson & Lieut Gover + 12 OR doing course of Instruction at Gas School.	
			ADMS 39 Div called for accommodation for patients at:	
			Main Dressing Station = under roof 49 OR 24 officers	
			with tents [struck through] 113	
			Lone farm for lying down cases at a push probably 90 using all available space.	
			At No 1 Southmoor Aid Post 8 lying down, could be built up for 16	
			" " 2 Lambeth Rd " " 5 " "	
			" " 3 Queens Rd " " 8 " "	
			I visited LONE FARM in afternoon.	
	14/6/16	23.50	2/Lt W. D. MADORE 254 Tun Coy RE adm with Orchitis acute	
			2/Lt A. YEADON " " " " Influenza	
			At 23 o'clock the watches &c of unit were advanced to midnight o'clock in accordance with Summer Time coming into force.	

T2134. Wt. W708—776. 500000. 4/15. Sir J. C. & S.

Instructions regarding War Diaries and Intelligence Summaries are contained in F. S. Regs., Part II. and the Staff Manual respectively. Title pages will be prepared in manuscript.

WAR DIARY
or
INTELLIGENCE SUMMARY.
(Erase heading not required.)

Army Form C. 2118.

46

Place	Date	Hour	Summary of Events and Information	Remarks and references to Appendices
ESSARS	14/6/16		Orders from ADMS 39 Div. that ADMS 33rd Div will send 1 officer + 10 OR to LOWE FARM on 15th inst to learn routine there preparatory to this ADS being taken over.	
			Later orders that 1 officer + 10 OR rank to proceed to R27C04 ZELOBES to learn routine of Fd. Amb. there particularly of ADS & accessory relay posts. That ADS LOWE FARM will be taken over by 33rd Div at an early date. That A Sect. & another section will take over Fd Amb. Site at ZELOBES at an early date. One section will remain at WHITE HOUSE.	
	15/6/16	10.00	Lieut G W GOWER + 10 OR left at 9.35 am. for ZELOBES as advance party.	
	16/6/16	22.15	Lieut WAYTE + 10 OR, proceeded to ADS RUE DU BOIS to learn routine of system there. Lieut HARRIS + 10 OR of 134 Fd Amb are also there as well as 2 officers +	

T2131. Wt. W708—776. 500000. 4/15. Sir J. C. & S.

Instructions regarding War Diaries and Intelligence Summaries are contained in F. S. Regs., Part II. and the Staff Manual respectively. Title pages will be prepared in manuscript.

WAR DIARY
or
INTELLIGENCE SUMMARY.
(Erase heading not required.)

Army Form C. 2118.

47

Place	Date	Hour	Summary of Events and Information	Remarks and references to Appendices
			a section of 106 Fd amb from whom I will take over. I went there today & also to MDS of 106 Fd amb to see accommodation.	
			~~Tonight~~ This afternoon orders came to take over their ADS tomorrow, I saw OC 106 Fd amb & arranged to have my full party there by 11 am 17th inst. Equipment went today.	
			Relief orders No 2 by ADMS 39 Div. Ref map BETHUNE Comb. Sheet	
			1. Information XI Corps front on night 16/17 June 35 Div will be withdrawn & Corps front be held by 3 Divs, 39th being centre, 33rd right & 61st left. Centre sector will be from GRENADIER Road (exclusive) to OXFORD STREET (inclusive) to be held with 2 Bdes in the line & one in Div^l reserve at VIELLE CHAPELLE.	
			2 Movements. 133 Fd amb less one section at WHITE HOUSE (W30 a 88) goes to ZELOBES (R26 d 93) to take over MDS from 106 Fd amb & ADS at RUE du Bois X17 d 55, ADS LOONE Farm to be taken over by 33rd Div.	
			4 Collection of sick 133rd - area W. of LOCON-LESTREM R^d inclusive ~~except~~ except LOCON village. WHITE HOUSE section will [illegible] units E of LOCON-LESTREM Road	

T2134. Wt. W708–776. 500000. 4/15. Sir J. C. & S.

Instructions regarding War Diaries and Intelligence Summaries are contained in F. S. Regs., Part II. and the Staff Manual respectively. Title pages will be prepared in manuscript.

WAR DIARY
or
INTELLIGENCE SUMMARY.
(Erase heading not required.)

Army Form C. 2118.

48

Place	Date	Hour	Summary of Events and Information	Remarks and references to Appendices
ESSARS	17-6-16	20	ordered to stand fast until 19th inst. 2/Lt D.M. RIGBY of Cheshire ad. with G.S.W. Scalp Comp. fract. Rt. Humerus, frac. Clavicle, wound Body + Chin. 2/Lt P. LAYARD 2/98/1 T.M. Bty 4 Suffolk frac. chin.	
	18-6-16	19	RE making a dump at ADS but I see no particular objection as it is not at all prominent. Saw ADMS 39 Div..	
ZELOBES	19-6-16	21	Arrived at new M.D.S with A Sec. + details of B + C. Genl. sanitation good except ditches which have much grass + weeds + are dammed in several places. Deep pit system of urinals + latrines in use. appears good. 40 men C section left at WHITE House with Capt. Robertson + Lt. Cooke. Billets for personnel are scattered + the horse lines rather far from Amb.. 1 NCO + 5 men gone to ADS for King George Relay Post	
	20-6-16	22	Major HILDRETH of ADMS inspected, thereafter he + I + San. Officer went to see RE re King George's Relay Post by junction of Kings Rd + King Georges Rd. Much structural alteration of proposed barn will be required. I am to supply a fatigue of 1 NCO + 20 men to work under RE.. The site is by a tram. line hence its object. In afternoon went to WHITE HSE, arranged for	

Instructions regarding War Diaries and Intelligence Summaries are contained in F. S. Regs., Part II. and the Staff Manual respectively. Title pages will be prepared in manuscript.

WAR DIARY
or
INTELLIGENCE SUMMARY.
(Erase heading not required.)

Army Form C. 2118.

49

Place	Date	Hour	Summary of Events and Information	Remarks and references to Appendices
			10 men to be returned to Hd. qtrs.	
			Capt A. HUNTER posted to unit.	
			Received orders to deal with crime of a combatant man attached to ESSARS Baths.	
ZELOBES	21/6/16	20	15 men sent to work at Relay Post in the making.	
			Visited GRUBB St. baths, tub system. Not at all inviting appearance. Also seems superfluous with LE TOURET baths in existence. Reported so to ADMS. DADMS XI Corps here.	
			2/Lt A.B.S. GIBB 159 Bde RFA adm with Gleet.	
	22/6/16	21	Conference at ADMS' office re possible move forward. My unit being to west of other ambs. will move first with 1st Group.	
			Visited R.A.P. with DADMS withdrew the 8 Ramc men of my unit from posts in front reserve line. In lieu 4 men will be kept at RAP to bring wounded to thence to A.D.S. Studied trambine as means of conveyance	

T2134. Wt. W708—776. 500000. 4/15. Sir J. C. & S.

Instructions regarding War Diaries and Intelligence Summaries are contained in F. S. Regs., Part II. and the Staff Manual respectively. Title pages will be prepared in manuscript.

WAR DIARY
or
INTELLIGENCE SUMMARY.
(Erase heading not required.)

Army Form C. 2118.

50

Place	Date	Hour	Summary of Events and Information	Remarks and references to Appendices
			2 stretchers go well on hand rail, 2 other men could be placed on floor of trolley. At present line is only of use from reserve line to RAP; later it will be of use for new Relay Post.	
			Capt HUNTER gone to ADS in relief of Lt. Taunton who rejoins at MDS	
	23/6/16	19	Fitted out 2 men, detailed by APM, with RAMC badges etc in order that they may watch suspected spies at A.D.S..	
			King George Relay Post changed to field alongside tram-line as farmer objects to his barn being cut down & altered. The new site is as good.	
			Very hot this morning, rain in evening relieved this.	
			2/Lt P.V. LAWS 1/ Sherwood ad. with S/W forehead.	
	24/6/16	9.45	Heavy rain last night. Went to see progress at KING GEORGES R.P	

T2134. Wt. W708—776. 500000. 4/15. Sir J. C. & S.

Instructions regarding War Diaries and Intelligence Summaries are contained in F. S. Regs., Part II. and the Staff Manual respectively. Title pages will be prepared in manuscript.

WAR DIARY
or
INTELLIGENCE SUMMARY.
(Erase heading not required.)

Army Form C. 2118.

Place	Date	Hour	Summary of Events and Information	Remarks and references to Appendices
ZELOBES	25/6/16	21	Visited ADMS + inspected section at WHITE HOUSE. Some rain. Gt. Western offensive has begun. Time & place of any operations kept secret.	
	26/6/16	20	Wet again but warm enough. Major HILDRETH ADMS here & visited new R.P. with him. Work progressing satisfactorily. 2/Lt SCRAGG A 16/Sherwoods adm abrasion R. Eye	
	27/6/16	21	Wet again. Conference at ADMS' office re action in event of advance &c + to consider ADMS' orders. Lt R.T. ROBINS GSW Face R hand + arm of London Artist Rifles 128 Bde att'd 17/KRR. 2/Lt L.W. DELPH 39 Div Signal Co GSW. R. leg.	
	28/6/16	22	Very wet with some sun. Lieut GOWER detailed to take charge of detachment 132 Fd Amb at CALONNE to relieve Lt CARLETON of 132. Court of Inquiry on No 65960 Sgt JARMAN S. RAMC of this unit. Court finds he is a cocaine taker. Placed under open arrest. King Georges R.P. much advanced but not completed. Capt B.O. ROBINSON 12/Sussex adm strain L. side	

Instructions regarding War Diaries and Intelligence Summaries are contained in F. S. Regs., Part II. and the Staff Manual respectively. Title pages will be prepared in manuscript.

WAR DIARY
or
INTELLIGENCE SUMMARY.
(Erase heading not required.)

Army Form C. 2118.

52

Place	Date	Hour	Summary of Events and Information	Remarks and references to Appendices
ZELOBES	29	22.40	16 transfers from 132 Fd Amb as they are clearing for casualties. Have 24 bearers with 6 stretchers ready to send them if required. My sector is not expected to take part actively, but I have made arrangements for sending a Ford Car to assist in clearing from R.A.P. to A.D.S., also supplemented stretchers at A.D.S.. Mostly fine & sunny. Some rain again this evening.	
	30/6/16	22.15	Bearers were asked for at 7am, seven sent to 132, also 2 officers to lend a hand. 62 slight cases were transferred to me from 132 Fd Amb & 50 patients admitted from ADS RUE DU BOIS. All bar one quite slight wound cases were evacuated by 6.30 pm to 32 CCS ST VENANT. One officer admitted viz Lt L.B. TURNER 13/ Sussex GSW thigh R arms & leg. DDMS & ADMS in frequently. A/General ? GOC XI Corps came as last 2 MAC cars were being filled, he was quite pleased at the evacuation being so quick.	
	1/7/16	21	At ADS Rue du Bois patients also came from Right Sector via RUE L'EPINETTE apparently having missed the correct ADS. from PATH HOUSE Regt-Post	

[signature] Williams
Major, 133 Fd Amb.

T2134. Wt. W708—776. 500000. 4/15. Sir J. C. & S.

39th Division

July 1916

133rd Field Ambulance

Instructions regarding War Diaries and Intelligence Summaries are contained in F. S. Regs., Part II. and the Staff Manual respectively. Title pages will be prepared in manuscript.

WAR DIARY
or
INTELLIGENCE SUMMARY.
(Erase heading not required.)

39.

Army Form C. 2118.

July

Vol. 5

Place	Date	Hour	Summary of Events and Information	Remarks and references to Appendices
			Confidential War Diary of 133 Field Ambulance Vol V July 1916	

T2134. Wt. W708–776. 500000. 4/15. Sir J. C. & S.

Instructions regarding War Diaries and Intelligence Summaries are contained in F. S. Regs., Part II. and the Staff Manual respectively. Title pages will be prepared in manuscript.

WAR DIARY
or
INTELLIGENCE SUMMARY.
(Erase heading not required.)

Army Form C. 2118.

52 a

Place	Date	Hour	Summary of Events and Information	Remarks and references to Appendices
ZELOBES	1/7/16	21	At ADS Rue du Bois patients also came from Right Sector via RUE L'EPINETTE apparently having missed the correct ADS.. from Path House Regimental Aid Post (patients)	

T2131. Wt W708—776. 500000. 4/15. Sir J. C. & S.

Instructions regarding War Diaries and Intelligence Summaries are contained in F. S. Regs., Part II. and the Staff Manual respectively. Title pages will be prepared in manuscript.

WAR DIARY
or
INTELLIGENCE SUMMARY.
(Erase heading not required.)

Army Form C. 2118.

5 3

Place	Date	Hour	Summary of Events and Information	Remarks and references to Appendices
	1/7/16		patients were conveyed to ADS by wheeled stretcher carrier & "Ford" car, the latter proving very useful at night. The trolley line from Rt sector was not used as it was not required, had there been many cases then it would have been useful. The Trolley between PATH HOUSE Aid Post & King Georges Relay Post was used & proved useful as a subsidiary means of evacuation. The road surface thence to LACOUTURE is very bad however for motor ambulances, they must proceed dead-slow. Evacuations from ADS proceeded without undue delay & were satisfactory. At 7 am 30 inst MO i/c [illegible] 1st Hants & OC 1/ Sherwoods applied for stretcher bearers for FACTORY Post, 15 names were immediately sent. They were employed till late at night to bring wounded from front line Trenches. The Regt! stretcher bearers being unable to cope with the cases alone.	
			Today I visited King Georges R.P. & found work was progressing well. It is sufficiently finished to be occupied. Owing to the good shell-proof nature of the building that is being aimed at the work to be done is large as regards sand-bagging.	

T2134. Wt. W708–776. 500000. 4/15. Sir J. C. & S.

Instructions regarding War Diaries and Intelligence Summaries are contained in F. S. Regs., Part II. and the Staff Manual respectively. Title pages will be prepared in manuscript.

WAR DIARY
or
INTELLIGENCE SUMMARY.
(Erase heading not required.)

Army Form C. 2118.

54

Place	Date	Hour	Summary of Events and Information	Remarks and references to Appendices
ZELOBES	2/7/16	15.30	Special order by Major Genl. R. DAWSON CB Commdg 39 Div. d/ 1.7.16 The Major Genl Commanding the Divn wishes to place on record his very high appreciation of the gallant manner in which 12/ & 13/ Sussex carried out the assault on enemy's lines on 30 ult & of the equally gallant manner in which the detachments of RE, Signal Coy, 11/Sussex, 13/ Glosters & R.A.M.C carried out the duties allotted to them. All concerned more than maintained the highest traditions of their Corps or Regt. Special order by ADMS 39 Div. The ADMS wishes to convey his hearty congratulations to officers NCOs & men concerned in care & evacn of wounded during the recent operations. The manner in which 132 Fd Amb & RMO's on duty at Plum St. Factory Post & Pope's Hse A.Posts performed their duties under very trying & arduous conditions is deserving of special commendation. The assistance rendered by all ranks of 133 & 134 Fd Ambs has not been lost sight of & is appreciated by me. Sd for Brigadier-Genl Col ADMS 39 Div 2/Lt W.E.C. SPENCE 12/Sussex adm accidental GSW foot rt. AF B117 submitted.	

T2134. Wt. W708—776. 500000. 4/15. Sir J. C. & S.

Instructions regarding War Diaries and Intelligence Summaries are contained in F. S. Regs., Part II. and the Staff Manual respectively. Title pages will be prepared in manuscript.

WAR DIARY
or
INTELLIGENCE SUMMARY.
(*Erase heading not required.*)

Army Form C. 2118.

55

Place	Date	Hour	Summary of Events and Information	Remarks and references to Appendices
Zelobes	3/7/16	20	The men of the unit employed in evacuating wounded from front line trenches appear to have worked well but as yet I have not been able to obtain any special note of conspicuous work by an individual. Conference at ADMS on recent operations. ADMS expressed his views on means of improvement in future actions. Visited King Georges R.P. & placed a 2nd car there. Also went to ADS. Regt M.O. at Kings Rd. A.P. is available in urgency for R.P. Capt Hunter & 23 OR of the unit sent to 134 Fd Amb for possible use in an operation tonight	
	4/7/16	21	Wet afternoon. Round SOMME region French & English are doing well – 14000 prisoners.	
	5/7/16	20	Lieut GOWER rejoined. Each section watercart sent to ADOS for alteration. Obtained reports from M.O's i/c units with whom my men were employed in attack of 30 ult. No individual action was remarked but collectively reports are good. 2/Lt E.J.L. BENNETT 184 Bde RFA adm Influenza	

Instructions regarding War Diaries and Intelligence Summaries are contained in F. S. Regs., Part II. and the Staff Manual respectively. Title pages will be prepared in manuscript.

WAR DIARY
or
INTELLIGENCE SUMMARY.
(Erase heading not required.)

Army Form C. 2118.

56

Place	Date	Hour	Summary of Events and Information	Remarks and references to Appendices
ZELOBES	6/7/16	11.45	Started to remove mud & dung at horse-lines. This was left by last unit in occupation. No opportunity for this work has arisen previously. Orders received to be prepared to move at 24 hours notice, later received orders to take over ECOLE MATERNELLE from 19 Fd. Amb. at BETHUNE. I proceeded there & arranged for taking over A.D.S CAMBRIN & site at Bethune at 9 am on 7th.	
			A/7 S/Capt H.E. ALLEN 1/4 Surrey ad. contusion thigh leg & back.	
BETHUNE	7/7/16	22	An officer of 2/3 Fd. Amb. 61st Div. reported at ZELOBES to take over site with 1 NCO + 4 men, also patients. I left Lt. MACARTHUR there with staff to look after patients until after patients' dinner. Marched off at 8 am, arrived at new site 10.45 am. Then had to stand-by until 19th moved clear at 2 pm. Sanitation of main site quite good. Usual trouble with 1 or 2 billeting people who were tired of the English viz Officers mess in fresh house & Sgts. old billet was unobtainable until interpreter at Town Major's brought a gendarme. Lieut T. J. TAUNTON posted to 47 Reserve Park A.S.C. in relief of Lt. A.H. MANFIELD	

T2134. Wt. W708—776. 500000. 4/15. Sir J. C. & S.

Instructions regarding War Diaries and Intelligence Summaries are contained in F. S. Regs., Part II. and the Staff Manual respectively. Title pages will be prepared in manuscript.

WAR DIARY
or
INTELLIGENCE SUMMARY.
(Erase heading not required.)

Army Form C. 2118.

57

Place	Date	Hour	Summary of Events and Information	Remarks and references to Appendices
			who is posted to this unit.	
			1 officer + 15 men 1 Sunbeam + 1 Ford + 1 Limber, 2 men at GRUBB ST Batts are at ADS Rue Du Bois.	
			2 officers & 34 men + 2 Sunbeams at ADS CAMBRIN.	
			GORRE Batts taken over by me. 2 men remain at ESSARS Batts; 1 NCO + 4 men at WHITE HOUSE; 1 man at Div! Bootmakers Shop.	
			I take patients from ADS. MARAIS of 134 Fd. Amb.	
			2/Lt O.E. GALLIE 167 Bde RFA 33rd Div admitted NYD, found wandering in trenches.	
			2/Lt C.B. DALLAS 17/KRR ad? G.S.W. Head.	
BETHUNE	8/7/16	20	Much cleaning up at ASC HT billets + horselines + stables.	
			Conference at ADMS' re large influx of patients as to registering them, keeping in touch with ADS + RAP, food to patients &c	
			2/Lt F PRIOR 13/Sussex ad? with Neurasthenia. Lt C WHILEY 16/RB also neurasthenia.	

T2131. Wt. W708—776. 500000. 4/15. Sir J. C. & S.

Instructions regarding War Diaries and Intelligence Summaries are contained in F. S. Regs., Part II. and the Staff Manual respectively. Title pages will be prepared in manuscript.

WAR DIARY
or
INTELLIGENCE SUMMARY.
(Erase heading not required.)

Army Form C. 2118.

58

Place	Date	Hour	Summary of Events and Information	Remarks and references to Appendices
BETHUNE	9/7/16	21	Visited ADS CAMBRIN, found much cleaning up proceeding & I saw it was needed. Studied system of working here. In afternoon went to ADS Rue du Bois. King Georges Relay Post & BATHHOUSE R.A.P. being taken over by 61 Div.. Reported to ADMS 39 Div.	
			Lt C E R FRASER 17/Sherwoods adm with Impetigo Contagiosa.	
			2/Lt R DARBY with GSW accidental of Forehead - shooting off his revolver reported to his O.C. & filled in AF B 117.	
	10/7/16	22.30	2/Lt V.A. SPINKS of Cheshires with Inflam" of Stomach.	
			2/Lt G W DOOGAN 11/Sussex GSW Rt Eyelid	
	11/7/16	22	Conference with ADMS 39 Div concerning active operations involving Rue du Bois ADS. I sent out 2 officers + 41 men to bring personnel to 3 O + 56 O.R., 4 Sunbeams + 2 Fords to be there, the latter to work between RAP + ADS specially. Warned & started personnel at MDS + prepared for influx of patients. Visited the ADS with ADMS	
			2/Lt O.A. GAMM 179 Bde RFA adm with Debility	

T2134. Wt. W708-776. 500000. 4/15. Sir J. C. & S.

Instructions regarding War Diaries and Intelligence Summaries are contained in F. S. Regs., Part II. and the Staff Manual respectively. Title pages will be prepared in manuscript.

WAR DIARY
or
INTELLIGENCE SUMMARY.
(Erase heading not required.)

Army Form C. 2118.

59

Place	Date	Hour	Summary of Events and Information	Remarks and references to Appendices
BETHUNE	13/7/16	21	First patient arrived at 2.10 am, Next at 3.30 am after which they came in together to a total of 3 officers 156 O.R.. The first car load arrived at MDS at 5 am & last at 10.55 am. 4 Sunbeams working satisfactorily, there was always one present at ADS.. There is no time for clerks to make out AF W 3210 as well as W 3118 at an ADS. This was the first opportunity we have had for trying the system. The patients all arrived well dressed from R.A.P.. 2/Lt V.G. DIXON 17/KRRC & 2/Lt C J HART adm with GSW Buttock. 2/Lt J.R. CHOLERTON 16/Sherwoods adm with GSW Head. 2/Lt WE MISKIN 186 RFA & Major WS NICHOLSON 186 Bde RFA adm with Neurasthenia	
	13/7/16	22	Cpl DEAN & Pte BEARD of this unit admitted with wounds which they received while attending patients with Pte Whiteley (very slight wound). All were buried under debris which they removed after which they removed patient to Aid Post. Pte Cavedasca went to fetch the other wounded man with a Hants. private. The trench was all the time being shelled. Reported to ADMS 39 Divn.. Pte Whiteley also slightly wounded but not admitted at same time. Pte Cavedasca relieved above men,	

T2134. Wt. W708—776. 500000. 4/15. Sir J. C. & S.

Instructions regarding War Diaries and Intelligence Summaries are contained in F. S. Regs., Part II. and the Staff Manual respectively. Title Pages will be prepared in manuscript.

WAR DIARY
or
INTELLIGENCE SUMMARY
(Erase heading not required.)

Army Form C. 2118.

60

Place	Date	Hour	Summary of Events and Information	Remarks and references to Appendices
BETHUNE	13/7/16		The former 3 men answered a call for Rame. Cpl Dean being hit in face & Cyle could not carry on but Ptes Head & Whitely removed one patient to Infant. Pte Head went for assistance & Pte Whitely & a Hants pte. removed second wounded man.	
			Lt H.F PAYNE 17/KRR HQ ad[d] with neurasthenia	
			2/Lt J E GRIFFITHS 184 Bde RFA with GSW buttock	
	14/7/16	20	Orders received to move at short notice. ADMS Office opens at LOCON on 15th at 10 am	
			New FRONT of 39 Div LA BASSÉE CANAL (exclusive) A15 d 10 6½ to FAUQUISSART - TRIVELET Rd (M24 b 88).	
			Later order same day that this amb. will not move.	
			Rame order No 3 of ADMS 39 Div.	
			39 Div Front Northern limit will be OXFORD St. S5 C44	
			Relief completed by 6 am 16 July.	
			132 Fd amb. go on 15th to MESPLAUX (X14 a 96).	
			133 " " remain at ECOLÉ MATERNELLE. Hands over CAMBRIN & retains ADS RUE du BOIS (X17 d 58)	

2449 Wt. W14957/M90 750,000 1/16 J.B.C. & A. Forms/C.2118/12.

Army Form C. 2118.

61

Instructions regarding War Diaries and Intelligence Summaries are contained in F. S. Regs., Part II. and the Staff Manual respectively. Title Pages will be prepared in manuscript.

WAR DIARY
or
INTELLIGENCE SUMMARY
(Erase heading not required.)

Place	Date	Hour	Summary of Events and Information	Remarks and references to Appendices
BETHUNE	14		2/Lt D. RILEY 1/Cambs adm with Malaria Lt L. G. GOLD 1/Herts " " G/SW Forehead	
	15	10.15	Capt. STEWART 2/4 Fd amb arrived last evening to learn routine at ADS Cambrin & proceeded there this morning. Gave orders for personnel	
		20	& equipment of this amb. to rejoin after handing over & being relieved. Major J. W. CROPPER XI Corps Cavalry adm with Scabies.	
	16	21	ADS Cambrin handed over. Lieut GOWER relieves Capt. Hunter at ADS Rue du Bois, latter returned to MDS. Visited ADS Rue du Bois. 2/Lt J. V. SMITH 4/8 Middsex attd 1/Herts G/SW Thigh Haemorrhage Capt. A M SPENCE 254 Tun. Coy RE Debility.	
	17	20	Staff at ADS Rue du Bois increased by 1 Officer (Lieut MANFIELD) + 18 OR, a total of 2 Officers + 30 OR, with 1 other OR i/c of clothing at GRUBB STREET Baths. Lieut LINDEMAN temporarily i/m/c 16/Sherwoods to relieve Capt MUNDEN. Close muggy day.	

2449 Wt. W14957/M90 750,000 1/16 J.B.C. & A. Forms/C.2118/12.

Instructions regarding War Diaries and Intelligence Summaries are contained in F. S. Regs., Part II. and the Staff Manual respectively. Title Pages will be prepared in manuscript.

WAR DIARY
or
INTELLIGENCE SUMMARY
(Erase heading not required.)

Army Form C. 2118.

62

Place	Date	Hour	Summary of Events and Information	Remarks and references to Appendices
BETHUNE	18/7/16	20	Pamphlet on Spies &c again read & explained to as strong as possible parade. Gas lecture in evening by Capt. ROBERTSON, lecture clearly & well given. Exchequer Bonds investment also explained again. F.G. Cm. on No 65960 Sgt S. JARMAN RAMC of this unit for drunkenness in self administering cocaine without medical advice. Letter No 39 in 4/316 d/ 17.7.16 from ADMS 39th Div, congratulating No 72006 Cpl DEAN, No 72091 Pte BEARD & No 72008 Pte Whiteley of this unit for devotion to duty under trying circumstances. As no supporting evidence is available recommendation for immediate reward is not possible but names are noted to be brought forward at the proper time.	
	19/7/16	21	1 officer 15 O.R. & 1 Sunbeam lent to OC 134 Fd. Amb. for possible rush night of 19/20.	

2449 Wt. W14957/M90 750,000 1/16 J.B.C. & A. Forms/C.2118/12.

Instructions regarding War Diaries and Intelligence Summaries are contained in F. S. Regs., Part II. and the Staff Manual respectively. Title Pages will be prepared in manuscript.

WAR DIARY
or
INTELLIGENCE SUMMARY
(Erase heading not required.)

Army Form C. 2118.

63

Place	Date	Hour	Summary of Events and Information	Remarks and references to Appendices
BETHUNE	20	2.30	Visited ADS, a dug-out entrance has been improved. The outside lean-to has been knocked down to make room for Cupolas under orders of A.D.M.S. 39 Div. PHG helmets arrived. Also went to WHITE HOUSE & ESSARS Baths – both correct & clean.	
	21	22	Lieut. COOKE & WAYTE & 50 O.R. went through the gas chamber this afternoon.	
	22	20	A.S.C. H.T. fired off 10 rounds each on 100x range. On the whole the shooting was satisfactory.	
	23/7/16	21	Rance order No 4 – I hand over ADS RUE DU BOIS to 132 Fd Amb & will take over ADS LOWE FARM from 134 Fd Amb, relief to take place on 24th & night of 24/25 by mutual arrangements between OC's the 3 Ambs. One section 133 to take over WHITE HOUSE W 30 a 88. I saw OC 134 & arranged for advance party of an officer & 21 men to proceed to LOWE FARM with equipment on 23rd evening & 10 & 12 OR on 24th morning	

2449 Wt. W14957/M90 750,000 1/16 J.B.C. & A. Forms/C.2118/12.

Instructions regarding War Diaries and Intelligence Summaries are contained in F. S. Regs., Part II. and the Staff Manual respectively. Title Pages will be prepared in manuscript.

WAR DIARY
or
INTELLIGENCE SUMMARY

(Erase heading not required.)

Army Form C. 2118.

64

Place	Date	Hour	Summary of Events and Information	Remarks and references to Appendices
			132 owing to handing over their ADS at St VAAST to 31 Div. agreed to relieve my unit at latest by 4 pm 24th	
			2/Lt N C CARTER 13/ Sussex admitted with G/W abdomen	
BETHUNE	24	18	B Section 2 O + 31 O.R. have taken over WHITE HOUSE with section Equipment & transport & one Ford car	
			C Section 2 O + 33 OR have taken over LONE FARM with requisite Equipment 2 Sunbeams + a push-bicycle. The working party of 134 Fd Amb to remain for tramline extension until information is received as to probable duration of work.	
			LE QUESNOY Bath to be restarted by me on 25th inst.	
		20	134 working party to return on relief by me on 25th as work on line will probably last another week.	
			Arrangements made for collection of sick from LES CHOQAUX ESSARS LE HAMEL & BETHUNE.	
			Capt. H.S. TRUMPLER 286 Coy ASC admitted on 23rd with Dislocation Acromio-Clavicular joint Right. Today Capt. Trumpler inspected Horses + wagons + reported all satisfactory. I asked his advice on cracked-hoof + he recommends home-made hoop rather than Govt. issue which are too narrow + grooves for nails are straight instead of being on a slope, also tarring as well as oil already used.	

Instructions regarding War Diaries and Intelligence Summaries are contained in F. S. Regs., Part II. and the Staff Manual respectively. Title Pages will be prepared in manuscript.

WAR DIARY
or
INTELLIGENCE SUMMARY
(Erase heading not required.)

Army Form C. 2118.

65

Place	Date	Hour	Summary of Events and Information	Remarks and references to Appendices
BETHUNE	25/7/16	24	Visited WHITE HOUSE on afternoon 24th. Found all satisfactory. Inventory made of requirements at M.D.S. site & billets at W 20 a 88 in view of another winter in these parts. Visited A.D.S. LONE FARM, accommodation for lying cases has been improved & the kitchen enlarged, otherwise things are as we left them. The Tram line extension to A.D.S. is being carried on by us now. It will be of use in evacuating patients provided it is not shelled. Also the question of whether it will lead to shelling of the A.D.S. has to be considered, this is being provided for by not bringing the line across the road but running it parallel to the WESTMINSTER BRIDGE Road. In the event of shelling prohibiting the use of road from Westminster Bridge to LE PREOL, another road is available towards a up to BEUVRY. Should the Bridge be broken the north canal bank can be reached by going across the fields behind the A.D.S. to the N. Canal bank.	Was duly considered & suitable arrangements to safeguard such a contingency. [illegible] Col

2449 Wt. W14957/M90 750,000 1/16 J.B.C. & A. Forms/C.2118/12.

Army Form C. 2118.

WAR DIARY
or
INTELLIGENCE SUMMARY
(Erase heading not required.)

Instructions regarding War Diaries and Intelligence Summaries are contained in F. S. Regs., Part II. and the Staff Manual respectively. Title Pages will be prepared in manuscript.

66

Place	Date	Hour	Summary of Events and Information	Remarks and references to Appendices
BETHUNE	25/7/16		Col. ? Urquhart + San. Officer 1st Army inspected M.D.S., Capt Robertson conducted them round. No adverse criticisms made. Lieut H. De B. BANNETT 17/Sherwoods ad^d with boils on buttock	
	26/7/16	18	No 1 Sunbeam car has been "armour-plated" with netting. The Driver has no means of signalling to vehicles behind + the rear-shield requires 2 men to place it in position as it is not hinged, consequently it is slow + tedious to fix. Reported to ADMS 39 Div.	
	27/7/16	21	Lieut. WAYTE ordered by ADMS 39th Div. to report for duty to OC 14/Hants in relief of Capt FERGUSON RAMC. This leaves 2 officers present with the unit who were at a Training Centre. ADMS inspected M.D.S. station today. Advised as to shoeing of an officer's rider; tarp canvas of amb. wagons to be scrubbed; grease of G.S. wagons to be wiped off as it oozes out; one man with stains on coat to take steps to erase them.	

2449 Wt. W14957/M90 750,000 1/16 J.B.C. & A. Forms/C.2118/12.

Army Form C. 2118.

67

Instructions regarding War Diaries and Intelligence Summaries are contained in F. S. Regs., Part II. and the Staff Manual respectively. Title Pages will be prepared in manuscript.

WAR DIARY
or
INTELLIGENCE SUMMARY
(Erase heading not required.)

Place	Date	Hour	Summary of Events and Information	Remarks and references to Appendices
BETHUNE	28/7/16	17	Lieut Wayte proceeded as ordered. No 65960 Pte S.W. JARMAN transferred to 16th Div. ADS Lone Farm visited by a "Staff Colonel Rance" accompanied by Capt. Fothergill 124 Fd Amb. he stated "an excellent ADS + beautifully kept". Capt W.D. DODGE of Cheshires adm ICT arm (L). Capt H.J. HOLKS 17/KRR with GSW arm (L) chest + face Lt. D.A. RECORCON 17/KRR with GSW back	
	29/7/16	21	By orders, reports o/c ADS, preparations are being made at ADS for retention of two men, under sent, who are to be shot at dawn on 30th inst..	
			A bomb was dropt near Hotel de France, one child came here for treatment.	
	30/7/16		Very hot	
	31/7/16	21	G.O.C. 33 Div inspected M.D.S. accompanied by ADMS. Expressed himself as quite satisfied. Orders as to action operations for night 31/1 received. To arrange for 100 casualties. Visited ADS in morning + advised as to details, orders issued by o/c – Capt A. HUNTER – for I had orders to reinforce RAP's by 4 men each, No 2 LAMBETH Rd A.P. asked later for 2 more these were supplied.	

2449 Wt. W14957/M90 750,000 1/16 J.B.C. & A. Forms/C.2118/12.

Army Form C. 2118.

Instructions regarding War Diaries and Intelligence Summaries are contained in F. S. Regs., Part II. and the Staff Manual respectively. Title Pages will be prepared in manuscript.

WAR DIARY
or
INTELLIGENCE SUMMARY
(Erase heading not required.)

68

Place	Date	Hour	Summary of Events and Information	Remarks and references to Appendices
BETHUNE	31/7/16		The trolley line just completed & running near A.P.'s was an asset of value especially so for serious cases as the motion is smoother than of wheeled stretcher carriers & better than of hand carriage. At ADS only AF W 3118 was prepared, this worked well. For transfers to No 33 CCS a manuscript transfer document was made out with duplicate for MDS. At MDS 2 clerks made out separately AF W 3210 these were collected & given to 2 clerks who entered up A&D book & A 36. This worked well. Evacuation worked excellently from RAP to ADS & on to MDS. Thus 29 patients arrived at MDS between 3.15 & 5.20 am & then 8 between 6.5 & 11.45 am. 10 patients were sent in their cars direct to No. 33 CCS en route to MDS. At the ADS 4 slightly wounded arrived at 1.45 am & 2 am 2 stretcher cases the majority of serious cases arrived after 3.30 am On arrival at MDS patients were found to be well dressed. They were given refreshment & smokes & then went to sleep. On waking they were bathed in tub or in wash-house. A total of 50 casualties were noted in my A&D book.	

2449 Wt. W14957/M90 750,000 1/16 J.B.C. & A. Forms/C.2118/12.

Instructions regarding War Diaries and Intelligence Summaries are contained in F. S. Regs., Part II. and the Staff Manual respectively. Title Pages will be prepared in manuscript.

WAR DIARY
or
INTELLIGENCE SUMMARY
(Erase heading not required.)

Army Form C. 2118.

69

Place	Date	Hour	Summary of Events and Information	Remarks and references to Appendices
BETHUNE	31/1/16		Lt M.A. KENT 17/Sherwoods adm GSW chest (R)	
			2/Lt LANGFORD do GSW arm (L), back (penetrating left lung + abdomen), case dangerous, sent direct to No 33 CCS	
			During night of 31/1 following admissions	
			Capt F.B. LUDLOW 17/Sherwoods GSW shoulder, humerus scapula + clavicle (R)	
			2/Lt L.T. FLINT do GSW hand R.	
			Admissions during month	
			Sick 476 Direct 72 Transfers	
			Wounded 219 " 69 "	
			Total admissions 836	
			There were 76 cases of Scabies. 4 self inflicted wounds, 4 venereal, 2 albuminuria	
			2 Died at ADS. 21 Civilians came for outpatient treatment, 3 were admitted + transferred to Civil & Military hospital.	
			Officers 32 {14 wounded, 18 sick (1 scabies)}	
			M. Williams, Major RAMC, OC 133 Fd Amb.	

2449 Wt. W14957/M90 750,000 1/16 J.B.C. & A. Forms/C.2118/12.

39th Div. Army Form C. 2118.

133 F Amb

Vol 6

Instructions regarding War Diaries and Intelligence Summaries are contained in F. S. Regs., Part II. and the Staff Manual respectively. Title Pages will be prepared in manuscript.

WAR DIARY
or
INTELLIGENCE SUMMARY
(Erase heading not required.)

Place	Date	Hour	Summary of Events and Information	Remarks and references to Appendices
Aug 1916			Confidential War Diary of 133 Field Ambulance August 1916	

Vol VI

Army Form C. 2118.

WAR DIARY
or
INTELLIGENCE SUMMARY
(Erase heading not required.)

Instructions regarding War Diaries and Intelligence Summaries are contained in F. S. Regs., Part II. and the Staff Manual respectively. Title Pages will be prepared in manuscript.

80

Place	Date	Hour	Summary of Events and Information	Remarks and references to Appendices
BETHUNE	1/8/16	11	Operations of night 31/1 completed on last day of month notes for July. G.O.C. visited to see wounded but they had just been evacuated to No 1 C.C.S. Very hot tropical weather. The G.O.C. 39 Div inspected on 31 ult the "armour-plated" motor ambulance & was shewn defects mentioned in Diary on 26.7.16. The same day 31 ult he inspected WHITE HOUSE with B section & spoke favourably of existing conditions.	
	2/8/16	17	Very hot indeed. One O.R. returned to RAMC Base for being underage. Warrant & order for Lieut G W GOWER to leave for WAR OFFICE on 3rd inst arrived. I greatly regret that this officer is unable to renew his contract as he is a most useful officer in every way.	
	3/8/16		Another grilling day. Lieut G W GOWER RAMC proceeded to ENGLAND on account of termination of his contract on 5th inst. ADMS 39th Division visited ambulance & made arrangements for purchase of dungaree suitings to preserve clothing of men in cook-house	

2449 Wt. W14957/M90 750,000 1/16 J.B.C. & A. Forms/C.2118/12.

…ons regarding War Diaries and Intelligence …mmaries are contained in F. S. Regs., Part II. and the Staff Manual respectively. Title Pages will be prepared in manuscript.

WAR DIARY
or
INTELLIGENCE SUMMARY
(Erase heading not required.)

Army Form C. 2118.

81

Place	Date	Hour	Summary of Events and Information	Remarks and references to Appendices
BETHUNE	3/8/16		A Pte. of this unit is to be tried by F.G.C.M. for attempted use of a code in a private letter to ENGLAND. B Section rejoined from WHITE HOUSE by sanction of ADMS 39 Div.; 1 NCO & 4 men with horse amb. wagon left there in charge to collect sick of units round there.	
	4/8/16	noon	S.S. 441 on Espionage read in as strong as possible parade, also DG no 28/2 of 10 May 1915. 'Confidence at arms'. Not so hot a day but almost. Issued AO VII Leakage of military information to all officers with unit.	
	5/8/16	72	DMS 1st Army visited amb. with a Fleet Surgeon & a Lt Col IMS. Showed DMS limber wagons fitted with a frame work & hooks to carry 4 stretchers each side of rear limber between body & wheels. Cooler. Capt A. H. CHURCH 251 Tun Coy RE ad. with appendicitis	

2449 Wt. W14957/M90 750,000 1/16 J.B.C. & A. Forms/C.2118/12.

Instructions regarding War Diaries and Intelligence Summaries are contained in F. S. Regs., Part II. and the Staff Manual respectively. Title Pages will be prepared in manuscript.

WAR DIARY
or
INTELLIGENCE SUMMARY
(Erase heading not required.)

Army Form C. 2118.

82

Place	Date	Hour	Summary of Events and Information	Remarks and references to Appendices
BETHUNE	6/8/16	17	Confidential letter re overdosing with morphia + question as to prevalence of individuals of this unit carrying morphia constantly. Not known to occur. Orders to be prepared to move on 10th or 11th August.	
	7/8/16	19	Shells fell in BETHUNE soon after midday + continued to about 2.15 pm; in all 11 shells were dropt. As each shell fell I sent a motorcyclist to see if aid was required + accordingly sent cars with orderlies + in addition a M.O. at times. OC 134 Fd Amb sent 2 O + 6 OR + a car for my disposal. Patients were evacuated to 134 Fd Amb. No 33 CCS was severely damaged several cars burnt + some deaths + casualties. DMS was then, later DDMS visited here. One O.R. of this unit Pte BROWN P.A. was badly hit in thigh + pelvis while tending wounded in Belfry Square. OC 96 Fd Amb reported here re taking over from me. My unit moves to AUCHEL on 11th Aug. MDS taken over on 11th; ADS 10/11. 2/Lt L. POPE 1st Siege Co (R. Anglesey) RE fracture of skull. Capt G.T. GIMLETTE Dame altd 12/Sussex suffn knee joint	

Instructions regarding War Diaries and Intelligence Summaries are contained in F. S. Regs., Part II. and the Staff Manual respectively. Title Pages will be prepared in manuscript.

WAR DIARY
or
INTELLIGENCE SUMMARY
(Erase heading not required.)

Army Form C. 2118.

83

Place	Date	Hour	Summary of Events and Information	Remarks and references to Appendices
BETHUNE	8/8/16	7	Town Major informs me that following Casualties occurred as result of shelling	
			Killed / Wounded	
			Officers 3 / 6	
			Sisters — / 4	
			Soldiers 46 / 46 — Total 138 as then known.	
			Civilians 2 / 31	
			Parties arrived to take over ESSARS Baths, WHITE HOUSE & LE QUESNOY baths, & a party for A.D.S. LOWE FARM.	
			Lt. I.V. DAWSON 126 Bde RFA adm. Neurasthenia	
			Lt LEVY 14 Hants G.S.W. head & thumb	
			2/Lt J.A. BAKEWELL 14/Hants G.S.W. knee (R)	
	9/8/16	noon	[illegible] on Pte BOLTON of this unit for using a code in a private letter.	
			A.D.S. LOWE FARM taken over by 96 Fd Amb.	
			1 O + 7 O.R. attended funeral of Pte. P.A. BROWN	
			Censorship G.R.O. read out on pay parade.	
			2/Lt H.F. CLEMETTS 14/Hants adm. Contusion toe (R)	

2449 Wt. W14957/M90 750,000 1/16 J.B.C. & A. Forms/C.2118/12.

Instructions regarding War Diaries and Intelligence Summaries are contained in F. S. Regs., Part II. and the Staff Manual respectively. Title Pages will be prepared in manuscript.

WAR DIARY
or
INTELLIGENCE SUMMARY
(Erase heading not required.)

Army Form C. 2118.

84

Place	Date	Hour	Summary of Events and Information	Remarks and references to Appendices
BETHUNE	10/8/16	22	advance party 7 96 Idaunt arrived for M.D.S. Personnel was distributed according to class. Billeting officer went to town major AUCHEL + arranged billets for unit. 2/Lt H.K. MATHEWS 1st Fd Survey RE Coy adm gonorrhoea. 2/Lt J D MACNELLAN 254 Tun Coy RE Contused wounds body	
AUCHEL	11/8/16	23	Pte Bolton given 28 days F.S. Pun. No 1 by F.G.C.M. 2/Lt BUCHANAN F.H. 4/5 Blackwatch transported by motor amb. being unfit to march, fetched from 3d amb MAISPLAUX. Marched off for AUCHEL passed LA CLARENCE River at 6.30 pm as ordered. arrived AUCHEL 9.20 pm. 1 OR fell out due fruit by heat. This was only casualty for the march. Men received cocoa immediately on arrival, prepared by advance party. Billets satisfactory. Hot day with long hill at end of march. Marching good.	
BAILLEUL AUX CORNEILLES	12/8/16		ordered to march off at 3.15 pm. + to follow No 4 Coy ASC. Held up by frequent stops + generally on steep hills. As units in front left very late for march at MAGNICOURT I halted for tea at 6.50 – 7.30 pm. to leave 8½ miles as final march. This was done to avoid exhausting the men by lack of food.	

2449 Wt. W14957/M90 750,000 1/16 J.B.C. & A. Forms/C.2118/12.

Instructions regarding War Diaries and Intelligence Summaries are contained in F. S. Regs., Part II. and the Staff Manual respectively. Title Pages will be prepared in manuscript.

WAR DIARY
or
INTELLIGENCE SUMMARY
(Erase heading not required.)

Army Form C. 2118.

85

Place	Date	Hour	Summary of Events and Information	Remarks and references to Appendices
BAILLEUL AUX CORNAILLES			Arrived in billets at 9.20 pm. One man only fell out, this was due to epistaxis. Water for horses very limited in well.	
			2/Lt BUCHANAN admitted, probably Trench Fever.	
	13/8/16	17	ADMS & DADMS 39 Div. visited unit about 2 hours after we had started to clean up & prepare for patients. As little as possible of equipment was opened but ADMS directed me to open out. Pointed out shortage of water to ADMS. Are now watering horses 2½ miles out. Usual sanitary arrangements made at 3 billets of men, yards cleaned & brushed, also road in front of unit.	
			Lt S. J. LINDEMAN struck off strength of unit.	
	14/8/16	17.15	Scabies cases to be treated here. Men did Squad Coy & Stretcher Drill.	
			2/Lt R. SIMPSON adm scabies - of 14/Hants	
			Capt. R. A. WILLIAMS 17 KRR infl'n middle ear.	
			2 heavy draught horses with laminitis & one with slight thrush. V.O. inspected. ADMS & DADMS inspected. Water cart wheel accidentally broken.	
	15/8/16	noon	Route marching drill &c.	
			Capt L. R. MEECH taken on strength of unit	
			Capt G L SIMPSON 14/Hants adm influenza & 2/Lt B. CLARKE 17/Sherwoods with urethritis.	

2449 Wt. W14957/M90 750,000 1/16 J.B.C. & A. Forms/C.2118/12.

Instructions regarding War Diaries and Intelligence Summaries are contained in F. S. Regs., Part II. and the Staff Manual respectively. Title Pages will be prepared in manuscript.

WAR DIARY
or
INTELLIGENCE SUMMARY
(Erase heading not required.)

Army Form C. 2118.

86

Place	Date	Hour	Summary of Events and Information	Remarks and references to Appendices
B Camp C	16/8/16	17	DDMS + ADMS inspected. Former made no observations. 2/Lt A.A. KIRKHAM 16/RB adm. Influenza	
	17	17.15	1 Heavy Draught with laminitis evacuated. Patients are all accommodated in tents. Fly proof latrines last day. Site of amb. is satisfactory, barns are made of biscuit boxes over a pit. Motor amb. have to be kept in the road. available in case of need.	
	18	17	Wet. ADMS + DADMS visited in afternoon.	
	19	18	Mostly fine.	
	18		2/Lt. G.S. ASH adm. with ICT (Ear)(R) + Capt R.W. McINTYRE 4/5 R. Highrs with Influenza. Persistent Pains.	
	19		Orders that 39 Div moves South abt. 24th to 6th Div Front. 118 Bde relieves 18 Bde from River ANCRE to MARY REDAN. 116 + 117 Bdes. probably leave present billets on 24th.	

2449 Wt. W14957/M90 750,000 1/16 J.B.C. & A. Forms/C.2118/12.

Instructions regarding War Diaries and Intelligence Summaries are contained in F. S. Regs., Part II. and the Staff Manual respectively. Title Pages will be prepared in manuscript.

WAR DIARY
or
INTELLIGENCE SUMMARY

(Erase heading not required.)

Army Form C. 2118.

87

Place	Date	Hour	Summary of Events and Information	Remarks and references to Appendices
Bailleul aux Cornailles	20		Interpreter JIQUEL transferred to 1st Indian Cavalry Division.	
	21		Interpreter PAUL JAMBEAU taken on strength of unit. 2/Lt W.G. TAYLOR attd 117 M G Coy – 16 RB – add Inflam^n Knee (L) Capt. J.S. CASSY 12/R. Sussex add^d Influenza	
	22		117 Inf Bde order No 48. Unit marches to DOULLENS area with B Group. Billeting officer to meet Capt COHEN at NUNCQ at 11am to take billets there. On arrival this officer was ordered to take billets at MAISNIL ST POL, he promptly held up unit on road & redirected us. Our "present billets" were given as ORLENCOURT. Two H.T. ambs. accompanied troops. In my opinion too many men are allowed to ride, they should march without their kit & equipment. Sent message off about 11.30 pm to Bde. Major to say where our present billets are. Got no answer	
MAISNIL St POL	23		Saw Bde Major before my breakfast & was told to march independent. Left billets at 11. am arrived Maisnil St Pol at 1.55 pm. Halted for lunch & feed horses at noon. Horse of Interpreter Jiquel died en route of colic. Lieut. WANKLYN-JAMES joined unit. Sunbeam detached to accompany Div^l Headquarters.	

Instructions regarding War Diaries and Intelligence Summaries are contained in F. S. Regs., Part II. and the Staff Manual respectively. Title Pages will be prepared in manuscript.

WAR DIARY
or
INTELLIGENCE SUMMARY
(Erase heading not required.)

Army Form C. 2118.

88

Place	Date	Hour	Summary of Events and Information	Remarks and references to Appendices
LE MARAIS SEC	24		Unit to march at 10.45 am, just under 20 miles. B group Commander gave me permission to halt for dinners at my discretion. We halted to feed men & horses at FM. CALONNE S. of FREVENT. I had arranged that 2 H.T. wagons should meet me at BOUQUEMAISON where infantry went into billets, but I had to commandeer one, after which I reported to B group Commander, who gave me tea. Arrived at billets at 7.35 pm. Men marched excellently. Only 3 fell out, 1 bilious attack, 1 chafe of fork of legs & 1 blistered feet. Lieut Curling (QM) SICK. Probably malaria.	
AUTHIE	25		10 mile march to AUTHIE, started at 10 am. Arrived billets 3.10 pm, joined up with Bde at FRESCHVILLERS. Billeting Officer reported as ordered by 117 Inf Bde order No 49 at Authie & I sent remainder of advance party to VAUCHELLES where ADMS 39 Div had ordered me to go. Bde Billeting Officer ordered us to Authie, as I was attached to Bde I went there.	
VAUCHELLES	26		Went to OC 17 Fd Amb at Vauchelles to arrange for an advance party to come here. On my return found orders for unit to come so we arrived abt. 4 pm. ADMS orders Chateau to be used only for sick Officers & not as such. Officers billets & mess as at present done for all. Arranged with proprietor for men to go into a barn. Officers in Tents. Are to take over by noon on 27th.	

2449 Wt. W14957/M90 750,000 1/16 J.B.C. & A. Forms/C.2118/12.

Instructions regarding War Diaries and Intelligence Summaries are contained in F. S. Regs., Part II. and the Staff Manual respectively. Title Pages will be prepared in manuscript.

WAR DIARY
or
INTELLIGENCE SUMMARY
(Erase heading not required.)

Army Form C. 2118.

89

Place	Date	Hour	Summary of Events and Information	Remarks and references to Appendices
VAUCHELLES	27		Took over by 12 noon but as Amb remains until tomorrow things are a bit mixed. Am running both a F.d Amb.t & a D.R.S. Very wet night & day.	
			2/Lt J. G BROOMAN 17 Sherwoods add Sprain ankle (L)	
			" A KERR " " " " (R)	
			" CD POUND 117 M. G. Coy " wound contused knee (R)	
			Lt P.U. LAWS 16 Sherwoods " Influenza	
	28		Ordered to report to ADMS 39 Div re active operations, on arrival was told I was not required as my unit is too far back. Saw OC 134 F.d Amb.t. ~~Arranged to lend more equipment [illegible] 2 tent subdivisions with him.~~ Arranged to lend certain articles on loan to 134. All sick to be sent or transferred to me that to be evacuated. One tent subdivision to report for duty to 134 on 29th.	
			Lt. R. ENGLAND 9/ Suffolks admitted with Pyrexia.	
	29		Capt MEECH & Lieut COOKE with 12 OR to go to ADS's to learn system of evacuation. Only a proportion could do so as a larger number would probably have drawn more fire than they did get. The two officers returned for night.	

Instructions regarding War Diaries and Intelligence Summaries are contained in F. S. Regs., Part II. and the Staff Manual respectively. Title Pages will be prepared in manuscript.

WAR DIARY
or
INTELLIGENCE SUMMARY
(Erase heading not required.)

Army Form C. 2118.

90

Place	Date	Hour	Summary of Events and Information	Remarks and references to Appendices
VAUCHELLES	29/8/16		Two tent-subdivisions went to 134 Fd Amb today. 6 GS wagons & 3 HT amb wagons. Very heavy rain. Saw OC 134 this morning. MT Sgt (PEEL) of this unit to direct convoy on future route; all my MT drivers, bar one Ford driver remaining with me, are learning route.	
	30/8/16		Capt ROBORTSON ordered to report in morning of 31st to OC 134 Fd Amb to take over ADS. I am to obtain an officer from 2nd S. Midland Fd Amb, as I am now left with 39 RAMC OR + one M.O. who joined unit on 23rd inst.. I may obtain personnel from above Amb.. Operations postponed 24 hours. Weather awful. Tropical deluge. Saw OC 134 Fd Amb he is very pleased with my two tent subdivisions who have been given duty of taking complete charge of all lying cases. Capt HUNTER is to take charge of the other ADS.. Send an orderly to report for duty to CO of a Camp at P2a for 600 to 500 O.R.. He went with a surgical haversack.	

2449 Wt. W14957/M90 750,000 1/16 J.B.C. & A. Forms/C.2118/12.

Instructions regarding War Diaries and Intelligence Summaries are contained in F. S. Regs., Part II. and the Staff Manual respectively. Title Pages will be prepared in manuscript.

WAR DIARY
or
INTELLIGENCE SUMMARY
(Erase heading not required.)

Army Form C. 2118.

91

Place	Date	Hour	Summary of Events and Information	Remarks and references to Appendices
Vauchelles	30 8/16		Lt. Col. S. SMITH 227 Fd. Coy RE admitted inflam. Nasopharynx. Sgt Major F. G. HERBERT posted to this unit to complete Establishment for Sgt major	
	31 8/16		Capt Robertson proceeded to 134 Fd amb. I saw OC 2/3. Mid Fd amb & he sent Capt. Cox to assist me. Operations will take place on 1st Sept. Later operations will take place on 2nd Sept. Two tents to be pitched one for Infectious British troops & other for Infectious German Prisoners of war. Admissions during the month Officers: Sick 24, Wounded 4 } Total 28 O.R.: Direct Sick 616, Wounded 52, Gassed 2 } 670 Transfers Sick 79, Wounded 5 } 84 Total 754 Detail: Scabies 75, Venereal 11, Self inflicted 2, Died 1, Infectious 4, Gas Poisoning 2, Civilians 3 [signature] Williams Major OC 133 Fd amb.	

2449 Wt. W14957/M90 750,000 1/16 J.B.C. & A. Forms/C.2118/12.

Army Form C. 2118.

140/1734

Instructions regarding War Diaries and Intelligence Summaries are contained in F. S. Regs., Part II. and the Staff Manual respectively. Title Pages will be prepared in manuscript.

WAR DIARY
or
INTELLIGENCE SUMMARY

(Erase heading not required.)

39th Div

Place	Date	Hour	Summary of Events and Information	Remarks and references to Appendices
Sept 1916			Confidential War Diary of 133 Field Ambulance September 1916 Vol VII	

2449 Wt. W14957/M90 750,000 1/16 J.B.C. & A. Forms/C.2118/12.

Army Form C. 2118.

92

WAR DIARY
or
INTELLIGENCE SUMMARY
(Erase heading not required.)

Instructions regarding War Diaries and Intelligence Summaries are contained in F. S. Regs., Part II. and the Staff Manual respectively. Title Pages will be prepared in manuscript.

Place	Date	Hour	Summary of Events and Information	Remarks and references to Appendices
VAUCHELLES	1/9/16		Fine. General clean up. Notified that active operations will take place on 3rd inst. Visited 134 Fd amb in evening re operations.	
	2/9/16		2 Bearer Subdivisions, less advance party, with Capt. MEECH + Lieut COOKE left for ADS's. Sent 1 horse sick to M.V.S. with abscess of fetlock. OC 1/2 S. Midland Field Amb. has lent me 10 + 19 OR. as I have 35 OR left for duty at Fd amb HQRS with 1 M.O. (Inevitable during heavy operations + quite sufficient for requirements. B-C ADMS) Capt. C.T.W FINCH 234 Fd Coy RE admitted with ? fatty heart. Diagnosed DAH.	Inevitable during heavy operations + quite sufficient for requirements. B-C ADMS
	3/9/16		Day quiet here, am using 22 sick to do light fatigues + sentry duties. Lieut James volunteered to go to 134 Fd amb in afternoon + again in evening to assist M.O's there. I carried on here. Lieut + QM CURLING still unable to do duty. During late afternoon + evening shell shock cases arrived as transfers + a few slightly wounded. Capt HUNTER + Capt ROBERTSON of this unit are each i/c of an ADS + Lieut MACARTHUR of patients arrived at M.D.S. 7 of my M.O.'s are working under OC 134 Fd amb.	

2449 Wt. W14957/M90 750,000 1/16 J.B.C. & A. Forms/C.2118/12.

Army Form C. 2118.

93

Instructions regarding War Diaries and Intelligence Summaries are contained in F. S. Regs., Part II. and the Staff Manual respectively. Title Pages will be prepared in manuscript.

WAR DIARY
or
INTELLIGENCE SUMMARY
(Erase heading not required.)

Place	Date	Hour	Summary of Events and Information	Remarks and references to Appendices
VAUCHELLES	4/9/16		40 odd Cas arrived by single amb. car loads during night. I heard unofficially that we have had 18 casualties among O.R of unit. Capts. HUNTER & MEECH + 13 O.R. arrived from A.D.S. Capt Hunter reports 27 battle casualties. Sgt Major HERBERT reported for duty & brought back 13 OR from M.D.S. Lieut Cooke has been kept at M.D.S of 134 Fd amb. Casualties reported are 5 killed + 22 wounded Total 27 but this requires Confirmation. Capt. Hunter reports that all ranks acted with great Gallantry & devotion to duty. Yesterday I sent a large amount of Equipment & dressings to 134 Fd amb., in fact I supplied everything asked for.	
	5/9/16		12 OR returned from M.D.S. 134 Fd amb. Lieut MacArthur came at 1.30 pm to take back some of Equipment sent back to me. 73 patients transferred to DRS + 5 officers. Lieut James to report for duty to OC 174 Bde RFA in relief of Capt FORD. He is detailed by name by ADMS X. I detailed Lieut AH MANFIELD for duty with a unit on order to name an officer.	[illegible]

2449 Wt. W14957/M90 750,000 1/16 J.B.C. & A. Forms/C.2118/12.

Instructions regarding War Diaries and Intelligence Summaries are contained in F. S. Regs., Part II. and the Staff Manual respectively. Title Pages will be prepared in manuscript.

WAR DIARY
or
INTELLIGENCE SUMMARY
(Erase heading not required.)

Army Form C. 2118.

94

Place	Date	Hour	Summary of Events and Information	Remarks and references to Appendices
VAUCHELLES	5/9/16		Lieut CRR GIDNAY 17 KRR adm with Shell Shock	
			2/ " R.C.H. LIMBERRY BUSE 11/ Sussex " " " "	
			2/ " C.S. CAUTHERLEY HAC + 1/Herts " " " "	
			2/ Lieut F.H.H. BUCHANAN 4/5 Black Watch " " Trench Fever	
			2/ " J.D. SECKER 11/ Sussex attd 1/Cambs adm with Infl. of Stomach	
	6/9/16		Lieut Cooke reports for reward for actions in recent operations the following men: 20738 Sergt T MILLS, 65988 Pte Vaughan, 72139 Pte RJ BAMBRIDGE 72030 Pte CA WILSON, 72073 Pte LE DENMAN, Pte 72117 Pte AC GREEN 65940 Pte S UNDERWOOD.	
			Capt MEECH likewise the following 72159 Pte W P BRANCHETT, 65983 Pte WG WILSON, 65994 T EUSTACE, 65995 P BENSON	
			Lieut R.C. COOKE posted to 17/ Sherwoods, Lieut AH MANFIELD to 11/Sussex + Lieut WANKLYN-JAMES to 774 Bde RFA	
			Lieut J.F. OKELL taken on strength of unit.	
			Capt RG TAYLOR 17/KRR adm with Shock Shell + Lt T F OKELL name with debility.	

2449 Wt. W14957/M90 750,000 1/16 J.B.C. & A. Forms/C.2118/12.

Army Form C. 2118.

WAR DIARY
or
INTELLIGENCE SUMMARY

(Erase heading not required.)

Instructions regarding War Diaries and Intelligence Summaries are contained in F. S. Regs., Part II. and the Staff Manual respectively. Title Pages will be prepared in manuscript.

95

Place	Date	Hour	Summary of Events and Information	Remarks and references to Appendices
VAUCHELLES	7/9/16		Capt G P SELBY RAMC (Regular) taken on strength. 2 HD horses evacuated - abscesses. ADMS 39 Div inspected. Desired a report as to huts required for a winter stay here. Fine	
	8/9/16		Remaining men rejoined from 134 Fd Amb MDS. Lieut MAC ARTHUR likewise & proceeded on 14 day leave. Fine	
	9/9/16		Capt SELBY struck off strength. Capt FERGUSON rejoined unit. 75 patients today including 34 scabies of which 20 are from Cheshire Rgt.	

2449 Wt. W14957/M90 750,000 1/16 J.B.C. & A. Forms/C.2118/12.

Army Form C. 2118.

WAR DIARY
or
INTELLIGENCE SUMMARY
(Erase heading not required.)

Instructions regarding War Diaries and Intelligence Summaries are contained in F. S. Regs., Part II. and the Staff Manual respectively. Title Pages will be prepared in manuscript.

96

Place	Date	Hour	Summary of Events and Information	Remarks and references to Appendices
Vauchelles	9/8/16		25 Casualties in recent operations 3 Killed & 23 wounded Killed: No 72034 Pte J.W. BRUNGER, No 65999 Pte W BARTON & No 69484 Pte W. CROMPTON Buried in Cemetery at Q 23 D 33 map 57 D 1:40000 FRANCE Wounded 23 O.R..	
	10/9/16		Divine Service. 20 men for working party at ADS MESNIL, this with 41 deficient makes one strength of 1 section deficient for working Fd amb patients, DRS, Scabies & Officers wards. * A large number of men fit for light duties are available to meet requirements as pointed out by D.M.S. & myself Huts, drains, latrines inspected. Specially with regard to making hutments for winter use. Only sitting officer patients are to be kept in the DRS. for officers. Shell Shock patients after 3-4 days observation are to be evacuated, if they are likely not to be well shortly. Scabies patients are employed in erecting a temporary wash-house, on guards & other general fatigues. L.D. patients on easier fatigues.	* in Div D.M.S. & myself B-C The D.M.S expressed dissatisfaction of the ... of the ...

2449 Wt. W14957/M90 750,000 1/16 J.B.C. & A. Forms/C.2118/12.

Instructions regarding War Diaries and Intelligence Summaries are contained in F. S. Regs., Part II. and the Staff Manual respectively. Title Pages will be prepared in manuscript.

WAR DIARY
or
INTELLIGENCE SUMMARY
(Erase heading not required.)

Army Form C. 2118.

97

Place	Date	Hour	Summary of Events and Information	Remarks and references to Appendices
Vauchelles	11/9/16		Difficulty in arranging change of clothing for scabies patients as there no means of disinfecting clothing or supplying a change. Reported to ADMS. Sanitary Officer (Major Sinclair) inspected. He explained method of separating sullage water by having a grease trap at chimney end of field kitchen & a pit to hold water under chimney end [illegible] soakage hole. The grease is thrown [illegible] the fire. Washing water can be cleared by passing through a mixture of lime & ashes.	
	12/9/16		Town Major, OC 3rd Amb & MO of Unit are all responsible for cleanliness of the billeting area, the last named for his own area. Town Major & I inspected today & found ground lately occupied by 1/6 R. Warwicks in a filthy state. Reported to ADMS 39 Div.	

Instructions regarding War Diaries and Intelligence Summaries are contained in F. S. Regs., Part II. and the Staff Manual respectively. Title Pages will be prepared in manuscript.

WAR DIARY
or
INTELLIGENCE SUMMARY
(Erase heading not required.)

Army Form C. 2118.

98

Place	Date	Hour	Summary of Events and Information	Remarks and references to Appendices
Varchelles	13/9/16		Capt MEECH temp^y attached to 39 Div Rt as MO i/c 25 men arrived as reinforcement. General physical condition good. Conference at ADMS for OC Fd Ambs.	
	14/9/16		an Rt officer of 48 Div came here re a hutting scheme, I pointed out the ground & showed him my scheme. He did not bring his scheme. British Red Cross officers came & took notes of what they considered should be supplied by them: Some articles I had in my possession as O.C., D.R.S. Foden Lorry arrived & immediately put in use to disinfect Scabies clothing blankets &c. A working party of 6 WARWICKS worked last night & cleared up refuse of past weeks & thereby disclosed decaying matter of months. Reported to ADMS in conjunction with Town Major. Distinctly cold after sundown	333 [illegible]

2449 Wt. W14957/M90 750,000 1/16 J.B.C. & A. Forms/C.2118/12.

Instructions regarding War Diaries and Intelligence Summaries are contained in F. S. Regs., Part II. and the Staff Manual respectively. Title Pages will be prepared in manuscript.

WAR DIARY
or
INTELLIGENCE SUMMARY
(Erase heading not required.)

Army Form C. 2118.

99

Place	Date	Hour	Summary of Events and Information	Remarks and references to Appendices
			Capts HUNTER + FERGUSON + 15 OR reported to OC Corps Collecting Station for duty for 24 hours. Active operations by French + British are to start & it is hoped that in the succeeding days the result may be that a winter campaign will be unnecessary.	
VAUCHELLES	15 9/16		4 G.S. wagons sent to RE yard. Re-erecting fd. kitchen & make an Evaporating sullage water pit.	
	16 9/16		Capts HUNTER & FERGUSON rejoined, the latter from an A.D.S.. The 15 OR at 134 Fd Amb still being kept. An R.E. Officer came to see about building baths here for amb. use.	

2449 Wt. W14957/M90 750,000 1/16 J.B.C. & A. Forms/C.2118/12.

Instructions regarding War Diaries and Intelligence Summaries are contained in F. S. Regs., Part II. and the Staff Manual respectively. Title Pages will be prepared in manuscript.

WAR DIARY
or
INTELLIGENCE SUMMARY
(Erase heading not required.)

Army Form C. 2118.

100

Place	Date	Hour	Summary of Events and Information	Remarks and references to Appendices
VAUCHELLES	17.9.16		Lt G.L.K. WISELY 174 Bde RFA att 39 Div Art. RFA HQ's admitted with Diarrhoea.	
			Went over new Divisional Collecting Station site at , working party of 132 Fd amb at work. At present only holes have been made in the chalk. The ground is well marked along route to be followed by walking patients. Water can be had at ENGLEBELMER. The road surfaces have a good many bad holes. Tracks lead all over the hills, they would probably not be passable for carts in wet weather.	
			DDMS V Corps inspected this morning. He accentuated that the DRS is for patients requiring REST & not for those requiring much dressing. Likewise Sick Officers wards for instance an officer with Diarrhoea & slight Fever should not be kept unless he is markedly better in the 24 to 36 hours. Anti-craft guns dropt caps & shrapnell around grounds when shooting at a German aeroplane. No damage done.	
	18.9.16		Very wet night & morning.	
			Orders from ADMS 39th Div.:– 39th Div. extends its front line northward taking over front now held by 2nd Div.. 39 Div will take evacuation from REDAN & SERRE section	

2449 Wt. W14957/M90 750,000 1/16 J.B.C. & A. Forms/C.2118/12.

Army Form C. 2118.

WAR DIARY
or
INTELLIGENCE SUMMARY
(Erase heading not required.)

Instructions regarding War Diaries and Intelligence Summaries are contained in F. S. Regs., Part II. and the Staff Manual respectively. Title Pages will be prepared in manuscript.

101

Place	Date	Hour	Summary of Events and Information	Remarks and references to Appendices
VAUCHELLES	18/9/16		133 Fd amb. to find working party daily for Div^l Collecting Station at Q 31 b 10.5 of 1 NCO + 20 OR & to work this station as required in active operations.	
			Remainder of personnel lent to 134 Fd amb rejoined.	
			Capt Ferguson + St. Sgt. Tustain attended instruction in new small Box Respirator.	
	19/9/16	9.25	Wet all yesterday + last night. Fine now.	
		18	All orders that have to be read out were read at as strong as possible parade.	
			Working party for Div. Collecting Station started work today.	
			Reinforcement of 17 men arrived.	
			Lt O.S. BROADHURST A.V.C attd 39 Div Train Adm adm. diarrhoea	
			Lt I.M. BAIN 4/5 R. Highlanders adm. from 134 Fd amb, with Ischio Rectal abscess.	
	20/9/16		Still wet. Inspected draft, 2 men are not fit one with piles + one with old deranged knee.	
			Many light duty patients are employed as working parties in amb grounds.	
			Lieut PATEY attached temporarily to 132 Fd amb H.Q.'s.	
			2/Lt C BARTLETT 13/Surrey adm with debility	

2449 Wt. W14957/M90 750,000 1/16 J.B.C. & A. Forms/C.2118/12.

Instructions regarding War Diaries and Intelligence Summaries are contained in F. S. Regs., Part II. and the Staff Manual respectively. Title Pages will be prepared in manuscript.

WAR DIARY
or
INTELLIGENCE SUMMARY

(Erase heading not required.)

Army Form C. 2118.

102

Place	Date	Hour	Summary of Events and Information	Remarks and references to Appendices
VAUCHELLES	21/9/16		DDMS + DADMS V Corps inspected the village wells. All water to be tested + notices affixed + provision made to prevent water running back into wells + a stand provided for bucket. Corps Sanitary Station was to communicate direct with ADMS. ... Finer day. ADVS inspected. 2/Lt G. A. BROOKE 117 M. G. Coy adm^d Shell Shock (S)	
	22/9/16		In view of my remarks that the horses + ASC generally were less well kept than formerly the OC 39 Div^l Train inspected + stated that all was most satisfactory. R E Officer came + viewed ground for erection of baths for patients + scabies. Site was selected + report sent to ADMS 39th Div. Fine day. Capt Ferguson gave a demonstration lecture on new Small Box Respirator to as strong as possible parade.	

2449 Wt. W14957/M90 750,000 1/16 J.B.C. & A. Forms/C.2118/12.

Instructions regarding War Diaries and Intelligence Summaries are contained in F. S. Regs., Part II. and the Staff Manual respectively. Title Pages will be prepared in manuscript.

WAR DIARY
or
INTELLIGENCE SUMMARY
(Erase heading not required.)

Army Form C. 2118.

103

Place	Date	Hour	Summary of Events and Information	Remarks and references to Appendices
Vauchelles	23/9/16		Two RE officers came about building bath-house.	
			DADMS V Corps came, concerning a patient whom he wished not to be evacuated if possible.	
			2/Lt J L BERRY 13/Glosters adm with Sp ankle (R)	
			2/Lt G McLAUGLAN 234 Fd Coy RE with debility	
	24/9/16		Capt MACARTHUR returned from leave; & Capt Meech & Lt. Paty from temp'y detached duty.	
			Capt G R DONALD 4/5 R.H. adm Influenza	
			2/Lt R GOUGH A/179 Bde RFA with gas Poisoning (shell HE) - very slight.	
	25/9/16		Capt Meech detailed by ADMS for temp'y duty with 174 Bde RFA & I am to detail an officer for permanent duty with 39 DAC. In my opinion Capt Meech is most suitable. I submitted names of Capts Macarthur & Ferguson, the former being junior but of incomparably more value in Fd. Amb owing to being a practising surgeon.	
			Capt Meech returned as he found M.O. he was to relieve had recovered.	

2449 Wt. W14957/M90 750,000 1/16 J.B.C. & A. Forms/C.2118/12.

Instructions regarding War Diaries and Intelligence Summaries are contained in F. S. Regs., Part II. and the Staff Manual respectively. Title Pages will be prepared in manuscript.

WAR DIARY
or
INTELLIGENCE SUMMARY
(Erase heading not required.)

Army Form C. 2118.

104

Place	Date	Hour	Summary of Events and Information	Remarks and references to Appendices
Vauchelles	25/9/16		Orders from ADMS to hold 2 sections ready for removal at a moments notice. I had wagons loaded. Also Capt Robertson under same orders went to D.S. COIGNEUX J 9 a 83 with 1 NCO + 2 men whom he left there as retaining party + to acquaint themselves with surroundings. Capt Robertson to go on to HQ BUTERNE K 15 b 64 + to get in touch with OC this post + find out thoroughly the collection + evacuation of the area + to return to HQ on completion. This was done + report sent in to ADMS on 26.9.16. ADMS came here + inspected. The site of Soden was not liked but I pointed out it is the only practicable place.	
	26/9/16	7 45 pm	Orders from ADMS: I am to prepare to run D.C.S. at Q 31 b 95 as from tomorrow morning but not to move until I get the word. To prepare for 5-700 men. One Tent subdivision plus fuids. Capts Robertson + Beech to be the officers detailed. All cases to be admissions there, no other record will be taken + cases sent as before to Corps Collecting Station.	

2449 Wt. W14957/M90 750,000 1/16 J.B.C. & A. Forms/C.2118/12.

Instructions regarding War Diaries and Intelligence Summaries are contained in F. S. Regs., Part II. and the Staff Manual respectively. Title Pages will be prepared in manuscript.

WAR DIARY
or
INTELLIGENCE SUMMARY
(Erase heading not required.)

Army Form C. 2118.

105

Place	Date	Hour	Summary of Events and Information	Remarks and references to Appendices
Vauchelles	26/9/16		That OC 132 Fd amb to ask[?] details of running DCS, Capt Robertson did this.	
			Two Bearer subdivisions will be required for duty at Mesnil & Cookers.	
			I shall be left alone here at HQ but MO's i/c DAC & ASC will be sent to me.	
			The posts prospected by Capt Robertson will not be taken over in this Event.	
		10 pm	Further orders: 2nd Div. will attack through 39 Div.	
			All casualties of 2nd Div pass through 39 Div to Corps Collecting Station.	
			DCS will have staff of clerks to take all particulars of 2nd Div men.	
			Capt Hunter will report to OC 132 Fd amb for duty at Left Collecting Station (BERTRANCOURT).	
			Bearer subdivisions not required but to be kept ready at a moments notice.	
			I did not send working party to DCS in view of orders to be ready at a moments notice. This proved to be a wrong action for in reporting to ADMS	
			2/Lt B V GANDER V Corps Cyclists add Inf. Knee joint (R)	

2449 Wt. W14957/M90 750,000 1/16 J.B.C. & A. Forms/C.2118/12.

Instructions regarding War Diaries and Intelligence Summaries are contained in F. S. Regs., Part II. and the Staff Manual respectively. Title Pages will be prepared in manuscript.

WAR DIARY
or
INTELLIGENCE SUMMARY
(Erase heading not required.)

Army Form C. 2118.

106

Place	Date	Hour	Summary of Events and Information	Remarks and references to Appendices
Vauchelles	27/9/16	Noon	Stand by orders still hold. Am sending G S wagons out to collect material from Rt. Shield batter here.	
	28/9/16	17	Operation Rame order No 8 received. Jinks new DCS + ADMS 2nd Div will supply clerks to do all clerical work for 2nd Div. I send one bearer subdivn to 34 + keep one in readiness here. Capt Hunter is at disposal of 132 Fd Amb. 6 Horse Ambs, 24 GS wagons + 5 motor lorries + 2 Char-a-bancs are under me for removal of walking from DCS. ADMS came here to see + men, 2 were passed fit. Some rain.	
	29/9/16	1.30	Much rain in night + wet this morning. 2/Lt E. HAY 1/Camb adm GSW chest (slt). but has a cough. Lt J. D. S. MENZIES 18 T M BY adm with scabies.	

2449 Wt. W14957/M90 750,000 1/16 J.B.C. & A. Forms/C.2118/12.

Army Form C. 2118.

Instructions regarding War Diaries and Intelligence Summaries are contained in F. S. Regs., Part II. and the Staff Manual respectively. Title Pages will be prepared in manuscript.

WAR DIARY
or
INTELLIGENCE SUMMARY
(Erase heading not required.)

107

Place	Date	Hour	Summary of Events and Information	Remarks and references to Appendices
VAUCHELLES	30/9/16		Order from ADMS 39th Div: operation referred Div Rance operation order No 8 are cancelled. Condition now normal. Warm day. Work in hand for building baths here. No 72117 Pte A. GREEN Rance of this unit has been awarded the Military Medal under Military Secretary's letter No MS/H/22 60 d/ GHQ 2 June 1916 Admissions during month: DRS 935 Fd amb 244. 166 cases Scabies treated [signature] Williams Major OC 133 Fd amb.	

2449 Wt. W14957/M90 750,000 1/16 J.B.C. & A. Forms/C.2118/12.

Army Form C. 2118.

Instructions regarding War Diaries and Intelligence Summaries are contained in F. S. Regs., Part II. and the Staff Manual respectively. Title Pages will be prepared in manuscript.

WAR DIARY
or
INTELLIGENCE SUMMARY
(Erase heading not required.)

140/1815

Place	Date	Hour	Summary of Events and Information	Remarks and references to Appendices
Oct. 1916			Confidential War Diary 2 133 Field Ambulance October 1916	
Vol VIII				

2449 Wt. W14957/M90 750,000 1/16 J.B.C. & A. Forms/C.2118/12.

M897

D.A.G.
3rd Echelon
BASE

Herewith War diary of 133 Fld Ambulance for October 1916.

[signature] Capt R.A.M.C.
Adjt. 133rd Field Ambulance.

Copy

O.C. 133 Field Ambulance

Confidential

Original of your War Diary for the month of September received. I desire again to point out to you that your War Diaries are not satisfactory. The information required in accordance with F.S. Reg. Pt II and the Staff Manual respectively as previously pointed out are not being followed.

I note that there are no appendices. War Diaries to be of any value from a professional or intelligence point of view should contain matter bearing on important subjects professional or otherwise such as meteorological conditions, brief reports on important medical or surgical cases and such like.

[illegible]
A.D.M.S.
39th Div.

3-10-16

Army Form C. 2118.

WAR DIARY
or
INTELLIGENCE SUMMARY
(Erase heading not required.)

Instructions regarding War Diaries and Intelligence Summaries are contained in F. S. Regs., Part II. and the Staff Manual respectively. Title Pages will be prepared in manuscript.

108

Place	Date	Hour	Summary of Events and Information	Remarks and references to Appendices
VAUCHELLES	1/10/16		Return to old time by putting clock back to midnight at 1am.	
			Orders from ADMS 39 Div to be in readiness to move in 36 hours.	
			No orders as to whom I hand over to. Probably I go to CLAIRFAYE & will take Rest Station Cases with me.	
			All surplus equipment taken over by me to be handed over to incoming unit.	
			Proceeded to Clairfaye. It is a DRS under canvas.	
			AA & QMG No 39/1146/A of 30 inst & ADMS 1/713 of 1st approves my wearing badges of rank of a Lt. Colonel under GRO No 1821 of 25 Sept 1916	

2449 Wt. W14957/M90 750,000 1/16 J.B.C. & A. Forms/C.2118/12.

Instructions regarding War Diaries and Intelligence Summaries are contained in F. S. Regs., Part II. and the Staff Manual respectively. Title Pages will be prepared in manuscript.

WAR DIARY
or
INTELLIGENCE SUMMARY
(Erase heading not required.)

Army Form C. 2118.

109

Place	Date	Hour	Summary of Events and Information	Remarks and references to Appendices
Vauchelles	2/10/16		39 Div HQ's move to site at Q 26 C 01 on 2nd Office of ADMS near by at Q 31 b 95 Map 57 D opening at noon. Later order ADMS' Office will be at HEDAUVILLE Later order " " " remain at ACHEUX Lieut E.D. RICHARDSON posted to unit. Capt Robertson with advance party proceeded to EAST CLAIRFAYE O29 b 88	
EAST CLAIRFAYE	3/10/16		Handed over DRS etc to 1/3 Highland Fd Amb. Paraded at 4.30 pm to move out, Sir Douglas Haig passed + came up, after a short conversation he rode down the ranks remarking that the men looked well. Brought 135 patients with us i.e. Fd Amb DRS + Scabies patients. Arrived at EAST CLAIRFAYE at 6.45 pm. Horse lines in a very muddy field.	
	4/10/16		Wet all night + this morning. Ready for patients at 10 am. Came in afternoon No 55 Fd Amb transferred 42 patients tres of 2nd Corps, mostly diagnosed Shell Shock. ADMS 18th Div came + said that all kinds of patients of his Divn would be coming here until noon tomorrow.	

2449 Wt. W14957/M90 750,000 1/16 J.B.C. & A. Forms/C.2118/12.

Instructions regarding War Diaries and Intelligence Summaries are contained in F. S. Regs., Part II. and the Staff Manual respectively. Title Pages will be prepared in manuscript.

WAR DIARY
or
INTELLIGENCE SUMMARY
(Erase heading not required.)

Army Form C. 2118.

110

Place	Date	Hour	Summary of Events and Information	Remarks and references to Appendices
CLAIRFAYE	4/10/16		Patient with shattered forearm had to have it removed here.	
			Adms 39 Div came in evening.	
			Rance Operation order No 10. 39th Div relieves 18th Div in SCHWABEN	
			Redoubt Section by evening of 5th inst. To be held by 117 Inf Bde with 1	
			batt from each 116 & 118. HAMEL & RAVINE Sections held by 116 & 118	
			132 & 134 Fd Ambs. take over ADS's & Cabstand respectively.	
			Walking & lightly wounded cases come to me for my ADS book	
			Lying & serious by 30 MAC to CCS	
			2/Lt. WR GWATHNEY 111 Bde RFA admitted with Gonorrhoea	
			2/Lt WB SOLLY 74 T.M.By with cellulitis knee (L)	
			Lt RK BORGE 7/E. Kents GSW shoulder (L)	
			2/Lt GE DILLON 8/Norfolks neuralgia	
			2/Lt NF HAZE 10/Staffs attd 9/L.N.Lancs GSW thigh (R)	
			2/Lt W MAITLAND 8/S. Lancs mucous colitis	

2449 Wt. W14957/M90 750,000 1/16 J.B.C. & A. Forms/C.2118/12.

Instructions regarding War Diaries and Intelligence Summaries are contained in F. S. Regs., Part II. and the Staff Manual respectively. Title Pages will be prepared in manuscript.

WAR DIARY
or
INTELLIGENCE SUMMARY
(Erase heading not required.)

Army Form C. 2118.

111.

Place	Date	Hour	Summary of Events and Information	Remarks and references to Appendices
CLAIRFAYE	5/10/16		Saw all Shell Shock cases. In my opinion many should have been Contusion (W) instead of Shell Shock (S) or Shell (Buried). A few had symptoms & were suitable for C.C.S.	
			Fine day but not much of a drying day.	
			2/Lt L.D. FRIENSHIP 6/Berks adm. Inflam. of Bursa (L)	
			Lt M.M. WOODS 132 Fd Amb R.D.O.	
			Lt G.S. MORLEY D/58 Bde RFA Sent with ? T.B.	
			2/Lt J.J. DALEY 3/Leinster Regt att. 2/R I Rifles Enteritis	
			2/Lt L.J. IRELAND 8/Middx att 1/Herts Diarrhoea	
			2/Lt A.W. ALLAN 1/1 Cambs S.W. head.	
			Lieut W. PATEY struck off strength on unit on posting to 179 Bde RFA as M.O. i/c	
	6/10/16		Wet again last night with showers. 390 patients in. R.N.D. Fd Amb taken over West CLAIRFAYE. I arranged with them for arranging train loads, in event of both getting 150 patients & inflow continuing to make load of 250.	
			Capt G.D. ROBERTSON 133 Fd Amb adm with Trench Fever	
			2/Lt A.D. LEWIS 8/Border Regt " " S.W. back	

2449 Wt. W14957/M90 750,000 1/16 J.B.C. & A. Forms/C.2118/12.

WAR DIARY
or
INTELLIGENCE SUMMARY
(Erase heading not required.)

Instructions regarding War Diaries and Intelligence Summaries are contained in F. S. Regs., Part II. and the Staff Manual respectively. Title Pages will be prepared in manuscript.

Place	Date	Hour	Summary of Events and Information	Remarks and references to Appendices
CLAIRFAYE	7/10/16		Lieut OKELL has gone to 9 CCS CONTAY for temp'y duty " Richardson " " " 44 CCS PUCHEVILLERS " " 14 O.R. sent to 44 CCS DDMS II Corps here this morning. Inspected whole camp & horse lines. Desires accommodation to be increased, by putting up huts or tents or both. Horse lines to be commenced. He sent his DADMS in afternoon, he went into question of horse-lines, improvement to huts, enlargement of accommodation. Orders from ADMS 39 Div to open a collecting Post at Mailly Maillet for sick & wounded of 2 left batts. of 39 Div. Posts to be manned at White City Q 4 a 5 3, 2nd Avenue Q 9 b 95 Thurles Dump Q 10 c 13 Q 9 d 95 Sunken Road Q 3 a 83 Auchonvillers Q 9 a 11, here a Ford car & wheeled stretcher carrier will be kept. Collecting Post is to be made in Mailly Maillet preferably at Hotel de Ville Body of Brig. Gen'l HOWELL arrived here for burial, arrangements to be made for funeral at 11 am tomorrow by order DDMS II Corps. Heavy shower in night & again this evening.	

2449 Wt. W14957/M90 750,000 1/16 J.B.C. & A. Forms/C.2118/12.

Instructions regarding War Diaries and Intelligence Summaries are contained in F. S. Regs., Part II. and the Staff Manual respectively. Title Pages will be prepared in manuscript.

WAR DIARY
or
INTELLIGENCE SUMMARY
(Erase heading not required.)

Army Form C. 2118

113

Place	Date	Hour	Summary of Events and Information	Remarks and references to Appendices
	7/10/16		Rev Major J S B BROUGH CF adm with Influenza 2/Lt A. Rice-Oxley 15 Sqd RFC adm with [illegible] forearm (L)	
Clairfaye	8/10/16		2/Lt A.W. GILFILLAN 15 Sqd. RFC adm with Int. Derangement knee joint (L). Saw O i/c IInd Corps wood dump re timber shuts for this place. He said I must see SORE. The former inspected the huts that require repair & advised on them, his method with saw timber. Damp day but not much rain. At 7 pm a patient with wound of chest started haemorrhage so he is being sent off to CCS forthwith. Capt Meech submitted a report & requires 4 more men, collecting post at BLARNEY (Q12 d65), aid Post at WHITE City Q4 a53 - 3 men, TENDERLOIN 300x E. of White City 1 man to retain post, SPIROCHAETE CORNER Q9 b95 4 men, THURLES DUMP Q9 d95, 2 men, SUNKEN ROAD Q3 a83 - 2 men, AUCHONVILLERS Q9 a11 2 men this is rendezvous where a Ford is kept. 12/ & 13/ Sussex M.O.'s seen by Capt Meech. One wheeled Stretcher Carrier at SUNKEN Road; 3 more wanted one for THURLES DUMP one for 2nd AVENUE & one for WHITE CITY.	

Army Form C. [illegible]

Instructions regarding War Diaries and Intelligence Summaries are contained in F. S. Regs., Part II. and the Staff Manual respectively. Title Pages will be prepared in manuscript.

WAR DIARY
or
INTELLIGENCE SUMMARY

(Erase heading not required.)

112

Place	Date	Hour	Summary of Events and Information	Remarks and references to Appendices
Clairfaye	9/10/16		Went to BLARNEY HOUSE, Sunken Road & Spinochate Corner.	
			DDMS V Corps came while I was away. I saw OC 63rd RND Fd amb who is to hand me over some ground for erection of tents.	
			Body of Colonel FOUKS Russian General Staff brought here by order of DDMS II Corps.	
			Lt. A. RAMSEY 7/ M.G. Coy adm. GSW back (slight). Lt. M.C. DRUMMOND ~~[illegible]~~ 13/Glo with Diarrhoea. 2/Lt AE COOLING 1/4 Notts & Derby with GSW neck. 2/Lt DC EVANS 10/Cheshires with GSW Shoulder (R&L). 2/Lt TW MASON 39 Bde RFA with GSW back. Capt J. SIMMONS 10/Cheshires with GSW thigh (L)	
			Col. FOUKS removed for burial.	
	10/10/16		Fine day.	
			Lt T H HARRISON 130 Fd Coy RE adm. GSW jaw (L)	
			Capt P. SNOW-TALLARD 39 DAC adm. Gastritis.	

2449 Wt. W14957/M90 750,000 1/16 J.B.C. & A. Forms/C.2118/12.

Instructions regarding War Diaries and Intelligence Summaries are contained in F. S. Regs., Part II. and the Staff Manual respectively. Title Pages will be prepared in manuscript.

WAR DIARY
or
INTELLIGENCE SUMMARY
(Erase heading not required.)

Army Form C. 2118.

115

Place	Date	Hour	Summary of Events and Information	Remarks and references to Appendices
Clairfaye	11/10/16		Saw SORE re timber for improving huts & make horse standings; an officer of 135 AT Coy RE came to inspect in evening.	
			Orders from ADMS that 134 Fd Amb will take over posts at Mailley Maillet tomorrow & my party will return to HQ's. Also orders to evacuate all possible cases. Applied for a train & sent off 280 by 9.30pm train. Difficulty is in issuing packs to so large a number, this is more difficult than making the nominal rolls.	
			DADMS here in morning of 25 Div, cases sent here by their Fd Ambs. are to be shown as transfers by me.	
			2/Lt C.K. WAIT 1/Wilts add ICT Knee (L)	
			2/Lt S I JAMES 12/Sussex with ICT Heel (R)	
			2/Lt L.J. MORGAN 12/ " " Int. Derangement knee joint (R)	
			Capt A. READE 8/ S.Lancs " GSW leg (R)	

2449 Wt. W14957/M90 750,000 1/16 J.B.C. & A. Forms/C.2118/12.

Instructions regarding War Diaries and Intelligence Summaries are contained in F. S. Regs., Part II. and the Staff Manual respectively. Title Pages will be prepared in manuscript.

WAR DIARY
or
INTELLIGENCE SUMMARY
(Erase heading not required.)

Army Form C. 2118.

116

Place	Date	Hour	Summary of Events and Information	Remarks and references to Appendices
~~EST~~ CLAIRFAYE	10 11 16		RE started work on huts, removed ~~tar~~ tarpaulin & put up wire & felt.	
			Started bringing chalk for horse-lines	
			Making road through Camp with stones brought by lorry.	
			orders for normal times received	
			orders in evening that active operations at 3.17 pm on 13th inst	
			Capt MEECH & 36 men to go on 13th to CABSTAND by 10 am 13th –	
			" " + 20 bearers go to LANCASHIRE DUMP ADS under OC 132 Fdamb	
			30 bearers in reserve at CABSTAND.	
			I am to prepare for large number of wounded.	
			II Corps Ramc orders No 21 sitting cases with come to EAST CLAIRFAYE & wait to transfers there. To be evacuated to BEAUVAL [illegible] ~~LEZ~~ ANCOURT by light railway under arrangement made by me with Ecns, who states only walking cases should go there. Lying & non-walking to go by Car - MAC.	
			Lt I.M. BAIN 4/5 R Highlanders ad Rectal abscess	

2449 Wt. W14957/M90 750,000 1/16 J.B.C. & A. Forms/C.2118/12.

Instructions regarding War Diaries and Intelligence Summaries are contained in F. S. Regs., Part II. and the Staff Manual respectively. Title Pages will be prepared in manuscript.

WAR DIARY
or
INTELLIGENCE SUMMARY
(Erase heading not required.)

Army Form C. 2118.

133RD FLD. AMB.

117

Place	Date	Hour	Summary of Events and Information	Remarks and references to Appendices
CLAIRFAYE	13/10/16		Saw OC R.N.D. Fd Amb as to forming 2 train loads between them & us.	
			Capt Meech + 36 OR proceeded as ordered.	
			Scotch mist rain this morning.	
			2/Lt G. BROWN 1/Cambs ad. & transfer with BW Land	
			2/Lt A.M. DIAMANT 174 Bde RFA " " PUO	
	14/10/16		Zero time 2.46 pm today. ADMS saw unfit men, one to return to duty with Varicose veins, flat-foot to H.Q. Div' Coy & one to be Evacuated.	
			Patients - wounded - began coming between 4 & 5 pm.	
			One hut is completed with new roof - wire strained felt -.	
			V Corps not participating in attack as 63 R.N.D. Fd Amb receiving no wounded.	

Instructions regarding War Diaries and Intelligence Summaries are contained in F. S. Regs., Part II. and the Staff Manual respectively. Title Pages will be prepared in manuscript.

WAR DIARY
or
INTELLIGENCE SUMMARY
(Erase heading not required.)

Army Form C. 2118.

133RD FLD. AMB.

118

Place	Date	Hour	Summary of Events and Information	Remarks and references to Appendices
Clairfaye	14/10/16		2/Lt P.L. CLARK 11/Sussex adm Strain shoulder (L)	
			Capt J. A. MOFFAT 4/5 B. Watch adm GSW Head	
			" J. R. STICKLAND 1/Cambs " GSW arm & shoulder (L), hand & shoulder (R)	
	15/10/16		Wounded continued training all night. There are 9am - 204 walking cases. No train can be provided until number reaches 300. Rain in night.	
			About 60 trivial wounded came in & 29 German prisoners of war.	
			Found that I have albuminuria.	
			2/Lt L.V. EVANS 14/Hants adm myopia.	
			Pte TAYLOR. J.N. wounded.	
			[signature] Lt Col. OC 133 Fd Amb.	

2449 Wt. W14957/M90 750,000 1/16 J.B.C. & A. Forms/C.2118/12.

Instructions regarding War Diaries and Intelligence Summaries are contained in F. S. Regs., Part II. and the Staff Manual respectively. Title Pages will be prepared in manuscript.

WAR DIARY
or
~~INTELLIGENCE SUMMARY~~
(Erase heading not required.)

Army Form C. 2118.

133RD FLD. AMB.

119

Place	Date	Hour	Summary of Events and Information	Remarks and references to Appendices
CLAIRFAYE	16 10/16	9 A.M	Weather very cold but fair. Barometer 12 noon 29.7.	
			ADMS 39 Div notified that Lt Col. A.S. WILLIAMS RAMC commanding this unit was sick with albuminuria, and that he would have to be evacuated. Instructions were sent that Capt. G.D. ROBERTSON RAMC would assume temporary command of the unit.	
			I therefore took over all monies, secret documents, maps, and censor's stamp from Lt Col A.S. WILLIAMS before he was evacuated to the Officers CCS 29 CCS GEZAINCOURT at 2.30 p.m.	
		11.15 Am	CAPT. W.A. REES RAMC(TC) reported for duty with this unit and was taken on the strength accordingly, being posted O.C. "B" Section.	
			19 O.R. reported at headquarters from temporary duty with 134 Field Ambulance 39 Div. 16 O.R. still remain with 134 Fld Amb.	
		12 noon	10 New Marquees H.P. small arrived for II Corps Collecting Station. Started to pitch the marquees - They are difficult to erect but sent an N.C.O. to No 11 CCS VARENNES to learn method - Two were pitched by 4 pm	
		4 pm	The DADMS II Corps visited this unit, and warned me to be prepared to give light refreshments to 2000 - 3000 walking wounded and to be able to accommodate 800 sitting and lightly wounded walking cases.	
			Many sick and wounded continue to arrive day and night.	
			Orders received from ADMS to send the 10 new Marquees to the 134 Fld Ambulance. Two were already pitched so I explained the difficulty to DADMS II Corps who instructed me to send 8 to 134 Fld Amb - This was complied with.	
			Officers admitted to unit:-	
			(i) Lt. Col. A.S. WILLIAMS RAMC 133 Fld Amb. - Albuminuria. - 29 CCS GEZAINCOURT.	
			(ii) 2nd Lt. D.R. MITCHELL 16th Royal Fusiliers attd 116 M.G.C. - Scabies - 11 CCS ~~GEZAINCOURT~~ VARENNES	
			I returned 2 Horse Ambulance wagons & 3 G.S. wagons to 132 Fld Ambulance.	
			I returned 2 Horse Ambulance wagons to 134 Fld Ambulance.	
			Admitted Officers 1 O.R. 123 Remained Officers 4 O.R. 459.	

Army Form C. 2118.

WAR DIARY
or
~~INTELLIGENCE SUMMARY~~
(Erase heading not required.)

Instructions regarding War Diaries and Intelligence Summaries are contained in F. S. Regs., Part II. and the Staff Manual respectively. Title Pages will be prepared in manuscript.

133 Field Ambulance. 120

Place	Date	Hour	Summary of Events and Information	Remarks and references to Appendices
CLAIRFAYE	17 10/16		Weather cloudy and damp. Camp very muddy – Barometer 29.5 steady. St Sgt WILLIAMS RAMC evacuated to C.C.S by train – Gonorrhoea – contracted in BOULOGNE. CAPT. L.R. MEECH. RAMC returned to Hdq. from duty with bearer division. LIEUT. E.D. RICHARDSON RAMC returned to Hdq from temporary duty with No 44 C.C.S. Pte EVANS RAMC evacuated to the Base from No 44 CCS and is struck off the strength of this unit – Officers admitted 2nd Lieut ALLEN, F.H. 8th BORDER REG. – G.S.W. forehead accidental – Daily state. Officers admitted 1 OR. 87 Remained Officers 4 OR. 465. Orders received from ADMS for party of 1 Officer & 20 OR to proceed to COUIN to strike & bring to Hdq 20 Marquees. 18.10.16. 14 new pattern Square ended 6 old pattern. The 6 old pattern to be put aside in reserve – 2 new pattern to go to 134 Fd Amb CABSTAND. 8-10 new pattern to be erected at EAST CLAIRFAYE. The remaining 4 – 2 new pattern to be in held in reserve. Active operations postponed for 24 hours. Shell shock cases continue to arrive showing very little sign of any shock to the nervous system especially cases notified as "buried and shell shock". All sick evacuated to ~~No~~ 54 Fd Ambulance VADENCOURT.	
	18 10/16		Weather fair barometer 30. There was much shelling of hostile aeroplanes – the pieces from the anti aircraft shell falling on this Camp. One German aeroplane was seen to fall from a considerable height nose first as if struck. No 72025 A/Cpl. BURNETT. W. appointed A/Sgt with pay. } both to take effect from 17.10.16 No 65980 L/Cpl. HEMMING C.A. appointed A/Cpl with pay. } No 72166 Pte COPPING L.W.A. detailed for anti gas course 19.10.16. Officers admitted. CAPT. COOPER A.T. 1/7 NOTTS & Derby. – Shell shock. CAPT MEECH RAMC detailed as officer i/c Bearer Subdivisions on 19.10.16. To leave early. Four Sunbeam cars detailed from this unit for duty with 134 Fd Amb. 2 Horse Ambulance wagons and 3 G.S. wagons reported here for duty from 132 Fd Amb. 2 Horse Ambulance wagons reported here for duty from 134 Fd Amb During active operations tomorrow clerking is to be reduced to a minimum – all cases for CCS that are capable of walking 400 yds are to be sent to EAST CLAIRFAYE with C.C.S on their card and they are not to be entered on our A & D books. They go to CCS as transfers from 132 & 134 Fd Amb. Cases capable of walking & who will be well in a few days, are to be marked D.R.S and are to be entered as transfers on our A & D books.	

Instructions regarding War Diaries and Intelligence Summaries are contained in F. S. Regs., Part II. and the Staff Manual respectively. Title Pages will be prepared in manuscript.

Army Form C. 2118.

WAR DIARY
or
~~INTELLIGENCE SUMMARY~~
(Erase heading not required.)

133RD FLD. AMB.

121

Place	Date	Hour	Summary of Events and Information	Remarks and references to Appendices
CLAIRFAYE	19/10/16		Weather very wet. Barometer 29.4 falling –	
			Tent party not returned from COVIN.	
			CAPT. MEECH R.A.M.C with one bearer subdivision less 16 men detailed to report today to O.C. 134 Fd Amb.	
			Forwarded 2 H.P. marquees to 134 Fd Amb	
			Detailed Staff Sgt TUSTAIN to proceed in 82nd Sanitary Sect. lorry to assist the striking of tents at COVIN	
		10 Am	Water column lorry No 27585 ran into the ditch in the camp road and was unable to proceed owing to a broken cardan shaft. Emergency road had to be made round it with bundles of wood.	
	*	11 Am	D.D.M.S. II Corps visited this unit & the following instructions given –	
			(1) 51st Div sick were not to be admitted.	
			(2) That no sick were to be admitted for treatment to EAST CLAIRFAYE from 12 noon. All cases of belonging to II Corps were to go to 54 Fd Amb 18th Div. VADENCOURT.	
			(3) Scabies, opthalmic & dental cases to return to their units until after active operations –	
			4) Cases to 54 Fd Amb to be shown as transfers.	
			He appeared satisfied with the accommodation for patients.	
			72090 Pte WENNER J. to attend Anti gas course in place of 72166 Pte COPPING L.W.A.	
			CAPT. N.A. REES returned from 132 Fd Ambulance.	
			Admissions officers. – NIL.	
			Daily State. admissions Officers 0 OR. 32 Remaining Officers 2 OR 77.	
	20/10/16		Weather fair Barometer 29.7 Steady.	
			2 marquees returned from COVIN & 20 OR.	
			6 Charabancs reported from II Corps headquarters – notified ADMS & ordered to detain them until they were taken over by No 28 MAC	
			Water column lorry still bogged.	
			Pte SPALL, BROWN, HUGHES } 133 Fd Amb wounded while temporarily detached with 132 Fd Amb.	
			They were replaced from Hdq of unit by Ptes CLAYSON, FINCH, TUCK.	

2449 Wt. W14957/M90 750,000 1/16 J.B.C. & A. Forms/C.2118/12.

Instructions regarding War Diaries and Intelligence Summaries are contained in F. S. Regs., Part II. and the Staff Manual respectively. Title Pages will be prepared in manuscript.

WAR DIARY
or
INTELLIGENCE SUMMARY
(Erase heading not required.)

Army Form C. 2118.

133RD FLD. AMB. 122

Place	Date	Hour	Summary of Events and Information	Remarks and references to Appendices
CLAIRFAYE	20/10/16		Pte BOWERS and Pte EDEN returned to Hdq sick from 132 Fd Amb –	
		4 pm	The DADMS II Corps visited this unit & suggested the following measures –	
			(1) To have reserve rations for 2000 men at railhead ACHEUX.	Carried into effect 21/10/16
			(2) To have sufficient means to mix with all liquid refreshments for wounded men.	
			(3) To have a reserve stock of coal & coke & paraffin –	
			The O.C. 39 Divisional Train visited this unit to inspect horse lines & vehicles – He expressed satisfaction at the condition of all the animals & the condition of all vehicles.	
			The new horse standing in course of construction by R.E is progressing favourably –	
			6 Small marquees sent to ADMS 18 Div. for TARA CAMP. 14 Marquees now remain in possession of this unit.	
			The following is a list of principal diseases coming through this unit for week ending 20.10.16	
			I.C.T. & boils 82 P.U.O. 50 Influenza 53 Myalgia 27 Debility 18 Tonsillitis 10 Bronchitis 11 Debility from want of dentures 11 Impetigo 7 Haemorrhoids 9 Diarrhoea 21.	
			Admissions officers LT. BECK J. 4th Norfolks att. 17 KRRC – contused back. W.	
			2LT. PALMER L.S. 3/4 Dorset att. 118 M.G.C. – undescended Testicle –	
			2LT. PEACEY H.M. 3rd att. 12 R.SUSSEX. – Neuritis	
			Daily state admissions officers 3 O.R. 0 Remained officers 5 O.R. 3.	
			2 Tents struck & 4 pitched.	
			Bombardment clearly heard & appears heavy –	
	21/10/16		Weather clear cold Barometer 30 Steady.	
			Pte JOBSON proceed on special leave 10 days.	
			ZERO hour 12.7 noon.	
			All possible arrangements made to deal with an inrush of wounded. Q.M. Sgt SUAR to be i/c Evacuations.	
			DRS cases will have a buff clip as a distinguishing mark pinned to them & will go to tents 18.17.16.15.14.19.10.9.8.20	
			CCS cases to go to tents 1.2.3.11.12.6.5.4.7.13 – to overflow to Theatre.	
			Officers 2 tents.	
			Sgt PEEL & six men to be guides & manage the M. transport on main road – no lorries to be on camp road.	

2449 Wt. W14957/M90 750,000 1/16 J.B.C. & A. Forms/C.2118/12.

Instructions regarding War Diaries and Intelligence Summaries are contained in F. S. Regs., Part II. and the Staff Manual respectively. Title Pages will be prepared in manuscript.

WAR DIARY
or
~~INTELLIGENCE SUMMARY~~
(Erase heading not required.)

Army Form C. 2118.

133RD F.. . AMB. 123

Place	Date	Hour	Summary of Events and Information	Remarks and references to Appendices
CLAIRFAYE	21/10/16		All ranks to be at their posts at 2.30 P.M. Orders given to collect all bomb cartridges & explosives from wounded.	
		12 noon	Rendered my report to ADMS on the circumstances relating to three Pte returned to Duty without rations or sufficient clothing. Report requested from G.H.Q.	
		5.30 pm	Cases started coming about 5.30 pm. They arrived in chars a bancs in batches of 25–30. They were very cold and were badly in need of refreshments.	
		6.30.	200 cases in for CCS including wounded German prisoners – notified EMO ACHEUX by despatch rider of the number and that they were coming in fast. Instructed to have 400 cases at the entraining point by 10 p.m. Ordered horse transport which consisted of 4 Horse Ambulances & 9 G.S. wagons capable of carrying in one load 210 cases. First 200 went off very well but the second 200 took longer owing to the fact that it was extremely dark and the German prisoners had undressed contrary to orders & were difficult to dress quickly – The arrangement of tents worked admirably & would have allowed of a greater number passing through without inconvenience of any sort – All refreshments were given prior to their being taken to the evacuating tents – A few cases arrived as walking which ultimately developed into walking or sitting and had to be detained for the M.A.C in the morning – but on the whole the selection was done carefully at the A.D.S.	
		12.30 AM	Cases coming in slowly – no necessity to apply for another train. 95 German wounded prisoners of War were admitted. One was too bad to evacuate by train & was sent to No 11 CCS VARENNES 1 German prisoner was sent in from the Camp at CLAIRFAYE with appendicitis & was sent to N.11 CCS 1 German prisoner retained by order of II Corps was evacuated by Order of II Corps – 6 Officers passed through as CCS cases. 120 cases were admitted to DRS	
	22/10/16	~~[illegible]~~	Weather fine. Barometer 30' steady 400 were evacuated by train at 3.15 pm 4 cases remaining for evacuation	
		9.15 pm	There was a fire in one of the Officers huts in the flying corps Camp close to our horse lines – no panic amongst the horses. Hut burned out.	

Army Form C. 2118.

WAR DIARY

or

~~INTELLIGENCE SUMMARY~~

(Erase heading not required.)

Instructions regarding War Diaries and Intelligence Summaries are contained in F. S. Regs., Part II. and the Staff Manual respectively. Title Pages will be prepared in manuscript.

133RD FLD. AMB. 124.

Place	Date	Hour	Summary of Events and Information	Remarks and references to Appendices
CLAIRFAYE	23/10/16		Weather cold and foggy.	
			CAPT W.A. REES returned to Hdq.	
			D.R.S admissions 16 evacuated 3	
			Fld Amb " 9 " 9	
			L/Cpl DYE returned to Hdq from D.D.M.S SENLIS.	
			Hardly any wounded arriving -	
	24/10/16		Very wet. Barometer 29'.	
			Camp very dirty and muddy - Sanitation as good as conditions permit.	
			Several of personnel reporting sick with colds & slight fever -	
		7.30 am	Winter clothing issued. Fur jackets socks & inner socks for boots Field Service boots for mounted troops Sheepskin waistcoats.	
			200 blankets put through Foden lorry for 26 Prisoners War Camp.	
		2 pm.	Sent Ford car to evacuate sick from 14th HANTS at SENLIS to 54 Fld Amb VADENCOURT.	
			Active operations postponed a further 24 hours -	
			Pte BAKER RAMC evacuated to C.C.S from 132 Fld Amb - Shell shock	
	25/10/16		Very wet Barometer 29'.	
		9 Am.	Approached O.C 15 Squadron R.F.C with a view to restraining R.F.C men from wandering round the area occupied by this Fld Amb.	
			Canteen doing well.	
		10 Am.	ZS. 316 Pte METCALF. E. 63. Div. accidentally wounded by .25 bullet fired through negligence by Sgt VALENTINE 4/5 Black Watch. Bullet entered knee below right patella & penetrated the knee joint. Court of Inquiry held by O.C. Fld Amb with CAPT. A. HUNTER RAMC & CAPT. W.A. REES RAMC as members. AFB 117 sent to A.P.M. 63 Div for completion & proceedings of Court of Inquiry forwarded to ADMS 29 Div.	
		3 pm.	Claim for 95 fr from owner of turnip field by horse standings. ADMS requires report - inspected the damage & satisfied myself that it was not caused by this unit. R.F.C & German Prisoners Camp fatigue party responsible -	

2449 Wt. W14957/M90 750,000 1/16 J.B.C. & A. Forms/C.2118/12.

Instructions regarding War Diaries and Intelligence Summaries are contained in F. S. Regs., Part II. and the Staff Manual respectively. Title Pages will be prepared in manuscript.

WAR DIARY
or
~~INTELLIGENCE SUMMARY~~
(Erase heading not required.)

Army Form C. 2118.

133RD FLD. AMB. 125

Place	Date	Hour	Summary of Events and Information	Remarks and references to Appendices
CLAIRFAYE	26/10/16	9 AM	Orders received that Captain C H. Bowle will take command of this unit temporarily – Weather wet. Barometer 29.7 rising.	
		12 noon	DADMS II Corps visited the unit and gave instructions to obtain more trench boards for this camp, also to endeavour to obtain permission to tap the main water pipe in order to fill our water tanks direct and so obviate the necessity for a daily visit of the water lorry.	
		4 pm	Capt. CW Bowle arrived to take over command.	
			Saw the officer i/c R.E dump VARENNES and arranged that a working party of 1 NCO + 5 OR could make trench boards for this unit at the dump.	
			L/cpl STREET detailed as NCO	
			Nothing could be arranged with regard to the water supply.	
			Many sick arriving.	
			Admissions Officers 0 O.R. 32 } Field Ambulance Remaining " 1 " 35 }	
			Admissions Officers 0 O.R. 97 } D.R.S. Remaining " 0 O.R. 265 }	
			~~Officers~~ 21823 Pte DE HERSANTH T.H. admitted to 39 D.R.S. VADENCOURT.	
			65964 Pte BRADDY. A.F. appointed L/cpl with pay from 26th 10 16 inclusive.	
			26/10/16 [signature] Capt RAMC O.C. 133 Fd Amb.	

2449 Wt. W14957/M90 750,000 1/16 J.B.C. & A. Forms/C.2118/12.

Army Form C. 2118.

WAR DIARY
or
~~INTELLIGENCE SUMMARY~~
(Erase heading not required.)

Instructions regarding War Diaries and Intelligence Summaries are contained in F. S. Regs., Part II. and the Staff Manual respectively. Title Pages will be prepared in manuscript.

133RD FLD. AMB. 126

Place	Date	Hour	Summary of Events and Information	Remarks and references to Appendices
CLAIRFAYE	27/10/16		Weather cold wet and windy. Barometer 29.4 falling	
			LIEUT BADO A.J. RAMC reported for duty with this unit and taken on the strength of the unit accordingly.	
			Pte HOLLAND proceed to AMIENS for examination of eyes and returned.	
		10 AM	F.G.C.M. held in this unit on Y2066 Cpl LEGG RAMC in that he when on Active Service, striking a soldier in camp 3-10-16. President Major T.D. MURRAY 4/5 Royal Highlanders Members CAPT. A. HUNTER RAMC 133 Fld Amb & Capt L.G GOLD 1/1 HERTS. Rg	
		2.30	CAPT. A.W. REES RAMC detailed for duty at NO 9 C.C.S CONTAY & is struck off the strength of this unit accordingly.	
			Admissions Officers 0 O.R 104. Remaining 329.	
	28/10/16		Wet weather – Camp very muddy.	
			~~Cpl~~ Y2006 Cpl DEAN RAMC proceeded on 10 days special leave.	
			Pte SIMPSON RAMC evacuated to C.C.S 27.10.16 and struck off the strength.	
			One Sunbeam car returned to Hdq for duty. Cars now at Hdq 2 Ford cars & 1 Sunbeam.	
			Horse standings progressing very slowly.	
			Several ~~huts~~ huts require re roofing. Indented for wire netting & tarpaulin –	
			Admissions Officers 0 O.R 13 Remaining 65. Field Amb	
			" " 0 OR 19 " 230 D.R.S	
			Evacuations Officers 2 OR 50.	
			Road through camp very bad. No authority arrived to draw loads of stones.	
			6 Stoves & piping arrived from R.E.	
			20 rolls of wire netting " "	

2449 Wt. W14957/M90 750,000 1/16 J.B.C. & A. Forms/C.2118/12.

Instructions regarding War Diaries and Intelligence Summaries are contained in F. S. Regs., Part II. and the Staff Manual respectively. Title Pages will be prepared in manuscript.

WAR DIARY
or
~~INTELLIGENCE SUMMARY~~
(Erase heading not required.)

Army Form C. 2118.

133RD FLD. AMB. 127

Place	Date	Hour	Summary of Events and Information	Remarks and references to Appendices
CLAIRFAYE	29 10/16		Weather very wet. Barometer 29.2. LIEUT C.M. ANDERSON RAMC reported for duty and taken on the strength of unit accordingly. LIEUT. E.D. RICHARDSON RAMC detailed to report to D.A.D.M.S Ambulance Trains and is struck off the strength accordingly. 6228 Pte Fox RAMC transferred from No 30 MAC is taken on the strength of this unit accordingly. 72166 Pte COPPING RAMC transferred to 30 MAC is struck off the strength of this unit. 90 bench boards made by working party of this unit yesterday. Admissions Officers 0 OR 4 Evacuated 9 Remaining 59. (Fld Amb) admissions " 0 OR 4 Evacuated 42 Remaining 192 (D.R.S) Handed over all money and secret documents & maps to Capt. C.W. BOWLE RAMC.	
	30 10/16		Weather wet & very windy. Barometer 29. steady. L/Cpl STREET RAMC returned to Hdq from R.E dump VARENNES & reports that the saw mill has broken down. Only 27 bench boards made during the day. Nominal roll of qualified dental surgeons required (including W.O. N.C.O. O.R.) – NIL return. Admissions Officers 1. O.R. 8 Evacuated 5 Remaining 62 (Fld Amb) Admissions Officers 0. O.R. 23 Evacuated 20 Remaining 195. (D.R.S) Officer. CAPT. HALL R.O. Gen. Staff 39 Div. – Trench fever. Special note from ADMS requesting that he may be retained for treatment & to notify O.C. when fit to travel. Indented on German prisoners camp VARENNES for labour for 31-10-16. Special water lorry detailed for supplying EAST CLAIRFAYE. Two bell tent boards arrived from R.E.	

2449 Wt. W14957/M90 750,000 1/16 J.B.C. & A. Forms/C.2118/12.

Instructions regarding War Diaries and Intelligence Summaries are contained in F. S. Regs., Part II. and the Staff Manual respectively. Title Pages will be prepared in manuscript.

WAR DIARY
or
~~INTELLIGENCE SUMMARY~~
(Erase heading not required.)

Army Form C. 2118.

133RD FLD. AMB.

128

Place	Date	Hour	Summary of Events and Information	Remarks and references to Appendices
CLAIRFAYE	31/10/16		Weather clear with sunshine & slightly frosty falling towards night. Barometer 29.5 [illegible]	
		11. Am.	DDMS II Corps visited unit. Mentioned improvements necessary for road, and drainage of sodden areas of camp.	
			Labour from German prisoners camp arrived 8 men. Put on to road repairing. OC Prisoners Camp approached with a view of obtaining a larger number of prisoners for work in this camp.	
		2pm.	Sentence of F.G.C.M on 72066 Cpl. LEGG RAMC promulgated before a Fld Amb parade; the sentence was that 72066 Cpl LEGG found guilty. Reduced to the ranks and to undergo 28 days Field Punishment No 1. Sentence confirmed but whole of Fld Punishment No 1 remitted by G.O.C 29 Div.	
			Dental Surgeon visited unit from no 49 C.C.S CONTAY.	
			Admissions Officers – 0 OR. 4 Evacuations 5 Remaining 51 (Fld Amb)	
			" " 0 OR 13 " 31 " 177 (D.R.S)	

C W Howle.
Capt. RAMC
Commanding 133RD FLD. AMB.

Confidential

Vol 9

War Diary

of

133RD FLD. AMB.

39th Div.

from 1st November to 30th November

(Volume 9)

C.W. Bowle

LT COL. R.A.M.C.

O. C. 133RD FLD. AMB.

Instructions regarding War Diaries and Intelligence Summaries are contained in F. S. Regs., Part II. and the Staff Manual respectively. Title Pages will be prepared in manuscript.

WAR DIARY
or
~~INTELLIGENCE SUMMARY~~
(Erase heading not required.)

Army Form C. 2118.

133RD FLD. AMB.

129.

Place	Date	Hour	Summary of Events and Information	Remarks and references to Appendices
CLAIRFAYE	1/11/16		Weather fine during morning - Slight rain later Barometer 29.8 rising	
		10 am	ADMS & DADMS 39 Div visited the unit - inspected and signed Admission and Discharge books & remarked on their improvement since last inspection. Examined two patients brought up before him as P.B. men. The ADMS also visited the horse lines.	
			CAPT. A. HUNTER RAMC ordered to entrain at ACHEUX at 5 AM 2-11-16 on the termination of his contract. He is struck off the strength of this unit.	
			CAPT. A.W. REES RAMC returned to duty from No 9 C.C.S CONTAY and is taken on the strength accordingly. Total in O.R.S 2 officers - 250 other ranks	
		2 pm	Colonel MAYNARD-SMITH. AMS visited the unit and inspected the surgery he asked if tourniquets were examined found on patients admitted to this unit - and if they were kept on until the cases reached C.C.S. - he advised their removal at the earliest opportunity. Orders have been issued - acting on his advice	
			Duckboards are being made by this unit - working at the Engineers Dump - all available men are cleaning up the roads - digging drains with a view to ameliorating the waterlogged condition of the Station.	
			Special care is being taken to rid the men of lice - the Thresh disinfector is working day and night.	
	2/11/16	[illegible]	Very busy getting down duckboards and attending to the drainage of the camp. - Disinfection of patients clothing and blankets is proceeding satisfactorily - The kitchen and precincts is receiving urgent attention - A bath has been placed in the Officers ward and arrangements are	

2449 Wt. W14957/M90 750,000 1/16 J.B.C. & A. Forms/C.2118/12.

Instructions regarding War Diaries and Intelligence Summaries are contained in F. S. Regs., Part II. and the Staff Manual respectively. Title Pages will be prepared in manuscript.

WAR DIARY
or
~~INTELLIGENCE SUMMARY~~
(Erase heading not required.)

Army Form C. 2118.

133RD FLD. AMB.

Place	Date	Hour	Summary of Events and Information	Remarks and references to Appendices
CLAIRFAYE	2/11/16	Cont:	being made to improvise baths for patients - I am also making arrangements to wash the clothing of patients and articles used in the Cookhouse.	Wet weather.
	3/11/16.		G.O.C. Division inspected the Camp - he appeared to be quite pleased with the arrangements which were being made and made no adverse criticism - I informed him of the neglected state of the Camp when I took over Command - he told me that he thought we were doing well D.A.D.M.S. II Corps also visited the Station. The bathing of the men and disinfection of their Clothes goes on uninterruptedly - A barbers shop has been started and means have been provided to sterilize instruments used. The laundry is in working order and good work is being done All men fit for light duty are being used for road mending and draining the Camp. Loads of chalk are being put down in the Stables - the whole length of the stables has been tarpaulined - all horses of the	

2449 Wt. W14957/M90 750,000 1/16 J.B.C. & A. Forms/C.2118/12.

Army Form C. 2118.

Instructions regarding War Diaries and Intelligence Summaries are contained in F. S. Regs., Part II. and the Staff Manual respectively. Title Pages will be prepared in manuscript.

WAR DIARY
or
INTELLIGENCE SUMMARY

(Erase heading not required.)

133RD FLD. AMB.

Place	Date	Hour	Summary of Events and Information	Remarks and references to Appendices
CLAIRFAYE	3/11/16	Cnt.	Mules are now under cover and their backs and legs are now kept dry - A special latrine for the A.S.C has been erected harness and corn and hay are now under shelter.	
			Totals in Station - Officers 5. O.R 290.	
	4/11/16		Roofing of huts is being attended to. The Ablution Room has been reorganised and duckboards put down - The Scabies bath has been canvassed round and whitewashed - and an overall supplied to the orderly - New tins for receiving urine have been placed in the latrines - Duckboarding and drainage continues.	
			Totals in D.R.S. - 7 officers 307. O.R.	
	5/11/16		12 loads of metal for the roads are coming in and the road of entrance to the D.R.S. is being cleared up preparatory to receiving same. - Sumps are being dug and the sides of the road drained by a big ditch - Lumps of chalk border the edge to guide ambulances at night. - A new signboard has been erected and trees whitewashed at the entrance	
			Interviewed O.C. 2nd R.N.D. F.A. CLAIRFAYE and arranged	

2449 Wt. W14957/M90 750,000 1/16 J.B.C. & A. Forms/C.2118/12.

Instructions regarding War Diaries and Intelligence Summaries are contained in F. S. Regs., Part II. and the Staff Manual respectively. Title Pages will be prepared in manuscript.

WAR DIARY
or
INTELLIGENCE SUMMARY
(Erase heading not required.)

Army Form C. 2118.

133RD FLD. AMB.

Place	Date	Hour	Summary of Events and Information	Remarks and references to Appendices
CLAIRFAYE	5.11.16.	Cont.	with him that he should immediately clean up the Common Entrance to the F.A.S. & that in future this entrance should be kept swept by us both on alternate days - he informed me that he would apply for stones to put down on this entrance	
			The R.F.C. Squadron opposite to us have encroached on my billeting area - interviewed the O.C. and informed him of my views on this matter - and asked him to withdraw his vehicles from my ground. - he did not apparently fall in with my views - I shall give him 2 days to remove his Cars & materials & shall then see him again	
			Lieut. L. R. MEECH. RAMC arrived in from THIEPVAL	
	6.11.16.		Totals in D.R.S. 7 officers. 343 O.R.	
			150 baths have now been given to patients coming in from the line	
			450 blankets have been freed from lice.	
			Proceeded to BOUZINCOURT to comply with an order received from A.D.M.S. 39th Div. - the interview lasted about 1½ hours.	
			The Road skirting the office and dressing room is now being	

Instructions regarding War Diaries and Intelligence Summaries are contained in F. S. Regs., Part II. and the Staff Manual respectively. Title Pages will be prepared in manuscript.

WAR DIARY
or
~~INTELLIGENCE SUMMARY~~
(Erase heading not required.)

Army Form C. 2118.

133RD FLD. AMB.

Place	Date	Hour	Summary of Events and Information	Remarks and references to Appendices
CLAIRFAYE	6.11.16		installed - much progress has been made with drainage and duckboards in spite of the weather - I am making a Drying Room for drying clothing which has been washed in the Laundry. Totals in D.R.S. - Officers 9. O.R. 408. - Men are now leaving the weather but	
	7.11.16		D.R.S. with clean free clothes, having had a bath & hair cut - Laundry, Baths, Hair Cutting, Disinfecting in full swing - a large amount of work under these headings is being done.	
	8.11.16		Interviewed O.C. R.F.C. Squadron - chance got him to remove his Cars from the areas in question - Interviewed O.C.s No. 4. & 11 C.C.S. with reference to obtaining stretchers as I am wanting to place them in the Marquees - for the patients to lie on - as there are no tent-boards - only damp tarpaulins An officer of the Canadian R.E. informed me that it was proposed to run a double gauge railway through this site. - The digging of drains and wiring of duckboards proceeds apace.	
	9.11.16		The A.D.M.S. 39th Div inspected the Camp & was shewn the improvements that have been effected. he expressed himself as satisfied	

2449 Wt. W14957/M90 750,000 1/16 J.B.C. & A. Forms/C.2118/12.

Instructions regarding War Diaries and Intelligence Summaries are contained in F. S. Regs., Part II. and the Staff Manual respectively. Title Pages will be prepared in manuscript.

WAR DIARY
or
~~INTELLIGENCE~~ SUMMARY
(Erase heading not required.)

133RD FLD. AMB.

Army Form C. 2118.

Place	Date	Hour	Summary of Events and Information	Remarks and references to Appendices
Clairfaye	9/11/16	(Cont.)	with the work which is being & has been done.	Bright Sunny day.
	10/11/16	–	D.A.D.M.S. II Corps visited the Camp	
			Admissions 9 am – 9 pm 1 officer & 58 O.Rs	Bright Sunny day.
			Evacuations. to duty – 7	
			to C.C.S. – 23	
			Remaining 8 officers 442 O.Ranks — 68 men received baths	
	11/11/16.		The drying room is nearly complete – this is to be used for drying clothes washed in the laundry when the weather does not permit of clothes being dried & bleached outside	
			Made arrangements for a Dining Hall in the Theatre – Started an enlargement of the wash house – as the one already in existence does not fulfil requirements – Some large shells fell in the vicinity of the Camp towards Acheux.	
			Admissions 9am – 9pm. 50 O.Rs. Evacuated. to Duty 16. – CCS. 170 O.Rs & 1 officer	
			Remaining – 7 officers & 380 O.Rs.	
	12/11/16.		We are evacuating patients rapidly. D.M.S. called in about 2 pm. and gave directions that patients were to be evacuated by charabancs	

2449 Wt. W14957/M90 750,000 1/16 J.B.C. & A. Forms/C.2118/12.

Instructions regarding War Diaries and Intelligence Summaries are contained in F. S. Regs., Part II. and the Staff Manual respectively. Title Pages will be prepared in manuscript.

WAR DIARY
or
~~INTELLIGENCE SUMMARY~~
(Erase heading not required.)

Army Form C. 2118.

133RD FLD. AMB.

Place	Date	Hour	Summary of Events and Information	Remarks and references to Appendices
CLAIRFAYE	12/11/16	cont.	to BEAUVAL. Admissions 9am–9am: 87 O.Rs Evacuations to Duty 21	
			Evacuation to C.C.S. 226. O.Rs and 8 officers. Dull day.	Barometer 30+
	13/11/16	5.45 am	A terrific bombardment – commenced at dawn –	
		10.15	Lightly wounded walking cases began to come into the Station	
			6 Charabancs arrived at 9 am to convey patients to BEAUVAL	
			D.M.S and D.D.M.S visited the Station and I received orders from the former that Charabancs were to be used for evacuation and that we were not to make use of the trains at ACHEUX	
			Many wounded Germans passed through our hands	
			The wounded are all given hot cocoa, sandwiches, chocolate, field post cards & cigarettes after having been passed through the Receiving Room – they fall asleep as soon as they reach their cots.	
			Wired to D.M.S for 3 more [illegible] buses – as one of the first 6 has broken down.	Misty morning
			Admissions — 156 O.Rs	
			Evacuations — 98 O.Rs	
			Remaining — 235	
			A lecture was given to officers – subject – "Duties of Officers Serving in a Field Ambulance"	

2449 Wt. W14957/M90 750,000 1/16 J.B.C. & A. Forms/C.2118/12.

Instructions regarding War Diaries and Intelligence Summaries are contained in F. S. Regs., Part II. and the Staff Manual respectively. Title Pages will be prepared in manuscript.

WAR DIARY
or
INTELLIGENCE SUMMARY
(Erase heading not required.)

133RD FLD. AMB.

Army Form C. 2118.

Place	Date	Hour	Summary of Events and Information	Remarks and references to Appendices
CLAIRFAYE	14/11/16		D.D.M.S. inspected the Camp & said that he was pleased with what he had seen	Dull day. Barometer 30.
		5pm	I have received orders to return the Cars to headquarters.	
		5.45pm	6 Cases are to proceed to TARA HILL - Albert-Bapaume Rd.	
	15/11/16		Orders were received from the Division to move to BEAUVAL & to take orders for the march from 116th Bg. H.Q. - Equipment was speedily packed - but no movement orders were received - A.D.M.S 39th was communicated with, also a wire sent to the Brigade telling them we were ready to move. - As no orders to move were received we remained the night at CLAIRFAYE	
	16/11/16		There are still no orders to move - but owing to a communication from Lt. BADO. RAME. who had been sent on to BEAUVAL as billeting officer it was decided to march to BEAUVAL - The F.A. marched out of ~~the~~ CLAIRFAYE at 10.30 a.m. arriving at BEAUVAL at 2.30 p.m. Under instructions from ADMS 39th Div. Capts. Robertson McCarthur and Lt + Q.M. Curling were left behind to look after patients remaining in hospital and to hand over Equipment-	

2449 Wt. W14957/M90 750,000 1/16 J.B.C. & A. Forms/C.2118/12.

Army Form C. 2118.

WAR DIARY
or
~~INTELLIGENCE SUMMARY~~
(Erase heading not required.)

133RD FLD. AMB.

Instructions regarding War Diaries and Intelligence Summaries are contained in F. S. Regs., Part II. and the Staff Manual respectively. Title Pages will be prepared in manuscript.

Place	Date	Hour	Summary of Events and Information	Remarks and references to Appendices
BEAUVAL	16/11/16	cont.	Good billeting accommodation was found on arrival in the Rue de CANDAS. - Visited 111th Bg Hq. and A.D.M.S at Doullens.	
	17/11/16		Capt's Robertson MacArthur and Lieut Cowling joined up with the unit and reported that they had handed over the patients and Equipment to the incoming unit at Clairfaye. 13 men rejoined the unit from C.C.S. Puchvillers. 14 Reinforcements were received the remainder of the Reinforcement party were handed over to 134 F.A. The Foden lorry has arrived. Very cold.	
	18/11/16		Snow has fallen & the wind is very cold. Moved out from BEAUVAL at 8 a.m. to march to CANDAS arriving about 11.30 a.m. Entrained in the evening for ESQUELBECQ. The entrainment was quickly and skillfully carried out - the train arrived about 11 o/c a.m. (19th) The Motor Ambulances travelled by road in Convoy with the other Divisional F.A.S Cars. The Foden lorry was despatched Early this morning. CAPT. REES was evacuated to 29 C.C.S	
	19/11/16		Arrived at ESQUELBECQ at 11 o/c disentrained rapidly and marched	

2449 Wt. W14957/M90 750,000 1/16 J.B.C. & A. Forms/C.2118/12.

Instructions regarding War Diaries and Intelligence Summaries are contained in F. S. Regs., Part II. and the Staff Manual respectively. Title Pages will be prepared in manuscript.

WAR DIARY
or
~~INTELLIGENCE SUMMARY~~

(Erase heading not required.)

Army Form C. 2118.

133RD FLD. AMB.

Place	Date	Hour	Summary of Events and Information	Remarks and references to Appendices
ESQUELBECQ	19/11	Cont.	through Esquelbecq to WORMHOUT and then on to HERZEELE arriving about 10 o/c pm : Good billets were found prepared for us and a good hospital in the Chateau - the men were soon fed and comfortably housed in Sheds.	
HERZEELE	20/11		A.D.M.S. visited and advised the procuring of a clipping machine for the horses. - Busy cleaning up. - and white washing. Lt. BADO went to No. 225 F.C. R.E.	
	21/11		Busy cleaning up. The ambulances and wagons, limbers and water carts are all being washed in the pond. and the making bricked standing and shelters for the horses proceeded with.	
	22/11		Carts and saddlery are being cleaned - the latter are being dubbined of which they are much in need. Lieut. Anderson returned from temporary duty with 134 F.A.	
	23/11		The work of cleaning up having been got well forward - the men spent the afternoon playing football.	
	24/11		A Belgian interpreter M. ETIENNE MINNE has joined up to replace M. JAMBEAUX who has been ordered to rejoin the French Mission. The men of A. Sect: went for a route march in the afternoon	

2449 Wt. W14957/M90 750,000 1/16 J.B.C. & A. Forms/C.2118/12.

Army Form C. 2118.

Instructions regarding War Diaries and Intelligence Summaries are contained in F. S. Regs., Part II. and the Staff Manual respectively. Title Pages will be prepared in manuscript.

WAR DIARY
or
INTELLIGENCE SUMMARY
(Erase heading not required.)

133RD FLD. AMB.

Place	Date	Hour	Summary of Events and Information	Remarks and references to Appendices
HERZEELE	25/11/16		[illegible] are being made - Orders are being given to move the latrine sites - as owing to their position on the low lying portion of the camp - they have become unfit for further use. The stables are being drained and a pathway made for use of piquets.	
	26/11/16		Two of the Sheds in the personnel billeting area are being used as overflow accomodation for patients - Small Stoves have been constructed and Straw is being supplied for filling paillasses	
	27/11/16		Duck boards are being put down - Kitchens are being whitewashed and roofing of the Stables is being completed. 30 patients in hospital	
	28/11/16		The Foden lorry went to 134 F.A. under instructions received from ADMS - Inspected Sites for Scabies Hospital. DDMS visited the F.A. Capt. MacArthur RAMC proceeded to BOULOGNE on 48 hours leave.	
	29/11/16		The latrines have been moved to a more favourable site. Horses are being clipped trace high - by hand machine - (rotary machine not being available). The work of sanitation and improvement continues. Inspected Sites for proposed Scabies Hospital. Report sent to ADMS.	
	30/11/16		Ablution benches have been constructed - 24 cases in hospital. Small box Respirators were issued to all ranks	

C.W. [illegible] Lt. Col. RAMC
Comdg. 133 F.A.

2449 Wt. W14957/M90 750,000 1/16 J.B.C. & A. Forms/C.2118/12.

140/98. Vol 10

Confidential

War Diary
of

33rd Div.

133RD FLD. AMB.

from December 1st 1916

to December 31st 1916

(Volume 10)

C.W. Howle
Lt-Col. R.A.M.C.
Cmdg. 133. F.A.

Army Form C. 2118.

WAR DIARY
or
~~INTELLIGENCE SUMMARY~~
(Erase heading not required.)

133RD FLD. AMB.

Instructions regarding War Diaries and Intelligence Summaries are contained in F. S. Regs., Part II. and the Staff Manual respectively. Title Pages will be prepared in manuscript.

Place	Date	Hour	Summary of Events and Information	Remarks and references to Appendices
HERZEELE	1/12/16	-	The drainage of the site of the Field Ambulance is receiving careful attention – a fatigue party is kept constantly at the work. Paths are being made. The stables now contain sufficient bricked standing for the horses to take all except mules – standing for mules is receiving attention.	
		9.30 am	The personnel were inspected and found to be efficient in the use of the box respirator. – Tests on the march are being carried out.	Frosty weather.
	2/12/16		The ablution shelter for personnel is now in working order.	
	3/12/16		A parade was ordered for the re-issuing of clothing. The personnel latrine close to the hutments has been moved to another site close to the duckboarding – and night-urinals have been provided and are stacked on a platform between the huts during the day.	
	4/12/16	10.30 am	A.D.M.S. & D.D.M.S. inspected the Field Ambulance & made various observations for the improvement of things in general. These were carefully noted down and are receiving immediate attention. Lt. LIMBERY RAMC reported for duty.	

2449 Wt. W14957/M90 750,000 1/16 J.B.C. & A. Forms/C.2118/12.

Instructions regarding War Diaries and Intelligence Summaries are contained in F. S. Regs., Part II. and the Staff Manual respectively. Title Pages will be prepared in manuscript.

WAR DIARY
or
~~INTELLIGENCE SUMMARY~~
(Erase heading not required.)

133RD FLD. AMB.

Army Form C. 2118.

Place	Date	Hour	Summary of Events and Information	Remarks and references to Appendices
HERZEELE	5 12/16	.	Nothing of importance occurred worthy of special mention. Capt. WARWICK R.A.M.C.	reported for ~~[illegible]~~ duty
	6 12/16	.	Reported to A.D.M.S. at ESQUELBECQ. - who gave directions as to correspondence in routine work. This matter is receiving careful attention & the necessary orders have been given.	
	7 12/16	.	A.D.M.S. 38th Division inspected the site of this Field Ambulance and expressed himself as pleased with the work done here as to improvements effected. He especially remarked on the improvements in the horse lines.	
			I am proceeding on leave on the 8th. In my absence the work is being carried on by Capt. Robertson R.A.M.C. C. W. Hawke Lt. Col. RAMC	
			Five reinforcements were received. Pte Cuff RAMC. reported to D.D.M.S. HAVRE.	
	8 12/16		Lt. Limbery reported for duty from the 38th Division	
			Lt. Bodo reported for duty from the 16th Notts & Derbys.	
	9 12/16	.	Lt Anderson returned from the 38th Division & reported for duty.	
		7. pm	A Concert was held in the evening. Was well attended & was a success.	

2449 Wt. W14957/M90 750,000 1/16 J.B.C. & A. Forms/C.2118/12.

Army Form C. 2118.

Instructions regarding War Diaries and Intelligence Summaries are contained in F. S. Regs., Part II. and the Staff Manual respectively. Title Pages will be prepared in manuscript.

WAR DIARY
or
~~INTELLIGENCE SUMMARY~~ 133RD FLD. AMB.

(Erase heading not required.)

Place	Date	Hour	Summary of Events and Information	Remarks and references to Appendices
HERZEELE	10/12/16	.	Capt Warwick RAMC reported for duty to 17th K.R.Rs	
			Lt. Bado RAMC reported to A.D.M.S. 38th Division for instruction in duties with C.R.E.	
	11/12/16	9.10 am	An Enemy aeroplane dropped a bomb mortally wounding Sgt. Barber and wounding Sgt. Burnett. Ptes Timms, Ealey, Jones E., Nation, Aylett and Jolly – All were evacuated to C.C.S. except Sgt. Burnett and Pte Jolly.	
			Lt. Limbery RAMC and advanced party of 1 N.C.O. & 11 O.Rs left for A.D.S. east of YPRES.	
			1 N.C.O. & 1 O.R. left for duty at R.E. yard.	
			S/Sgt. Justain. Ptes Holland & North left for Bde Headquarters in connection with a Concert party.	
	12/12/16		Lt. Anderson RAMC reported for duty to 134 F.A.	
	13/12/16	10. am	The Unit moved from HERZEELE to A.28 a 3.6. arriving at 3.10 pm. Notification received that Sgt. Barber of this unit had died of wounds (13.12.16.)	

2449 Wt. W14957/M90 750,000 1/16 J.B.C. & A. Forms/C.2118/12.

Army Form C. 2118.

WAR DIARY
or
INTELLIGENCE SUMMARY

(Erase heading not required.)

133RD FLD. AMB.

Instructions regarding War Diaries and Intelligence Summaries are contained in F. S. Regs., Part II. and the Staff Manual respectively. Title Pages will be prepared in manuscript.

Place	Date	Hour	Summary of Events and Information — Map. 28 1/40.000. Ed. 3.	Remarks and references to Appendices
A.28. a 3.6.	13/12/16	10 p.m.	Capt. Robertson & Capt. Meech inspected the A.D.S. —	100 Sand bags indented for.
	14/12/16		The day was spent in cleaning up and making arrangements for the reception of Sick & wounded.	
	15/12/16	.	Capt. Meech reported to the Town Major YPRES. to arrange for the collection of bricks to repair the approach road which is in urgent need of repairs. 1 NCO & 6 men sent to billets in YPRES. - a good cellar has been found. Wagons fetch the bricks back to camp after dark.	
	16/12/16	.	Lt. Anderson rejoined from 134 F. A. - Capt. Robertson visited A.D.S. to make arrangements for evacuation of Sick & wounded	
	17/12/16	.	Orders were issued that boots were to be always kept well-dubbined - Sgt. Earle returned from the Gas School.	Should have been signed by Capt. Robertson if Acting. RB
	18/12/16	12.30 am	A.D.M.S. VIII Corps inspected the F.A.	
	19/12/16		Lt. Col. C.W. Bowle RAMC returned from leave.	
	20th	.	A.D.M.S. visited the Camp & made various suggestions for alterations and improvements especially as regards airing & lighting of rooms. - these were noted & steps taken to act upon them.	

2449 Wt. W14957/M90 750,000 1/16 J.B.C. & A. Forms/C.2118/12.

Army Form C. 2118.

WAR DIARY
or
INTELLIGENCE SUMMARY

(Erase heading not required.)

133RD FLD. AMB.

Place	Date	Hour	Map 28. 1:40.000 Ed 3. Summary of Events and Information	Remarks and references to Appendices
A. 28. a. 8. 8	21/12/16	.	Capt. Robertson R.A.M.C. departed to take over Command temporarily of 134. F.A.	Very wet.
	22/12/16	.	A thawing room with cement flooring is being made The Shoemakers shop has been extended.	
		10.30 pm	I made a reconnaissance for an A.D.S. in the vicinity of Outskirts Farm. – found a suitable place near the Wds X Rd. also another place at LA, BRIQUE – but this latter place is only splinter proof. whereas the former is proof against a 5.9. – a report on these places is being sent in to the A.D.M.S. I attended 2nd Army Med. Society discussion at HAZEBROUCK in the afternoon.	
	23/12/16	.	G.O.C Division inspected the Ambulance – he noted that night-duty men were lying about in the huts – I am having a night orderlys room set-apart for these men.	Windy day
	24/12/16	2.30	Attended a conference at the A.D.M.S.'s Office – his remarks were carefully noted e.g. Training of officers, dress, airing of rooms etc. A window has been placed in the MAIN WARD. – this is a great improvement.	

Army Form C. 2118.

Instructions regarding War Diaries and Intelligence Summaries are contained in F. S. Regs., Part II. and the Staff Manual respectively. Title Pages will be prepared in manuscript.

WAR DIARY
or
~~INTELLIGENCE~~ SUMMARY
(Erase heading not required.)

133RD FLD. AMB.

Place	Date	Hour	Summary of Events and Information	Remarks and references to Appendices
A 28. a. 3.6.	24/12/16	Cont.	A case of Scarlet Fever has been admitted to hospital disposed of to C.C.S. at PROVEN. - The necessary disinfection steps have been taken.	
	25/12/16	"	Capt. MEECH. M.C. RAMC has been given leave to go to Canada. he departed at mid-day on 42 days leave. A good dinner was provided for the men. The A.S.C. dined separately - I visited all dinners - all the men were delighted & satisfied with what had been prepared for them - many cheers were given	
	26/12/16	"	Cpl. Pack and 1 O.R. reported to A.D.M.S. for duty with Batts. Pte. Aylett who was wounded on the 13th inst. was returned to duty by C.C.S. Another party has gone to YPRES to collect bricks for the repair of roads. in relief of the party already there. 12 men were bathed last night. (Personnel)	
	27th/12/16.	10 a.m.	The D.D.M.S. inspected the Unit - he suggested that there should be a separate place for Medical Stores in the Dispensary. I am taking necessary steps to make provision for this - he paid special attention	

2449 Wt. W14957/M90 750,000 1/16 J.B.C. & A. Forms/C.2118/12.

Army Form C. 2118.

WAR DIARY
or
~~INTELLIGENCE SUMMARY~~

(Erase heading not required.)

133RD FLD. AMB.

Instructions regarding War Diaries and Intelligence Summaries are contained in F. S. Regs., Part II. and the Staff Manual respectively. Title Pages will be prepared in manuscript.

Place	Date	Hour	Maps A 28 1/40.000 & ?E. Summary of Events and Information	Remarks and references to Appendices
A. 28. a. 3.1.	27/12/16	Cont.	to drains - all of which were working well - he also suggested new oil cloth for the table in the Hospital Ward. - this has been changed.	
	28/12/16	10.30 am	A.D.V.S inspected the horse lines & was apparently quite satisfied with the condition of our horses.	
		6 pm	I inspected ~~my~~ A.D.S. at OUTSKIRT FARM and found everything correct - & well cared for. Whitewash is being liberally used and the structure reinforced with sandbags. Went up to the Regimental Aid Post - & found that my men were comfortable in a good dugout. I suggested to the M.O. that he might strengthen the dug out with more sandbagging.	
	29/12/16		I am building a new bath house close to the wards - which will be convenient for the patients - I propose having a hair dressers shop here too adjoining the ablution room. Received orders to open up an A.D.S. at Larry Farm (B.9 c 2 3). An Engineer officer visited me with reference to the repair and upkeep of my approach road - he has the matter in hand meanwhile I am repairing with bricks from YPRES. A Conference was held here - & was attended by 7. R.M.Os - various subjects discussed.	Wrt. letter

2449 Wt. W14957/M90 750,000 1/16 J.B.C. & A. Forms/C.2118/12.

Instructions regarding War Diaries and Intelligence Summaries are contained in F. S. Regs., Part II. and the Staff Manual respectively. Title Pages will be prepared in manuscript.

WAR DIARY
or
~~INTELLIGENCE SUMMARY~~

(Erase heading not required.)

133RD FLD. AMB.

Army Form C. 2118.

Place	Date	Hour	Summary of Events and Information	Remarks and references to Appendices
A28 a 36	30 12/16	10 AM	Busy morning inspecting the precincts of the camp and attending to correspondence. The butchers shop has been cemented and now has an excellent floor which can be well drained & kept clean. A thawing chamber is in process of construction. The tailors shop has been enlarged. Many repairs have been executed by the Carpenters. Many dilapidations had occurred owing to the recent storms.	Dull day.
		2-30 pm	Visited the A.D.M.S. at H.Q. His remarks were carefully noted. He handed over 2 baths for my use of which use is being made.	
			Lt Anderson prospected LARRY FARM and BOESINGHE CHATEAU.	
	31 12/16	11 Am	Inspected the A.D.S party for LARRY FARM. Sgt GOODSMARK is N.C.O. i/c. Some of the mens boots were not well dubbined. Orders were given to rectify this.	Dull day
		11.30 am	CAPT WARWICK R.A.M.C. reported for duty. 200 blankets have arrived. The window in the Ward has been finished – a good job has been made of it & a great improvement is noticeable.	

C. W. Dowle Lt Col RAMC
Cmdg. 133. Field Amb.

2449 Wt. W14957/M90 750,000 1/16 J.B.C. & A. Forms/C.2118/12.

Confidential

War Diary

of

133RD FLD. AMB.

from January 1st 1917
to January 31st 1917

(Volume 11)

C.W. Bowle
LT. COL. RAMC.
O. C. 133RD FLD. AMB.

Original
Vol XI

Instructions regarding War Diaries and Intelligence Summaries are contained in F. S. Regs., Part II. and the Staff Manual respectively. Title Pages will be prepared in manuscript.

WAR DIARY
or
~~INTELLIGENCE~~ SUMMARY
(Erase heading not required.)

Army Form C. 2118.

133RD FLD. AMB.

Place	Date	Hour	Map A 28 1.40000 Summary of Events and Information	Remarks and references to Appendices
A.28.a.3.6.	1/1/17		Capt. WARWICK RAMC. Sgt. MACKIE and Cpl HEMING and 12 O.Rs proceeded to OUTSKIRTS FARM to relieve Lt. LIMBERY RAMC & the 14 men who have been doing duty there.	
		4 pm	I inspected A.D.S at LARRY FARM and walked up to the R.A.P. at BOESINGHE CHATEAU on the YSER CANAL - I found my men were sleeping in a very damp dug out and suggested to the M.O. of 11th Sussex that steps should be taken to rectify this. I gave instruction to Senior N.C.O. at LARRY Farm to strengthen the Aid Post with sand bags.	
	2/1/17		Drew 800 francs to pay the men.	
		2.30 p.m.	Visited A.D.M.S. - brought back some rat traps and 2 Zinc Baths.	
			Lt LIMBERY RAMC reported for duty at HQ from A.D.S.	
			About 20 men had a change of clothing at the Baths.	
			Capt. ROBERTSON reported for duty from 134 F.A.	
			One man died in Hospital of wounds received. (11th R. Sussex)	
	3/1/17		Capt MacArthur RAMC. delivered a lecture ~~of~~ on Care of Feet at Div Schools VOLKERINGHOVE.	
			Rev. HAWKINS C of E. visited us - conducted a service and was informed of the death of a soldier in Hospital.	

2449 Wt. W14957/M90 750,000 1/16 J.B.C. & A. Forms/C.2118/12.

Instructions regarding War Diaries and Intelligence Summaries are contained in F. S. Regs., Part II. and the Staff Manual respectively. Title Pages will be prepared in manuscript.

WAR DIARY
or
~~INTELLIGENCE~~ SUMMARY
(Erase heading not required.)

Army Form C. 2118.

133RD FLD. AMB.

Place	Date	Hour	Summary of Events and Information — Map A 28. 1.40,000	Remarks and references to Appendices
A.28.a.3.1	3/1/17	Cont.	Capt. ROBERTSON R.A.M.C. proceeded on 14 days leave to England. The Cook house is being improved – a cement floor has been laid in the pantry. – A patients bath house with cement floor is being made.	
			A great deal of work is being done on the approach road daily, the holes are being filled in with bricks and drainage is receiving attention	Very mild weather
			26 men received Baths & changes of underclothing.	
	4/1/17	10 a.m.	Rev. HAWKINS conducted a funeral on a Soldier of the 11th Sussex Regt. (Pte Cooper) at Elverdinghe Cemetery.	Very wet
			L/Cpl. Street reported to the Unit from C.C.S.	
			Lt. LIMBERY R.A.M.C. prospected a site for a Collecting post at BRIELEN. Am making a pergola at entrance of F.A. to take some red X lights – all will be whitewashed and should look well	Bright morning
	5/1/17		Great enemy aeroplane activity. – Advice was given to air all blankets in the sun. Prospected a dug-out in BRIELEN for the accommodation of wounded.	Bright morning
			Inspected A.D.S. at Outskirts Farm and Lacey Farm.	
			A Case of Measles was admitted from 38th Division Schools. – YPRES heavily shelled	

2449 Wt. W14957/M90 750,000 1/16 J.B.C. & A. Forms/C.2118/12.

Instructions regarding War Diaries and Intelligence Summaries are contained in F. S. Regs., Part II. and the Staff Manual respectively. Title Pages will be prepared in manuscript.

WAR DIARY
or
~~INTELLIGENCE SUMMARY~~
(Erase heading not required.)

Army Form C. 2118.

133RD FLD. AMB.

Place	Date	Hour	Summary of Events and Information	Remarks and references to Appendices
A 28. a 3.8.	6/1/17	10 am.	Presided at a Board on P. B. men —	[illegible]
			Visited 134 F.A.	
			No. T4/+5-7892 S/Sgt. FRASER J.N. promoted to permanent rank (A.S.C.)	
	7/1/17	12 am.	Lt Bissel R.F.C. wounded in the head whilst flying over the Salient was attended to & sent direct to C.C.S. — I fear he will not recover.	
		2.30 pm	Football match played against D.A.D.O.S team.	
	8/1/17	.	Enemy shelled YPRES. a man of my brick plague party was wounded by a shell (Pte Jones, J.)	
			Visited O.C. 2/1 WESSEX F.A. The College POPERINGHE.	
	9/1/17	.	Inspected A.D.S. LARRY FARM — also tried to confirm a report by A.D.M.S. that another Aid Post existed near BOESINGHE CHATEAU — no such post exists.	
	10/1/17	2.30 pm	Heavy bombardment. POPERINGHE shelled —	
		3 pm	Bombardment continued until 6.30 pm — an aeroplane fell near our Camp. and a captive balloon was seen to explode.	
			6 Reinforcements received — two only retained remainder sent on to 134. F.A.	
		2.30 pm	Conference Regt. M.O.s at H.Q. 133. F.A.	

2449 Wt. W14957/M90 750,000 1/16 J.B.C. & A. Forms/C.2118/12.

Army Form C. 2118.

Instructions regarding War Diaries and Intelligence Summaries are contained in F. S. Regs., Part II. and the Staff Manual respectively. Title Pages will be prepared in manuscript.

WAR DIARY
or
~~INTELLIGENCE SUMMARY~~

(Erase heading not required.)

133RD FLD. AMB.

Place	Date	Hour	Summary of Events and Information	Remarks and references to Appendices
A28 a 3.1.	11/1/17	2.30 pm	Attended a Conference at 2-30pm at ADMS's office. his remarks noted.	
			Lt Limbery RAMC made a reconnaissance of our new advanced posts to be shortly taken over. 1 N.Co. & 4 men accompanied him and are remaining at the ~~A.D.S~~ Asylum YPRES.	
			Visited the COLLEGE POPERINGHE and made arrangements with the O.C. 2/1 Wessex F.A.	
	12/1/17	11 am	Visited O.C. 2/1 Wessex F.A. and arranged times of relief to be made. Busy getting out orders for the move	
			1 horse. H.D. evacuated sick to M.V.S.	
	13/1/17	6 pm	Took over the ASYLUM - YPRES. - A.D.S. M.O. i/c Lt LIMBERY. RAMC and the necessary personnel relieved the outgoing F.A. at time stated	
			Inspected R.A.Ps at St JEAN and the EMBANKMENT - also the two C.P.s at MENIN Rd and the CANAL BANK - and found them complete in personnel and Equipment -	Ray Cold [illegible]
			One Sunbeam car was hit by shell fire - the steering wheel was knock completely off - the radiator was smashed and the body riddled with bullets - the driver contrived to escape in some miraculous way.	

2449 Wt. W14957/M90 750,000 1/16 J.B.C. & A. Forms/C.2118/12.

Instructions regarding War Diaries and Intelligence Summaries are contained in F. S. Regs., Part II. and the Staff Manual respectively. Title Pages will be prepared in manuscript.

WAR DIARY
or
~~INTELLIGENCE SUMMARY~~

(Erase heading not required.)

Army Form C. 2118.

133RD FLD. AMB.

Place	Date	Hour	Map. A28. 1:40,000 Summary of Events and Information	Remarks and references to Appendices
A28. a.3.6.	13/1/17		Capt Warwick Rame rejoined H.Q. from A.D.S. Ferskens Farm. with personnel and Equipment.	
			Sgt. Goldsmark Rame rejoined H.Q. from A.D.S. LARRY Farm.	
	14/1/17	10.15 am	The unit moved from M.D.S. A28 a.3.6. to the COLLEGE POPERINGHE. and found the place very dirty. - much time will have to be spent cleaning it up - it is a large rambling place with many passages and stairs a little room for its size - all the windows are broken - Two enemy shells fell - one within 10 yds. and the other within 40 yds of the Officers Mess. on the 10th 1.17.	
	15/1/17		Busy cleaning up and getting straight	a fall of Snow.
	16/1/17		Busy cleaning up. - A bad case of fractured Base admitted & I ordered that he should be kept in the F.A. & not evacuated - as his case seemed hopeless.	
		2.30 pm	Officers of the unit attended a lecture at the Corps School of Sanitation - Subject: - Horrocks Water Cart. - Water Clarification and Sterilization.	
	17/1/17		Divisional Chaplain visited us.	

Instructions regarding War Diaries and Intelligence Summaries are contained in F. S. Regs., Part II. and the Staff Manual respectively. Title Pages will be prepared in manuscript.

WAR DIARY
or
~~INTELLIGENCE SUMMARY~~

(Erase heading not required.)

133RD FLD. AMB.

Army Form C. 2118.

Place	Date	Hour	Summary of Events and Information — Maps. A28 1/40000.	Remarks and references to Appendices
POPERINGHE	18/1/17		A.D.M.S. visited the Field Ambulance his remarks were carefully noted & orders were issued to comply with his suggestion for improvements.	
			Capt Robertson RAMC rejoined for duty - coming off leave.	
	19/1/17		Lt Curling RAMC proceeded on 10 days leave.	
			1 Douglas Motor Cycle sent to the Base - & has been struck off the strength	
	20/1/17		Capt Robertson RAMC took over the duties of MO i/c A.D.S Asylum YPRES. vice Lt Limbery RAMC	
	21/1/17		Lt Anderson RAMC proceeded on duty to 17. N.&D. Regt.	
			A new pack store is being made - to accomodate 100 kits & rifles	Frosty weather
			The interiors are being limewashed & latrine utensils tarred.	
	22/1/17		Lt Limbery rejoined from A.D.S. YPRES.	
			Lt. Bado. - on instructions received from ADMS - has been struck off the strength of the Ambulance.	Frosty
	23/1/17		Visited the A.D.S. - made a few minor suggestions - found everything clean & well cared for.	
			Maj Genl. Cuthbert visited the horse lines & was apparently pleased with his inspection	Frosty weather
			Officers went to a lecture. delivered by Rev. Brough.	
	24/1/17	2.30	Instructional Conference of M.O.s - poor attendance. report sent to ADMS	

2449 Wt. W14957/M90 750,000 1/16 J.B.C. & A. Forms/C.2118/12.

Army Form C. 2118.

Instructions regarding War Diaries and Intelligence Summaries are contained in F. S. Regs., Part II. and the Staff Manual respectively. Title Pages will be prepared in manuscript.

WAR DIARY
or
~~INTELLIGENCE SUMMARY~~

(Erase heading not required.)

133RD FLD. AMB.

Place	Date	Hour	Summary of Events and Information — Maps 28 1:40 000.	Remarks and references to Appendices
Poperinghe	25/1/17	12 noon	D.D.M.S VIII Corps visited the F.A. – he remarked on the fact that a bombproof shelter had been removed by the Corps School of Sanitation – he also remarked on the necessity of providing fresh vegetables for patients and personnel.	Very Cold Frost
			Capt DENNIS RAMC T.C. joined up from No 10 C.C.S	
	26/1/17		Capt Warwick RAMC relieved Capt Robertson RAMC at the A.D.S. YPRES	Very Cold Frost
			Two dud aeroplane shells dropped in the area occupied by this unit. Orders were issued to the effect that the watching of aeroplane shelling by men was prohibited and that they were to take cover when shelling was in progress.	
	27/1/17		Capt S D Robertson RAMC reported to A.D.M.S for duty with 82nd Sanitary Section. – Everything is frozen up. The pipes of a water cart have burst.	Frost
	28/1/17		Capt Anderson RAMC reported himself at H.Q from temporary duty with 17th Sherwoods. – I attended Divine Service in the Canteen about 20 other ranks were present.	Frost
	29/1/17	9.30 am	A.D.M.S visited the Unit. – I personally conducted him over the cellars he suggested braziers being kept in them to dry them up – this is being done – his other remarks were carefully noted for compliance	

2449 Wt. W14957/M90 750,000 1/16 J.B.C. & A. Forms/C.2118/12.

Instructions regarding War Diaries and Intelligence Summaries are contained in F. S. Regs., Part II. and the Staff Manual respectively. Title Pages will be prepared in manuscript.

WAR DIARY
or
~~INTELLIGENCE SUMMARY~~
(Erase heading not required.)

133RD FLD. AMB.

Army Form C. 2118.

Place	Date	Hour	Summary of Events and Information	Remarks and references to Appendices
			Map A28. 1/40.000	
Poperinghe	30/1/17	.	The water cart which had burst a pipe owing to the frost returned from having been repaired by the I.O.M. The new pack store is now in use and provided with a desk for the clerk and a long rifle rack. The wall to which the old one was affixed is being repaired	Frost — A little snow has fallen
	31/1/17	.	Brigadier General Gordon was treated for a minor disability — Sgt Mason who had fallen sick during a Course of Sanitation was ordered to re-attend	Frosty & some snow
			Reported to ADMS that a further accommodation in the matter of cellars had been found under the Y.M.C.A. building in this street.	
			C W Bowle Lt Col. RAMC Cmdg. 133. F.A.	

2449 Wt. W14957/M90 750,000 1/16 J.B.C. & A. Forms/C.2118/12.

Vol 12

140/995

CONFIDENTIAL

War Diary

of

133RD FLD. AMB.

39th Div.

from February 1st 1917

to February 28th 1917

(Volume 12)

H F Warwick
Capt RAMC
for O C 133 F Ambulance

Instructions regarding War Diaries and Intelligence Summaries are contained in F. S. Regs., Part II. and the Staff Manual respectively. Title Pages will be prepared in manuscript.

WAR DIARY
or
INTELLIGENCE SUMMARY
(Erase heading not required.)

133RD FLD. AMB

Army Form C. 2118.

No 1
Not numbered consecutively
190

A. 28 1.40,000

Place	Date	Hour	Summary of Events and Information	Remarks and references to Appendices
Poperinghe.	1/2/17	11.30 am	D.D.M.S. inspected the F.A. he remarked that the sick rate of the Division was high. his remarks were carefully noted and M.O.s subsequently warned not to be too sympathetic in the treatment of minor ailments. I visited A.D.S. & C.P.s found all correct.	
	2/2/17	.	The cold is intense. A German aeroplane dropped a bomb near us last night. no damage done - one man wounded in the buttock	
	3/2/17	2.30	Interviewed A.D.M.S. - his remarks were carefully noted. The pack store is now complete with rifle rack.	
	4/2/17	.	D.M.S. D.D.M.S. A.D.M.S. inspected the F.A. discussed the high rate of sick - afterwards visited the wards and saw some "feet" cases. Held a Board on P.B. men. Capt Dennis and Capt MacArthur members	
	5/2/17	10.30	Spr T. Bird R.E. was buried by R.C. Chaplain at the Cemetery.	
	6/2/17	.	O.R. from Div! Baths rejoined H.Q. - A water cart was damaged by fire. I convened a Court of Inquiry to report on and allocate the blame if any. A.D.M.S. visited the F.A. Saw Capt Robertson who is in hospital - he also came to see me as I was unable to attend on him.	

2449 Wt. W14957/M90 750,000 1/16 J.B.C. & A. Forms/C.2118/12.

Instructions regarding War Diaries and Intelligence Summaries are contained in F. S. Regs., Part II. and the Staff Manual respectively. Title Pages will be prepared in manuscript.

WAR DIARY
or
~~INTELLIGENCE SUMMARY~~
(Erase heading not required.)

Army Form C. 2118.

No 2

Place	Date	Hour	A 28 140.000. Summary of Events and Information	Remarks and references to Appendices
Poperinghe.	6/2/17	7.30 pm	Enemy aeroplane dropped a bomb in the back garden did no damage. blew a large brick on to the Cookhouse roof alarmed the officers whilst at Mess.	Frost – white.
		11.30 pm	More bombs dropped – no damage. – none very near us.	
	7/2/17	.	Sgt Wishart reported for duty from VIII C. H.Q. – he is a dispenser. Instructional Conference held at the College. – Capt Dennis presided as I was unable to attend through sickness.	Frost – white
			Capt S.D. Robertson RAMC evacuated to No. 12 C.C.S. – sick	
	8/2/17	.	Sgt Herbert being sick. I brought Sgt Burrow down from the Menin Rd C.P. & sent up Sgt Burnett in his place.	
			Lt Anderson RAMC proceeded on temporary duty to 134 F.A.	
			3 Reinforcements taken on strength (RAMC)	
	9/2/17		Pte Kilby came back from leave.	
	10/2/17	.	2 Reinforcements ASC H.T. reported for duty from 39th Div Train.	
			M. Minne Belgian Interpreter proceeded to U.K. on leave	
	11/2/17		Capt Miller MC RAMC took over command of this Ambce vice self.	

2449 Wt. W14957/M90 750,000 1/16 J.B.C. & A. Forms/C.2118/12.

Instructions regarding War Diaries and Intelligence Summaries are contained in F. S. Regs., Part II. and the Staff Manual respectively. Title Pages will be prepared in manuscript.

WAR DIARY
or
~~INTELLIGENCE SUMMARY~~
(Erase heading not required.)

133RD FLD. AMB

Army Form C. 2118.

No - 3

Place	Date	Hour	Summary of Events and Information	Remarks and references to Appendices
Poperinghe	11/2/17		admitted to Hospital with Bronchitis C.W. Bowle Lt Col. RAMC. Odpave taken over temporary charge of this Ambulance vice Lt. Col. C.W. Bowle R.A.M.C. admitted to hospital ~~today with~~ Bronchitis. Sinclair Miller Capt ~~R.A.M.C. S.R.~~ Lieut. C. M. Anderson R.A.M.C. rejoined this unit today from temporary duty with 134 Fd. Amb. No 1 Sunbeam car returned today from WORKSHOPS.	Front continues
	12/2/17		All the necessary preparations were completed for the Evacuation of wounded in connection with the proposed raid tonight. ~~Lieut R.T. Lim~~ Lieut R.T. Lim[illegible] R.A.M.C. + 16 stretcher bearers proceeded to the A.D.S. Asylum today to reinforce the Staff there and at the collecting posts. Weather warmer. A.D.M.S. 39th Div. visited the F.A. + saw Lt. Col. BOWLE R.A.M.C. Gifts of tobacco, sweets and matches were received from the Red Cross Society. Sergt. Major HERBERT admitted to Hospital sick.	

2449 Wt. W14957/M90 750,000 1/16 J.B.C. & A. Forms/C.2118/12.

Instructions regarding War Diaries and Intelligence Summaries are contained in F. S. Regs., Part II. and the Staff Manual respectively. Title Pages will be prepared in manuscript.

WAR DIARY
or
INTELLIGENCE SUMMARY
(Erase heading not required.)

Army Form C. 2118.

133RD FLD. AMB.

No. 4

Place	Date	Hour	Summary of Events and Information	Remarks and references to Appendices
Poperinghe	13 2/17		The raid was quite successful last night and all objectives were gained. There were 3 casualties. These were evacuated to the No 10 C.C.S. this morning. There is another raid to-night – a small affair. Lt LIMBERT and party are therefore staying up at the asylum for another day.	
			D.D.M.S VIII Corps visited the Ambulance to see Lt Col BOWLE, and advised his removal to the Corps Rest Station. He also examined the Trench feet cases, raising the question of diagnosis between trench foot, frostbite, chilblains and ulcers.	
			A Field General Court Martial was held as per instructions Div' Routine Order No 622 dated 11 2/17.	
			No 72135 Pte NELSON. W. R.A.M.C. proceeded to ABBEVILLE for duty under instructions A.A. & QMG 39th Division and is struck off the strength accordingly.	
			3 Reinforcements reported from the BASE for duty and are taken on the strength of the Unit from Feb. 13th	
			Warmer today.	
	14 2/17		Lt Col. C W BOWLE, R.A.M.C was transferred to VIII Corps Officers Rest Station WORMHOUDT. Lt LIMBERT rejoined Unit from A D S. Asylum. also 17 O.R. POPERINGHE was shelled during the afternoon. The patients were removed to the cellars. There was no casualties in the town.	

2449 Wt. W14957/M90 750,000 1/16 J.B.C. & A. Forms/C.2118/12.

Instructions regarding War Diaries and Intelligence Summaries are contained in F. S. Regs., Part II. and the Staff Manual respectively. Title Pages will be prepared in manuscript.

WAR DIARY
or
INTELLIGENCE SUMMARY
(Erase heading not required.)

133RD FLD. AMB.

Army Form C. 2118.

No. 5

Place	Date	Hour	Summary of Events and Information	Remarks and references to Appendices
Poperinghe	15/2/17		Capt. S. MILLER. R.A.M.C. M.C. (SR) rejoined his unit 132nd Fld Amb. under instructions from A.D.M.S. Capt A.W. DENNIS. R.A.M.C. takes over temporary command of the ambulance. 1 N.C.O. and 2 O.R. proceeded to WATOU. A.D.S. at Asylum was heavily shelled tonight, and two cars damaged but able to proceed. Thaw is setting in.	
	16/2/17		Capt. L.R. MEECH. R.A.M.C.; M.C, returned off leave. S/M Herbert discharged Hospital. No. 72066 Pte W. LEGG. R.A.M.C evacuated to the BASE 8th inst. & is struck off the strength. Arrangements for the move are now completed. Lt LIMBERT with 6 O.R. proceeded to WATOU as an advance party to take over from 1/3 West Lancs Fd Amb. Capt. WARWICK and 30 O.R arrived from A.D.S. having handed over to 2/1 Wessex Fld Amb. The relief was completed at 9 p.m. The body of Spr MILLER. R.O.D att R.E. brought into HD.	
WATOU	17/2/17		The Fld Amb. moved from the COLLEGE, POPERINGHE ~~and~~ to WATOU departing at 10 a.m. and arriving at 11.45 a.m. 3 men of the 82nd Sanitary Section attached to us for rations. Thaw precautions. 1 Douglas m/cycle received from Workshop 39th Supply Column, completing establishment. Certificates handed over to 2/1 WESSEX Fd Amb. and received from 1/3 West Lancs. Fd Amb. Body of Spr MILLER. R.O.D. att. R.E. handed over	

2449 Wt. W14957/M90 750,000 1/16 J.B.C. & A. Forms/C.2118/12.

Instructions regarding War Diaries and Intelligence Summaries are contained in F. S. Regs., Part II. and the Staff Manual respectively. Title Pages will be prepared in manuscript.

WAR DIARY
or
INTELLIGENCE SUMMARY
(Erase heading not required.)

Army Form C. 2118.

133RD FLD. AMB

No 6

Place	Date	Hour	Summary of Events and Information	Remarks and references to Appendices
PRATOU.	18 2/17.		The Sanitation of the Camp was proceed with. Parties were working round the Horse Lines. Hospital Yard, and Billets. Cars proceeded to D. E. G + P camps to collect sick. and and Medical Officers i/c of Regmts quartered here were informed of that cars would call every morning at 10.30 am. 227 Coy R.E at ELVERDINGHE told to wire when they had cases for Hospital.	
		X	Lt ANDERSON detailed to report upon a case of TYPHOID FEVER at A23 C28 (Hut 28) Report sent into A D M S tonight.	A. W. Dennis Capt RAMC (T.C.)
			Lt Col BOWLE returned from VIII Corps Rest Station and takes over command of the Fld Amb.	
			Took over command of the F.A. from Capt Dennis R.A.M.C. having rejoined the unit from Corps Rest Station.	
	19 2/17		Lieut C M ANDERSON proceeded to attend Course of Sanitation at HAZEBROUCK. – Sent in an indent for roofing and timber for the purpose of repairing the horse lines.	
	21 2/17		A.D.M.S visited & inspected the F.A. his attention having been invited to some cases of "TRENCH FOOT" which had been accumulating in the hospital – he ordered me to send them along to C.C.S – I had already	

2449 Wt. W14957/M90 750,000 1/16 J.B.C. & A. Forms/C.2118/12.

Instructions regarding War Diaries and Intelligence Summaries are contained in F. S. Regs., Part II. and the Staff Manual respectively. Title pages will be prepared in manuscript.

WAR DIARY
or
~~INTELLIGENCE SUMMARY.~~
(Erase heading not required.)

133RD FLD. AMB.

Army Form C. 2118.

No. 7

Place	Date	Hour	Summary of Events and Information	Remarks and references to Appendices
			Maps. ~~Sheet~~ 27 1/40000.	
WATOU F.28.d.5.3.	20.2.17		Sent a serious case of moist gangrene on to C.C.S. the night before. Men were checked for not wearing overalls when whitewashing by A.D.M.S and he also expressed his displeasure at the condition of the horse lines, and at a general want of organisation. I represented the fact that an indent had already gone in for horse lines structures and I was doing my best to train all ranks of the personnel of the Ambulance. (The men having been one year on service are trained. More supervision & disciplinary measures only needed B.C.)	X More supervision & disciplinary measures only needed B.C
			Capt McARTHUR RAMC was transferred to Corps Rest Stat. in WORMHOUDT.	
			Capt Dennis RAMC proceeded to 132 F.A. for temporary duty.	
			250 blankets and 8 kits sent to 82nd Sanitary Section for disinfection.	
	21.2.17		Capt DENNIS RAMC rejoined unit from 132 F.A.	409.
			Instructional Conference held at Watou 5 officers attended	
	22.2.17		Capt S.D. Robertson RAMC on being evacuated from Corps area is struck off the strength of the Unit.	705.
			Capt R.F. BOLT RAMC reported for duty.	
			A foot inspection of the personnel of the Unit was carried out.	

Instructions regarding War Diaries and Intelligence Summaries are contained in F. S. Regs., Part II. and the Staff Manual respectively. Title pages will be prepared in manuscript.

WAR DIARY
or
~~INTELLIGENCE~~ ~~SUMMARY.~~
(Erase heading not required.)

Army Form C. 2118.

133RD FLD. AMB.

N°. 8

Map Sheet 27 1/40.000

Place	Date	Hour	Summary of Events and Information	Remarks and references to Appendices
WATOU	23.2.17		O.C. unit proceeded to new Site of Ambulance to make a reconnaissance	Area
			Two officers attended 2nd Army Med. Society meeting at HAZEBROUCK.	Foggy day.
			Capt. Dennis RAMC proceeded to RENINGHELST for duty with the 69th Heavy Artillery Group.	
			Capt. Bolt RAMC proceeded to ABEELE to report to DDMS X Corps.	
			50 men were bathed at HERZEELE.	
			Interpreter E MINNE rejoined unit from leave.	
	24.2.17	1pm	Capt. Meich and Lt. Carling and 28 O.R.s proceeded to the new area with orders to report to O.C. 70th FA – as an advance party with a small amount of Equipment.	Warmer.
	25.2.17	1pm	Lt. Col Bowle and Capt. Warwick visited the various A.D.S.s & R.A.P.s on the 39th Divisional Front.	Bright, clear & warm
	26.2.17		The unit marched from WATOU leaving at 10 a.m. to VLAMERTINGHE MILL arriving at 1.15 pm & took over from 70th Field Ambulance.	Bright & sunny
			Interpreter MINNE E. remained at Watou & is struck off the strength of this unit from 26th inst.	

T2134. Wt. W708–776. 500000. 4/15. Sir J. C. & S.

Instructions regarding War Diaries and Intelligence Summaries are contained in F. S. Regs., Part II. and the Staff Manual respectively. Title pages will be prepared in manuscript.

WAR DIARY
or
INTELLIGENCE SUMMARY.
(Erase heading not required.)

Army Form C. 2118.

No. 9.

Place	Date	Hour	Summary of Events and Information	Remarks and references to Appendices
THE MILL	26th		The undermentioned men rejoined unit from VIII Corps School of Sanitation No 72088 Pte SYKES, 43601 Pte Grady. 72002 Pte KENDRICK, 8365 Pte HINES	
	27th		Capt MacArthur J rejoined unit having been discharged from VIII Corps Officers rest Station. Lt Col. BOWLE CW admitted to Hospital. One NCO & five men took over the G.B.D.R. YPRES.	Weather dull but fine
"	28th	11am	DDMS Xth Corps inspected the Ambulance. Lt Col BOWLE CW. evacuated to No 2 CCS. A.D.M.S. inspected the Ambulance & made several suggestions regarding improvements. CAPTAIN SINCLAIR MILLER took over temporary command of this Amb^ce.	Weather clear & bright

H F Warwick Cap RAMC

for. O.C. 133rd F.A.

T2134. Wt. W708–776. 500000. 4/15. Sir J. C. & S.

39

CONFIDENTIAL

Original Vol 13

WAR DIARY

OF

133RD FLD. AMB.

from:- 1st March 1917

140/2042 to:- 31st March 1917

(Volume 13)

39th Div.

J.S. Manford Capt. Ramc
~~LT. COL.~~
O. C. 133RD FLD. AMB.

Mar. 1917

Instructions regarding War Diaries and Intelligence Summaries are contained in F. S. Regs., Part II. and the Staff Manual respectively. Title pages will be prepared in manuscript.

WAR DIARY
or
~~INTELLIGENCE SUMMARY.~~
(Erase heading not required.)

133RD FLD. AMB.

Army Form C. 2118.

No. 1

Place	Date	Hour	Sheet 28 1–40,000 Summary of Events and Information	Remarks and references to Appendices
VLAMERTINGHE	1/3/17		Improvements at the MAIN Dressing Station commenced; ablution bench for personel reconstructed; ward for officers equipped. Also fitted up a dining hall for patients making the necessary tables and forms. I visited the A.D.S. at the Asylum & found everything correct. Suggested some improvements which the O/c is carrying out. I also visited the collecting post at the LILLE gate. Also the A.D.S. at the BUND. The cookhouse is not satisfactory there and I made arrangements with the O/c A.D.S. The BUND for the construction of a new one. Also whitewashing &c. to be done. I visited the collecting post at COW FARM. No cooking or heating arrangement at COW FARM save a BRAZIER. Arranged with O/c A.D.S. The BUND for the fitting up of a Stove ~~Hear~~ at COW FARM. Also visited R.A.P. at ZILLEBEKE. YPRES badly shelled. Pte Dye of this unit wounded at LILLE gate	Weather bright and dry.
	2/3/17		Two officers from the 234 R.E. Coy. called here this morning. I made arrangements with them for further improvements. A new	Weather foggy.

T2134. Wt. W708–776. 500000. 4/15. Sir J. C. & S.

Instructions regarding War Diaries and Intelligence Summaries are contained in F. S. Regs., Part II. and the Staff Manual respectively. Title pages will be prepared in manuscript.

WAR DIARY
or
~~INTELLIGENCE SUMMARY.~~
(Erase heading not required.)

Army Form C. 2118.

No 2

Place	Date	Hour	Summary of Events and Information	Remarks and references to Appendices
VLAMERTINGHE	Cont'd 2/3/17		path laid down along EASTERN side of main dressing station. BUTCHER'S Shop reconstructed + whitewashed. One N.C.O. + 2 O.R.'s detailed to proceed to INFANTRY BARRACKS YPRES to take over the baths there. I visited A.D.S. Ypres and the COLLECTING POST, LILLE GATE YPRES Arranged for erection of sand-bag wall in front of CANTEEN at LILLE GATE — PERMISSION from TOWN MAJOR YPRES — Also to increase accommodation at the COLLECTING POST, LILLE GATE. VLAMERTINGHE shelled. I also visited the baths + the FOOT preparation Room in the INFANTRY BARRACKS YPRES and found neither of them satisfactory	
	3/3/17		Capt Sinclair Millar having rejoined 182 Field Ambulance handed over temporary Command of the Ambulance to Capt H F Warwick RAMC. The undermentioned men proceeded to ADS THE BUND for duty. PTE LIGHTLE, PTE GALSWORTHY, PTE MASON + Pte SLODEN. One Ford car reported here for duty from 134 F Ambulance. Two pairs + one single trench waders collected from No 10 CANADIAN CCS per instructions from ADMS. NO 40662 PTE GOURLEY awarded 28 days No 2 Field	Weather foggy

Instructions regarding War Diaries and Intelligence Summaries are contained in F. S. Regs., Part II. and the Staff Manual respectively. Title pages will be prepared in manuscript.

WAR DIARY
or
~~INTELLIGENCE SUMMARY.~~
(Erase heading not required.)

Army Form C. 2118.

No 3.

Place	Date	Hour	Summary of Events and Information	Remarks and references to Appendices
VLAMERTINGHE			Punishment for drunkeness. No 3302 Gunner GORDON 21st Siege Bat[y] RGA (patient in hospital) was placed under close arrest & charged with drunkeness	
	4.3/17		CAPT BOLT. R.F. RAMC rejoined the unit from DDMS X[d] Corps. I proceeded to the ADS ASYLUM & inspected the Dressing room, mens quarters cook house etc & found everything satisfactory. I then proceeded to the ADS the BUND & found the personnel busy constructing a new cook house, Recommended the Offr in charge to put up a shelter of sand bags in front of the doors of the Dressing room & Officers ~~room~~ to prevent fragments of shell from coming back through the doors from shells exploding in front. Both the above mentioned places require whitewashing but lime not available at present, otherwise ADS. Satisfactory. Improvements at MDS being continued windows being put in roof of mens billets, bricks brought down for new incinerator, fresh duckboards being put down, filtering apparatus at ablution benches constructed & tested & drains being cleared. A.F.s W 3121 forwarded for two recommendations in triplicate viz Pte STREDWICK RAMC & Pte DYE. H. RAMC. church parade was held	Weather bright

T2134. Wt. W708—776. 500000. 4/15. Sir J. C. & S.

Instructions regarding War Diaries and Intelligence Summaries are contained in F. S. Regs., Part II. and the Staff Manual respectively. Title pages will be prepared in manuscript.

WAR DIARY
or
INTELLIGENCE SUMMARY.
(Erase heading not required.)

Army Form C. 2118.

No 4.

Place	Date	Hour	Summary of Events and Information	Remarks and references to Appendices
VLAMERTINGHE	4 3/17		at 2pm & was well attended. One horse H.Q was wounded at ASYLUM YPRES	
	5 3/17		L/Cpl THOMAS & Pt MESSENGER relieved from MENIN RD & reported to head quarters, Pte DOUGLAS transferred from ADS. THE BUND. sick, to head quarters. NO 65688 Staff Sgt TUSTIAN promoted to Q.M.S. from 1.2.17, vide RAMC orders 1.2.17.	Weather dull
	6 3/17		One Stewart horse clipping machine received tested & found to work in a satisfactory manner. Notification received NO 65971 Cpl WILLMER of this unit was evacuated to Base from No 2 Canadian C.C.S 24.2.17 by Hospital train No 10. & is Struck off the Strength of this unit. I proceeded with Sgt Major Herbert to inspect A.D.S. ASYLUM & ADS THE BUND & found everything Satisfactory. Also inspected the Gum boot drying room YPRES (Infantry Barracks) the Baths & the foot preparation room both in the same building. Baths & Gum Boot D.R. found to be working Satisfactorily. Nothing being done in F.P. room as no one ever came to it. As it adjoins the baths it would be a good procedure to have this room attached to the baths as a changing room	Weather cold, snow

T2134. Wt. W708-776. 500000. 4/15. Sir J. C. & S.

Instructions regarding War Diaries and Intelligence Summaries are contained in F. S. Regs., Part II. and the Staff Manual respectively. Title pages will be prepared in manuscript.

WAR DIARY
or
INTELLIGENCE SUMMARY.
(Erase heading not required.)

Army Form C. 2118.

No 5

Place	Date	Hour	Summary of Events and Information	Remarks and references to Appendices
VLAMERTINGHE			Instructional conference held at M.D.S. 9 was attended by five Medical officers. The following subjects were discussed. Re-inoculation against Typhoid & Para-Typhoid Ulcerative Stomatitis, Disposal of men Suitable	
	7 3/17		No 72020 L/Cpl Drinkwater proceeded to the 39th Divisional R.E. for duty. VLAMERTINGHE was heavily shelled for a couple of hours this morning. No 72027 Pte EVERITT proceeded to the 39th Divisional Supply Column for purpose of testing his capabilities as a Mechanic under instructions from H.Q. Second Army No A/2101/3	Cold Weather dull
	8 3/17		Visited A.D.S. Asylum & found everything in a satisfactory condition Also visited Gum Boot Drying room & baths. Ford Car which was lent temporarily to this unit from 134 Field Ambulance was returned to-day. C of E Service held here @ 6.30 p.m. There was a good attendance.	Cold Weather bright

T2134. Wt. W708—776. 500000. 4/15. Sir J. C. & S.

Instructions regarding War Diaries and Intelligence Summaries are contained in F. S. Regs., Part II. and the Staff Manual respectively. Title pages will be prepared in manuscript.

WAR DIARY *or* INTELLIGENCE SUMMARY.

(Erase heading not required.)

Army Form C. 2118.

No 6.

Place	Date	Hour	Summary of Events and Information	Remarks and references to Appendices
VLAMERTINGHE	9/3/17		Holy Communion C of E held at 7 a.m. 65954 Pte BOLTON. H. W. evacuated to base from No 10 C.C.S. & is struck off the strength of this unit from that date. No 64911 PTE. HOPE, A.T. RAMC to be acting Sergeant from 23.2.17. Authority DDMS B 1450/S. 19.	Weather Bright & frosty
			Capt A.W. DENNIS, RAMC rejoined unit from 132 Field Ambulance & proceeded to Asylum, YPRES to relieve Capt LIMBERY. at A D S.	
			CAPT. MACARTHUR. J. RAMC. gave a lecture on Chiropody to personnel of unit. M2/132126 PTE COUSINS, M. ASC MT proceeded on 10 days special leave to U.K. Authority X Corps No. A348 d. 24. 2. 17	
	10/3/17		DDMS Xa Corps inspected Field Ambulance. I proceeded with DDMS Xa Corps to the ADS THE BUND which he inspected, & then proceeded to the RAP at HALF WAY HOUSE & from there we went to the Collecting post at COW FARM & thence back to LILLE GATE.	Weather Dull, hazy & warm
			CAPT. K.T. LIMBERY RAMC proceeded on fourteen days special leave.	
			No 4937 PTE. DUNKLEY H. having been instructed to report to the base for	

Instructions regarding War Diaries and Intelligence Summaries are contained in F. S. Regs., Part II. and the Staff Manual respectively. Title pages will be prepared in manuscript.

WAR DIARY
or
INTELLIGENCE SUMMARY.
(Erase heading not required.)

Army Form C. 2118.

No 7

Place	Date	Hour	Summary of Events and Information	Remarks and references to Appendices
VLAMERTINGHE			transfer to Railway CONSTRUCTION Co. & struck off the strength of the unit from this date. One Bay man (rider) transferred to 50th MVS	
	11 3/17		ADMS 39th Division visited and inspected Field Ambulance this afternoon. Suggested site where Hospital marquees should be pitched. Also suggested that window should be inserted in eastern wall of small isolation ward. Inspected several cases of Trench Feet & gave instructions regarding their disposal. Also inspected two cases of Hernia & Examined one case of suspected phthisis. The following church parades were held. (a) for Non-Conformists at 10 a.m. for C of E at 2 p.m.	Weather fine
	12 3/17		Thirteen O.R's RAMC inoculated TAB. Personnel at ADS ASYLUM changed. Visited the ADS. ASYLUM, & Gum Boot Drying room INFANTRY BARRACKS, YPRES & found everything in a satisfactory condition	Weather dull

T2134. Wt. W708–776. 500000. 4/15. Sir J. C. & S.

Instructions regarding War Diaries and Intelligence Summaries are contained in F. S. Regs., Part II. and the Staff Manual respectively. Title pages will be prepared in manuscript.

WAR DIARY
or
INTELLIGENCE SUMMARY.
(Erase heading not required.)

Army Form C. 2118.

NO 8

Place	Date	Hour	Summary of Events and Information	Remarks and references to Appendices
VLAMERTINGHE	13 3/17		Notification received from No 10 CCS. of the undermentioned men evacuated to Base & struck off the strength of this unit from 3 3/17 No 65965 PTE STREDWICK. J. RAMC. No 57252 PTE DYE. H. RAMC.	Weather bright & dry.
			QMS TUSTIAN. C.R rejoined unit from 39th Divisional Concert party.	
			I attended a Conference of CO's F.A's at 134 F.A where ADMS. 39th Div. gave particulars regarding our dispositions & duties in case of active operations taking place in future.	
	14 3/17		Capt F. PIERCE GROVE RAMC & Lieut W L JOHNSTON RAMC reported their arrival for duty with this unit & were taken on the strength accordingly	Weather dull
	15 3/17		No 72138 L cpl DAISH. C.J. rejoined unit having been discharged to duty from D.R.S. Notification received No 52726 PTE KITCHENS. C transferred to No 2 Canadian C.C.S from D.R.S 7 3 17	Weather wet & cold

T2131. Wt. W708—776. 500000. 4/15. Sir J. C. & S.

Instructions regarding War Diaries and Intelligence Summaries are contained in F. S. Regs., Part II. and the Staff Manual respectively. Title pages will be prepared in manuscript.

WAR DIARY
or
INTELLIGENCE SUMMARY.
(Erase heading not required.)

Army Form C. 2118.

NO 9

Place	Date	Hour	Summary of Events and Information	Remarks and references to Appendices
VLAMERTINGHE	16/3/17		Capt J MACARTHUR RAMC transferred to Etaples for duty (authority) DMS 2nd Army 850/17. I proceeded to BRANDHOEK to make arrangements for carrying out work at proposed site of Corps Collecting Station at that place. Inspected the ground & met ADMS & DADMS. Received instructions from ADMS regarding the clearing up of the ground, draining it & removing trees & other debris, also position for incinerator & latrines. Sgt KELLY of this unit was thrown down by a motor cyclist & sustained a fractured arm. He was transferred to CCS	Weather cold wet &
	17/3/17		DDMS IX Corps visited & inspected the ambulance. He then proceeded to the ADS THE ASYLUM & inspected it. Two horses (Heavy Draught) supplied from No 2 Co's Train (ASC) to complete establishment. L'Cpl DRINKWATER rejoined unit from RE 39th Division having been relieved by L'Cpl Daish. Pte Gellibre rejoined unit from DRS. Fatigue party proceeded to site of new Corps Collecting Station & the work of clearing away debris from that place. No 65372 Pte WOOLNER C	Weather frosty

T2131. Wt. W708–776. 500000. 4/15. Sir J. C. & S.

Instructions regarding War Diaries and Intelligence Summaries are contained in F. S. Regs., Part II. and the Staff Manual respectively. Title pages will be prepared in manuscript.

WAR DIARY
or
INTELLIGENCE SUMMARY.
(Erase heading not required.)

Army Form C. 2118.

No 10

Place	Date	Hour	Summary of Events and Information	Remarks and references to Appendices
VLAMERTINGHE			RAMC transferred to CCS 22 2/17 is struck off the strength of this unit from that date. No 72038 Pte MAXWELL E.R. & No 36142 Pte HUDSON H.F. evacuated to base from No 17 CCS & are struck off the strength of this unit from this date. Six men reported from 134 Field Ambulance for duty at site of Corps Collecting Station at BRANDHOEK.	
	18 3/17		I visited the ADS. ASYLUM, the Gum boot drying room & the Canteen at LILLE GATE & found everything satisfactory. Have had brick floorings put down & two marquees pitched at MDS. Brick paths put down between the marquees. Nonconformist parade at 10 a.m. Capt DENNIS RAMC ADS ASYLUM instructed to see sick of 225 & 227 Co^s^ R.E. on morning of 19 3/17	Weather cold
	19 3/17		No 65717 Pte SCHOLES S.L. returned to duty from Ophthalmic Hospital Hazebrook. No 72168 Pte CLAYSON F.E. & No 060832 Pte HAMER F both of A.S.C. M.T. attached to this unit discharged to duty from DRS 19 3/17	Weather frosty

T2134. Wt. W708–776. 500000. 4/15. Sir J. C. & S.

Instructions regarding War Diaries and Intelligence Summaries are contained in F. S. Regs., Part II. and the Staff Manual respectively. Title pages will be prepared in manuscript.

WAR DIARY
or
INTELLIGENCE SUMMARY.
(*Erase heading not required.*)

Army Form C. 2118.

No 11

Place	Date	Hour	Summary of Events and Information	Remarks and references to Appendices
VLAMERTINGHE	20 3/17		The undermentioned men having reported as reinforcements for duty are taken on the strength of this unit NO 68284 Sgt MACKIE J S. No 26647 Cpl ORMAN R NO 100701 PTE COMPTON R.R., NO 100706 PTE COBB J.H., NO 100704 PTE CRABTREE W. & No 28580 PTE COOPER F. No M/2 05-3354 PTE EVANS W.C ASC M.T. att^d reported for duty from No 39 D.S.C. & is taken on the strength of the unit from this date	Weather clear & cold
	21 3/17		No 104667 PTE LEEMING J, No 3365 HINES J., No 52726 KETCHEN C. No 62594 Sgt O'REILLY J., No 105338 PTE MESSENGER, F. No 222517 TOLLINGTON ASC M.T. att^d The above men having been evacuated to the Base from CCS are struck off the strength of this unit. Conference of CO's Field Ambulances held at office of ADMS 39th Division & instructions given regarding the work to be done by the various ambulances in view of future operations. One patient NO 7853 PTE SYMONDS died in this Field Ambulance. His unit was the 1st Cambs & he was buried in the Cemetery VLAMERTINGHE on 22 3 17 by C of E Chaplain HAWKINS	Weather cold & frosty

T2134. Wt. W708—776. 500000. 4/15. Sir J. C. & S.

Instructions regarding War Diaries and Intelligence Summaries are contained in F. S. Regs., Part II. and the Staff Manual respectively. Title pages will be prepared in manuscript.

WAR DIARY
or
INTELLIGENCE SUMMARY.
(Erase heading not required.)

Army Form C. 2118.

No 12

Place	Date	Hour	Summary of Events and Information	Remarks and references to Appendices
VLAMERTINGHE	22 3/17		One horse (rider) received from Camp Commandant. Visited the ADS ASYLUM & the Canteen at LILLE GATE. As complaints had been received that the Canteen was gathering a lot of soldiers in the vicinity of LILLE GATE acting under instructions from the A D M S. I ordered it to be closed & went with Lieut E.C. Curzon to the TOWN Majors Office who recommended a new site. This was a cellar in the RUE DE LILLE which we inspected & as it seemed to be the best place in the neighbourhood I decided to transfer the Canteen there & gave orders for this to be done.	Cold Weather Snowing
	23 3/17	[illegible]	No 132126 Pte Cousins M. ASC MT rejoined unit from 10 days special leave on 22. 3. 17. Permission got for six loads of bricks to be sent to new Corps Collecting site at BRANDHOEK & this was proceeded with	Snowing
	24 3/17		Summer time adopted at 11 p.m. to night & clocks & watches ordered to be advanced from 11 pm. to 12 midnight. Pte FINDING RAMC rejoined unit from No 12 CCS HAZEBROOK. Capt R.F. BOLT. RAMC proceeded	Snowing

T2134. Wt. W708—776. 500000. 4/15. Sir J. C. & S.

Instructions regarding War Diaries and Intelligence Summaries are contained in F. S. Regs., Part II. and the Staff Manual respectively. Title pages will be prepared in manuscript.

WAR DIARY
or
INTELLIGENCE SUMMARY.
(Erase heading not required.)

Army Form C. 2118.

No 13

Place	Date	Hour	Summary of Events and Information	Remarks and references to Appendices
VLAMERTINGHE			to England on ten days special leave from 24 3/17 to 2 4/17 inclusive	
	25 3/17		CAPT A.W. DENNIS RAMC detailed from this unit for temporary duty with 17th Notts & Derby's to replace Capt. COOK evacuated sick. Capt PIERCE GROVE proceeded to A.D.S. ASYLUM to replace CAPT DENNIS.	Weather cold with occasional snow showers.
			Capt C.B. ROBERTSON RAMC rejoined unit from CAP MARTIN & took over command of the Ambulance.	
	26 3/17		No 65962 Pte Wakefield RAMC rejoined unit from No 3 Coy 39 Div. Train ASC. 30660 Pte Mott RAMC proceeded to replace Pte Wakefield.	
			Weather dull - wet.	
	27 3/17		Visited Asylum ADS and found all correct. Forwarded report on state of health of Pte Weller "a soldier under arrest" to ADMS, also report on proposed site for a lorry loading point at H12 C4.6 Sheet 28. There is at this point a ~~lorry loading~~ machine gun emplacement out of repair which could be added to to make a suitable splinter proof resting place for 20 men.	
	28 3/17		Capt K.T. LIMBERY RAMC rejoined Unit from 14 days special leave to England	

T2134. Wt. W708–776. 500000. 4/15. Sir J. C. & S.

Instructions regarding War Diaries and Intelligence Summaries are contained in F. S. Regs., Part II. and the Staff Manual respectively. Title pages will be prepared in manuscript.

WAR DIARY
or
INTELLIGENCE SUMMARY.
(Erase heading not required.)

Army Form C. 2118.

1014

Place	Date	Hour	Summary of Events and Information	Remarks and references to Appendices
VLAMERTINGHE	28 3/17		During the afternoon enemy shelled the A.D.S at the BUND with shrapnel and 4.2'	
			Causing considerable damage and obtaining a direct hit on the elephant dug	
		3.30 pm	out used as the dressing room. A telephone message was received about 3.30 pm	
			stating what had occurred and I immediately proceeded to the BUND to ascertain	
			the damage. I reported the matter to A.D.M.S who approached the 225 Coy RE with	
			a view to having the damage put straight. A later telephone message stated that	
			2 sections of steel were already in & the outside was being renewed.	
			No personal damage was done.	
			Earlier in the afternoon I visited the new site at BRANDHOEK and satisfied	
			myself that all the ground had been prepared for the commencement of	
			erection of tents etc.	
	29 3/17		CAPT. J.S MANFORD RAMC (T.F.) from No 5 MAC posted to command this unit.	
			Personnel of Asylum and BUND relieved.	
			CAPT. K.T. LIMBERY RAMC proceeded to the BUND in relief of CAPT. L.R. MEECH RAMC	
			who returned to H.d.q.	
			No 65688 Q.M.S. TUSTAIN RAMC transferred to 134 Fld Ambulance for duty	8

Instructions regarding War Diaries and Intelligence Summaries are contained in F. S. Regs., Part II. and the Staff Manual respectively. Title pages will be prepared in manuscript.

WAR DIARY
or
INTELLIGENCE SUMMARY.
(Erase heading not required.)

Army Form C. 2118.

No 15.

Place	Date	Hour	Summary of Events and Information	Remarks and references to Appendices
VLAMERTINGHE			is struck off the strength of the unit accordingly.	
			Cpl PACK RAMC + Cpl THOMAS RAMC proceeded for a course at the Anti gas School.	
			No 65727 S/Sgt. SMITH J. A. RAMC transferred to unit from 134 Fld Ambulance and is taken on the strength of the unit accordingly.	
			E D Robertson Capt RAMC.	
	30/3/17		No 88602. Pt. Skinner RAMC of this Unit was evacuated to No 7 G.H. suffering from Measles. All necessary precautions were taken re disinfection &c.	
			No 6919 Pte Garrett proceeded to MO i/c 2 Can^dn Tunnelling Co for duty. Authority ADMS. 39^d Div	
			Capt Dennis RAMC rejoined Unit from temporary duty with 17th Notts & Derby Reg:	
			Capt Temp Lt Col. C W BOWLE RAMC evacuated sick Feb. 28th relinquished rank as Lt. Col: & command of this Unit on 1/3/17 Authority D G M S. 227/21 15/4/16.	
			I proceeded with DADMS & Capt to ADS. asylum YPRES where arrangements were made for the strengthening of that station & against direct hits by placing suitable protection on the floor above the cellars. Arrangements were also made with reference to the construction of a shelter on the roadside outside YPRES for	J. S. Mumford

T2134. Wt. W708—776. 500000. 4/15. Sir J. C. & S.

Instructions regarding War Diaries and Intelligence Summaries are contained in F. S. Regs., Part II. and the Staff Manual respectively. Title pages will be prepared in manuscript.

WAR DIARY
or
INTELLIGENCE SUMMARY.
(Erase heading not required.)

Army Form C. 2118.

No 16.

Place	Date	Hour	Summary of Events and Information	Remarks and references to Appendices
VLAMERTINGHE	30/3/17 continued.		the shelter of walking wounded awaiting transport by supply wagons &c.	
	31/3/17		I visited the CP at LILLE GATE, the ADS, at THE BUND the Foot Preparation Room at THE BUND and the Collecting Post at COW FARM and found all in order. A shell exploded on road about 150 yars from this Unit.	Weather Showery
			J. S. Manford Capt. RAMC T.	

T2134. Wt. W708—776. 500000. 4/15. Sir J. C. & S.

CONFIDENTIAL

Original

133 F. A.

Vol 14

WAR DIARY

OF

133RD FLD. AMB.

From 1st April 1917

To 30th April 1917

Volume No. 14.

I. S. Manford LT COL. RAMC.

O. C. 133RD FLD. AMB.

April 1917

Instructions regarding War Diaries and Intelligence Summaries are contained in F. S. Regs., Part II. and the Staff Manual respectively. Title pages will be prepared in manuscript.

WAR DIARY
or
~~INTELLIGENCE SUMMARY.~~
(Erase heading not required.)

Army Form C. 2118.

133rd Field Ambulance

Page I

Place	Date	Hour	Summary of Events and Information	Remarks and references to Appendices
	1/4/17			
VLAMERTINGUE			Capt. Dennis proceeded for temporary duty to 132nd F Amb:	
			" J.D. MacKinnon RAMC from 132 F Amb: reported here for instructional duties at A.D.S.	
	2/4/17.		I had interview with DADMS. 39th Div with reference to X scheme. X Corps.	
	3/4/17.		Outdoor work impossible owing to weather.	Heavy Snow.
			Capt the Rev. H.J. Hawkins rejoined the Unit from St OMER	
			I had an interview with ADMS (acting) at 134 F Amb:	
			Lt Johnston RAMC proceeded to 11th R Sussex Reg for temporary duty.	
	4/4/17		DMS. Second Army accompanied by DADMS. X Corps inspected this M D Station and expressed approval of progress made in constructional work in gas wards.	Very Cold.
	5/4/17		Capt Bolt RAMC rejoined the Unit from leave.	
	6/4/17		I visited Horse Transport Lines at POPERINGUE wh. were in satisfactory condition. One of the huts had been hit by shrapnell. About twenty holes in felting of roof but curiously ~~none~~ no piece of casing had penetrated the wire netting under the felt. Capt MacKinnon, attached, proceeded to A.D.S. Asylum.	

J.S. Manford Lt. Col.

T2134. Wt. W708—776. 500000. 4/15. Sir J. C. & S.

Instructions regarding War Diaries and Intelligence Summaries are contained in F. S. Regs., Part II. and the Staff Manual respectively. Title pages will be prepared in manuscript.

WAR DIARY
or
INTELLIGENCE SUMMARY.
(Erase heading not required.)

Army Form C. 2118.

133 Field Ambulance

Page II

Place	Date	Hour	Summary of Events and Information	Remarks and references to Appendices
	6/4/17			
VLAMERTINGUE			Work on general improvements at M.D.S. progressing satisfactorily also at A.D.S. - Asylum. where the floor above the Officers mess & sleeping quarters & offices has been covered with broken bricks. upon wh. have been placed large pieces of stone the cellar roofs have been strengthened by 12 inch pit props supporting cross pieces This portion of ADS was ~~first~~ completed first as it is the strongest part of the building having the shortest "span" of roof. & all personelle can be accomodated there if necessary. The dressing room wh has a "span" of 24 feet is now in process of strengthening in the same way.	
	ǂ.		I proceeded with Capt Robertson RAMC of this Unit to locate & inspect the proposed "rail head" at KRUISSTREET. We walked down the light railway from VLAMERTINGUE to it junction at first named place. It is a suitable place for off loading except that the proposed road for Motor Ambulances proceeding to the main YPRES - POPERINGUE road is much in need of repair. This road was used for traffic both ways in 2nd Battle of YPRES There are many. gun emplacements on each side of it. I first road on left after passing Asylum on road to POPERINGUE has a much better surface.	

I. S. [signature]

T2134. Wt. W708-776. 500000. 4/15. Sir J. C. & S.

Instructions regarding War Diaries and Intelligence Summaries are contained in F. S. Regs., Part II. and the Staff Manual respectively. Title pages will be prepared in manuscript.

WAR DIARY
or
~~INTELLIGENCE~~ SUMMARY.
(Erase heading not required.)

133 Field Ambulance

Army Form C. 2118.

Page III

Place	Date	Hour	Summary of Events and Information	Remarks and references to Appendices
VLAMERTINGUE				
	7/4/14		Nothing to report.	
	8/4/14		On instructions from Acting ADMS Capt Bolt proceeded to 134th F. Amb. for duty. He rejoined the Unit later in the day. The personnel attached to 234 Field Co RE were relieved & substituted, and 4 o.rs. RGA reported for course of Ambulance training I had an interview with DDMS. X Corps. with reference to x scheme X Corps.	
	9/4/14		Notified that Lt ANDERSON, RAMC M.O. 12 Royal Sussex is struck off strength of this Unit from this date Capt R F BOLT proceeded to WATOU to report to "B" Battery for duty & is struck off strength of this Unit from this date. Capt. DENNIS rejoined from 132 F Amb. Activity near divisional front about 30 casualties passed through MDS. Capt. WARWICK rejoined from 134 F Amb	

I. S. Ulanford.

T2134. Wt. W708—776. 500000. 4/15. Sir J. C. & S.

Instructions regarding War Diaries and Intelligence Summaries are contained in F. S. Regs., Part II. and the Staff Manual respectively. Title pages will be prepared in manuscript.

WAR DIARY
or
~~INTELLIGENCE SUMMARY.~~
(Erase heading not required.)

133rd Field Ambulance

Army Form C. 2118.

Page IV

Place	Date	Hour	Summary of Events and Information	Remarks and references to Appendices
	10/4/17			
VLAMERTINGUE			Total casualties passed through M.D.S. since night of 9th inst. 78	Stormy
			Enemy shelled this village during the morning. No casualties reported	Snowing
	12/4/17		ADMS 39th Div visited this M.D.S. & made general inspection.	
	13/4/17		Green Discs distributed to personnel and AB. 64 placed in groups as directed in Army Order 93. 1917. Hostile shelling during evening.	Fine
	14/4/17		I proceeded to POPERINGUE with Capt ROBERTSON & arranged re "taking over" with the O.C. 2/1 WESSEX F Amb. at the College.	
	15/4/17		One NCO & four men proceeded to CANAL BANK Collecting Post & the same number to OUTSKIRT FARM Collecting Post to take over from 130th Field Amb.	
			I visited 130th F Amb & interviewed the OC with reference to taking over ESSEX FARM tomorrow. He had received no definite instructions to hand over.	

J. S. [signature]

T2134. Wt. W708—776. 500000. 4/15. Sir J. C. & S.

Instructions regarding War Diaries and Intelligence Summaries are contained in F. S. Regs., Part II. and the Staff Manual respectively. Title pages will be prepared in manuscript.

WAR DIARY
or
INTELLIGENCE SUMMARY.
(Erase heading not required.)

133 Field Ambulance.

Army Form C. 2118.

Page V

Place	Date	Hour	Summary of Events and Information	Remarks and references to Appendices
POPERINGUE				
	16/4/17		This Unit moved from THE MILL, VLAMERTINGHE. to the College POPERINGHE	Fine
			The transport were moved to new standing with exception of one horse (sick)	
			Capt WARWICK proceeded with 20 men to ESSEX FARM. ADStation & took over from 130th F Ambulance	
			Capt ROBERTSON visited the ADS. ESSEX FARM & the Collecting Posts during the evening.	
	17/4/17		ADMS visited this MDS.	
			I attended a conference of Administrative Medical Officers & F Amb: Commanders at 130 F Amb.	
			A supply of Area stores (Sanitary) were received & stored under directions of ADMS with instructions not to issue them without his authority.	Dull. Cold
			Foden lorry Disinfector arrived from 82nd Sanitary Section	
	19/4/17		No 88221 Pt Lanham RAMC proceeded to 38 Parliament St London re taking temporary commission in Infantry & is struck off the strength.	

I. S. Mumford.

T2134. Wt. W708—776. 500000. 4/15. Sir J. C. & S.

Instructions regarding War Diaries and Intelligence Summaries are contained in F. S. Regs., Part II. and the Staff Manual respectively. Title pages will be prepared in manuscript.

WAR DIARY
or
~~INTELLIGENCE SUMMARY.~~
(Erase heading not required.)

133 Field Ambulance

Army Form C. 2118.

Page VI

Place	Date	Hour	Summary of Events and Information	Remarks and references to Appendices
POPERINGHE				
	20/4/17.		Telephone installed into this Office. this will be a very great advantage to the working of the Ambulance.	
			I attended with Capt LIMBURY. the Lecture at Second Army Medical Society.	
	21/4/17.		Gen: Court Martial held at the COLLEGE - Capt L.R. MEECH. MC. RAMC of this Unit was tried on charges of drunkenness & assault.	Weather good
			LIEUT TOWNSEND of 39. DSC. inspected the Ambulances & Cycles.	
			The preparation & planting of available ground for potatoes &c is nearly completed	
			The ADS. Asylum was heavily shelled from 11 p.m to 11.30 p.m. Little damage was done to the ADS. but the Asylum buildings suffered heavily. No casualties.	"
	22/4/17.		ADMS. 39th Div visited ADS Asylum & advised that a further supply of blankets be kept	
			A Foden Lorry disinfector was attached this day to the Unit ~~with~~ instructions received from ADMS re fumigating clothing of Units &c.	

J. S. Manford

T2131. Wt. W708–776. 500000. 4/15. Sir J. C. & S.

Army Form C. 2118.

Instructions regarding War Diaries and Intelligence Summaries are contained in F. S. Regs., Part II. and the Staff Manual respectively. Title pages will be prepared in manuscript.

WAR DIARY
or
~~INTELLIGENCE~~ SUMMARY.
(Erase heading not required.)

133rd Field Ambulance

Page VII

Place	Date	Hour	Summary of Events and Information	Remarks and references to Appendices
POPERINGHE				
	24/4/17.		The sentence upon Capt MEECH of this Unit for the G C Martial held on 21st inst was promulgated by me. The sentence was to lose seniority & take rank as Capt as if his appointment to that rank bore date 21st April 1917 and to be severely reprimanded.	Fine
			Lt Curling QM to this unit evacuated through. CCS to Base suffering from Malaria.	
	26/4/17.		I inspected the 23rd Div Baths & reported to ADMS 39th Div.	
	27/4/17		I inspected the 39th Div Baths at D Camp & reported to ADMS 39 Div.	
	28/4/17		Received instructions to prepare to assist ~~at~~ the Medical Service of 38th Div if necessary during the next 72 hours. Instructions of ADMS forwarded to Capt WARWICK at ESSEX FARM immediately on receipt. (1.40 p.m)	
	29/4/17		I inspected the A.D.S. at the ASYLUM & at ESSEX FARM & found all was in order should assistance be required by 38th Div. The water supply (pipe) for ESSEX FARM is completed & is expected to be in use tomorrow.	

T2134. Wt. W708—776. 500000. 4/15. Sir J. C. & S.

Instructions regarding War Diaries and Intelligence Summaries are contained in F. S. Regs., Part II. and the Staff Manual respectively. Title pages will be prepared in manuscript.

WAR DIARY
or
~~INTELLIGENCE SUMMARY.~~
(Erase heading not required.)

133rd Field Ambulance

Army Form C. 2118.

Page VIII

Place	Date	Hour	Summary of Events and Information	Remarks and references to Appendices
POPERINGHE				
	30/4/17.		ADMS 39th Div visited M.D.S. Activity on 38th Div front night 29/30th. Fifteen wounded were received during the night. A heavy bombardment by the enemy took place about 11. p.m. last night. it appeared to be in the region of RENINGHELST. no shell dropped in this town.	

I. S. Manford. Lt Col RAMC
O.C. No 133 Field Amb.

Original

CONFIDENTIAL

Vol 15

WAR DIARY OF

140/2101

133RD FIELD AMBULANCE

From 1st May 1917.

To 31st May 1917.

VOL. XIV.

I. S. Manford LT COL. R.A.M.C. T.
O. C. 133RD FLD. AMB.

ma[illegible]

Instructions regarding War Diaries and Intelligence Summaries are contained in F. S. Regs., Part II. and the Staff Manual respectively. Title pages will be prepared in manuscript.

WAR DIARY
or
~~INTELLIGENCE SUMMARY.~~ 133rd Field Ambulance.

(Erase heading not required.)

Army Form C. 2118.

VOL XIV

Page I

Place	Date	Hour	Summary of Events and Information	Remarks and references to Appendices
POPERINGHE				
	1/5/17.		The ADS Asylum was heavily shelled today. One of the Sunbeam Motor Ambulances was damaged necessitating it being sent for extensive repairs.	weather warm & fine.
	2.5.17		POPERINGHE shelled by HV gun between 4pm & 6pm. Nine shells fell near horse-lines. Gas Alarm received abt 10 15pm & "alarm" given at once. Notified about ½ hour later that the gas was not travelling in this direction. Capt Warwick RAMC. M.O/c ADS. Essex Farm reports that raids by 38th Div on nights 29.30 April 30 Apl. 1 May. were both most successful & casualties lighter than expected. 16 wounded cases were ~~#~~ treated in his ADS. including 1 officer and also 1 wounded prisoner. during first night & 12 cases including 2 prisoners during second night. 17 Prisoners taken & report from Bdgs: states "many enemy were killed.	do
	3.5.17		ADMS. 39th Div visited this Ambulance. Another gas alarm at 11.30pm. Nothing materialized	
	5.5.17		POPERINGHE shelled between 10.30 p.m. & 1 am 6th inst. shells again falling close to horse lines	do
	6.5.17		I attended at ADMS. Office this morning. Town again shelled. The horse lines were evacuated & horses removed into the open country on Proven road.	do
	7.5.17		Heavy bombardment of town from 9.45 to 11 pm.	
	8.5.17		I attended conference at ADMS Office. D camp. Capt A.W. DENNIS. RAMC. posted to 16th RB. & struck off strength of this unit	

J. S. Mumford

T2134. Wt. W708—776. 500000. 4/15. Sir J. C. & S.

Instructions regarding War Diaries and Intelligence Summaries are contained in F. S. Regs., Part II. and the Staff Manual respectively. Title pages will be prepared in manuscript.

WAR DIARY
or
INTELLIGENCE SUMMARY. 133rd Field Ambulance.
(*Erase heading not required.*)

Army Form C. 2118.

Page 11.

Place	Date	Hour	Summary of Events and Information	Remarks and references to Appendices
POPERINGHE				
	9/5/17.		Capt S. J. L. LINDEMAN. RAMC taken on strength of this Unit today. Authority ADMS. 10/674	
			Owing to shortage in issue of fresh vegetables I ordered lime juice to be issued to patients & personnel in presence of an Officer.	
			Sports (Divisional Medical) held at 132 Fld Amb also competition for Horse Transport.	
	10/5/17		Notification of death of ~~Capt~~ Lt & QM Curling of this Unit, on 2nd inst.	
			ASC. M.T. returned to their horse lines there having been no more shelling.	
	12/5/17		ADS. ASYLUM heavily shelled this morning. A direct hit was obtained through the staircase into the dressing room killing 4 and wounding two of my medical orderlies. Lt Johnston was uninjured but shaken & he was relieved by Capt Lindeman who went to ADS Canal Bank wh. is under construction. The Asylum ADS being untenable. ~~[illegible]~~	
	13/5/17.		Definite orders to vacate this COLLEGE, received & transferred my AMBULANCE to the CLOISTERS POPERINGHE. ADMS. visited Ambulance. Transfer took place about midday. The Cloisters is a much more suitable building for Hosp. work & if the whole building should be acquired would make an excellent C.C.S.	dull.
	14/5/17		All available men employed in cleaning re this building wh is very dirty.	
			DDMS. VIII Corps visited the Ambulance.	

J. S. Manford

T2134. Wt. W708—776. 500000. 4/15. Sir J. C. & S.

Instructions regarding War Diaries and Intelligence Summaries are contained in F. S. Regs., Part II. and the Staff Manual respectively. Title pages will be prepared in manuscript.

WAR DIARY
or
INTELLIGENCE SUMMARY.
(Erase heading not required.)

133rd Field Ambulance

Army Form C. 2118.

Vol. XIV

Page iii

Place	Date	Hour	Summary of Events and Information	Remarks and references to Appendices
POPERINGHE				
May	15·	17.	ADMS. 39th Div visited the MDStation & inspected it	
			A German prisoner captured by 39th Div was passed through this Ambulance	
			The necessary furniture to equip 15 beds for the Officers ward was received from B.R.C.	
"	16·	17	D.D.M.S. VIII Corps visited the MDStation & expressed approval of progress in work of cleaning & constructing &c.	
			Capt. E F MANSFIELD. RAMC. taken on strength of this Unit.	
			Conference of Regimental MOs held here.	
"	17·	17	Lt Lindeman RAMC rejoined HQ from ADS "Duhallow" & brought all personnel & equipment with him. 134th F.A. took over ADS. "Duhallow."	
			Capt. E. F MANSFIELD proceeded to 39th Div Train for temporary duty.	
"	19·	17	Progress in constructional work proceeding satisfactorily.	
"	20	17	ADMS visited & inspected MDS.	
"	21	"	~~Capt~~ Capt ROBERTSON proceeded to Essex Farm ADS. to relieve Lt BULLOCK who rejoined his own unit (134th FA).	
			Capt. MEECH rejoined from (134th F.A)	
			All NCOs & men paraded for inspection of Box respirators	

Instructions regarding War Diaries and Intelligence Summaries are contained in F. S. Regs., Part II. and the Staff Manual respectively. Title pages will be prepared in manuscript.

WAR DIARY
or
INTELLIGENCE SUMMARY.
(Erase heading not required.)

133rd Field Ambulance

Army Form C. 2118.

Vol XIV.

Page. IV

Place	Date	Hour	Summary of Events and Information	Remarks and references to Appendices
POPERINGHE				
May	22nd 17.		DADMS VIII Corps visited & inspected MDS. & expressed approval of progress made	
"	23. 17		Five enemy shells fell in the town.	
			Lt & QM. AUDUS, W.C. taken on the strength from this date.	
"	24 17		The town was shelled about 8 p.m.	
"	25. 17		The town again shelled about 6. a.m. After consultation with ADMS. 39th Div. I made tour of inspection to find a suitable place for an emergency camp should we be compelled to vacate owing to shelling. A suitable place was found about 3/4 of a mile along the Rue de DUNKIRK.	
"	26 17		Temporary camp to accomodate about 70 men erected & arrangements made for accomodation, in case of emergency, of 50 men in a school house near the camp.	
"	27 17		Heavy Bombardment in sight of sector during greater part of night.	
	28 17		"Gas alert" received from 24th Div at 2.15 am. Slight trace of gas noticed.	
			3 Shells dropped in town.	
			I visited Essex Farm A.D.S. & made inspection	
"	30. 17		ADMS & DADMS visited MDS.	
			Instructional conference of regimental MOs.	

T2134. Wt. W708—776. 500000. 4/15. Sir J. C. & S.

Instructions regarding War Diaries and Intelligence Summaries are contained in F. S. Regs., Part II. and the Staff Manual respectively. Title pages will be prepared in manuscript.

WAR DIARY
or
INTELLIGENCE SUMMARY.
(Erase heading not required.)

133rd Field Ambulance

Army Form C. 2118.

Vol. XIV

Page V.

Place	Date	Hour	Summary of Events and Information	Remarks and references to Appendices
POPERINGHE				
May	31.17		Major Gen: CUTHBERT. CB CMG Commanding 39th Div inspected this M.D.S. + expressed approval of what he saw. The town was shelled at intervals during the afternoon and evening.	

I. S. Wayford. Lt. Col: RAMC.T.
OC. 133rd Fld. Amb

T2131. Wt. W708–776. 500000. 4/15. Sir J. C. & S.

Original

Vol 16

CONFIDENTIAL

War Diary

of

140/2220

133RD FLD. AMB.

from 1-6-17.
to 30-6-17.

Volume XVI

I S Manford LT COL.
O. C. 133RD FLD. AMB.

9

June 1917

B.E.F.

SUMMARY OF MEDICAL WAR DIARIES OF 133rd F.A. 39th Div. 18th Corps

5th ARMY.

Western Front Operations June 1917.

Officer Commanding - Lt.Col. J.S. Manford.

SUMMARISED UNDER THE FOLLOWING HEADING:-

Phase "D". Battle of Messines. June 1917.

133rd F.A. 39th Div. 18th Corps. 5th ARMY. Western Front. June 1917.

Officer Commanding - Lt.Col. J.S. Manford.

PHASE "D". Battle of Messines. June 1917.

Headquarters at Poperinghe.

June 10th. Transfer. To 5th ARMY.

13th. Evacuation. No patients evacuated to D.R.S. and Field Ambulance became congested in consequence.

15th. Ops. Enemy.) Poperinghe shelled.
Casualties.) Fair number.

16th-19th. Shelling and bombs on Poperinghe.
R.E. yard shelled, many casualties.

22nd. Casualties. M.D.S. and D.R.S. full - mostly Corps Troops.
Ops. Enemy. Heavy shelling in line.

25th. Casualties. R.A.M.C. Capt. Meech wounded.
0 & 2 killed.) 134th F.A. (At Duhallow A.D.S.
0 & 2 wounded.)

29th. Moves. To Red Farm (now called Gwent Farm.)

B.E.F.

SUMMARY OF MEDICAL WAR DIARIES OF 133rd F.A. 39th Div. 18th Corps

5th ARMY.

Western Front Operations June 1917.

Officer Commanding - Lt.Col. J.S. Manford.

SUMMARISED UNDER THE FOLLOWING HEADING:-

Phase "D". Battle of Messines. June 1917.

133rd F.A. 39th Div. 18th Corps. 5th ARMY. Western Front.
June 1917.

Officer Commanding - Lt.Col. J.S. Manford.

PHASE "D". Battle of Messines. June 1917.

Headquarters at Poperinghe.

June 10th. Transfer. To 5th ARMY.

13th. Evacuation. No patients evacuated to D.R.S. and Field Ambulance became congested in consequence.

15th. Ops. Enemy.) Poperinghe shelled.
Casualties.) Fair number.

16th-19th. Shelling and bombs on Poperinghe.
R.E. yard shelled, many casualties.

22nd. Casualties. M.D.S. and D.R.S. full - mostly Corps Troops.
Ops. Enemy. Heavy shelling in line.

25th. Casualties. R.A.M.C. Capt. Meech wounded.
O & 2 killed.) 134th F.A. (At Duhallow A.D.S.
O & 2 wounded.)

29th. Moves. To Red Farm (now called Gwent Farm.)

Instructions regarding War Diaries and Intelligence Summaries are contained in F. S. Regs., Part II. and the Staff Manual respectively. Title pages will be prepared in manuscript.

WAR DIARY
or
INTELLIGENCE SUMMARY.
(Erase heading not required.)

133rd Field Ambulance

Army Form C. 2118.

Vol. XVI

Page I.

Place	Date	Hour	Summary of Events and Information	Remarks and references to Appendices
POPERINGHE				
	June 1.17		Considerable progress made in the preparation of this Building for the reception of patients.	
	3.17		Poperinghe & district shelled, causing fires in places. Macintosh Capes called in. These have not been worn at all since issue in beginning of May.	
	4.17		Town rather heavily shelled.	
	5.17		39th Div. Supply Officer inspected ambulance cars. Vicinities of town shelled	
	6.17		Capt S J LINDEMAN evacuated, sick, to No 2 C.C.C.S. Town shelled during night	
	7.17		IX & X Corps attacked south of YPRES with considerable success. This MDS assisted in the evacuation of wounded to CCSs. About 160 cases passed through between 6.30pm & 8.30pm. Arrangements have been made to utilise this Fld. Amb MDS to assist in the evacuation of wounded from 47th Div.	J.S. Mumford Lt Col
	8.17		LIEUT. DOWNES. RAMC from 132 Fld Amb sent to ESSEX FARM in relief of Capt. G.D. Robertson who returns to HdQ	

T2134. Wt. W708—776. 500000. 4/15. Sir J. C. & S.

Instructions regarding War Diaries and Intelligence Summaries are contained in F. S. Regs., Part II. and the Staff Manual respectively. Title pages will be prepared in manuscript.

WAR DIARY
or
~~INTELLIGENCE SUMMARY.~~
(Erase heading not required.)

133 Fld Ambulance

Army Form C. 2118.

Vol. XVI
Page II

Place	Date	Hour	Summary of Events and Information	Remarks and references to Appendices
POPERINGHE	9.7		Sgt Goddard RAMC rejoined on completion of gas course.	
			778 L/Cpl Thomas 6904 Pte Harvey 4713 Armstrong H. proceeded on 10 days leave –	
			Field Ambulance Sports held at 132 Fld Ambulance PROVEN.	
			Work progressing favourably. Still a great deal to be done –	
	10.7		39971 Pte Frost 64780 Pte Scott granted 10 days leave.	
			Unit transferred to Fifth Army XVIII Corps. Weather fine & close – water question for horses becoming serious as all sources are drying up.	
	11.7		Capt L R Heech rejoined unit from temporary duty with 23 Div.	
			Work progressing	
	12.7		78729 Pte Veitch rejoined unit from 10 days leave – Col Manford RAMC T. proceeded 10 days leave	
	13.7		65727 Staff Sgt Smith returned from Base after wounds, & is taken on strength of unit	
	14.7		Car shelter at A.D.S. Dose Farm completed.	
	15.7		Lieut & Qr M Andrews RAMC proceeded on 10 days leave to U.K.	
			No 72152 Sgt Herbert RAMC proceeded on 10 days leave to U.K.	
			Lieut Johnston RAMC proceeded to 132 Fld Amb for temporary duty.	
			No patients evacuated to D.R.S. & Fld Amb becoming full in consequence –	

Instructions regarding War Diaries and Intelligence Summaries are contained in F. S. Regs., Part II. and the Staff Manual respectively. Title pages will be prepared in manuscript.

WAR DIARY
or
~~INTELLIGENCE SUMMARY.~~ 133 Fd Amb.
(Erase heading not required.)

Army Form C. 2118.

Vol. XVI
Page 3

Place	Date	Hour	Summary of Events and Information	Remarks and references to Appendices
POPERINGHE.			D.A.D.M.S. XVIII Corps visited the Fd Amb, & expressed satisfaction at the work done.	
			He also visited a new camp used as a D.R.S. in consequence of 134 Fd Amb & 137	
			Fd Amb being shut down. Arrangements to open same - A.D.M.S. 39 Div.	
			Poperinghe shelled in region of station - four number of casualties	
	16.7		Poperinghe again shelled - few casualties - Work in Fd Amb very heavy.	
	17.7		Enemy aeroplane dropped bombs in region of Unit horse lines & wounded	
			3 horses slightly & ~~injured~~ damaged one G.S. wagon 'B' Section. Time 4 a.m.	
			No casualties in personnel. Constructional work almost complete.	
			A.D.M.S. 39 Div visited M.D.S and saw some T.U. men. He also informed	
			Capt J.P. Gore that he was being transferred to 38 Div. as a permanent measure.	
	18.7		Capt J.P. Pierce from RAMC proceeded to report for duty to A.D.M.S. 38 Div. & posted to	
			130 Fd Amb. He is struck off the strength of this unit from 17-7-17.	
			88907 Pte Sullivan & 72056 Pte Richardson of this unit proceeded to 2nd Army Rest	
			camp for 14 days at AMBLETEUSE.	
			Capt L.R. Mutch proceeds to Essex Farm to relieve Capt Warwick RAMC who	
			returned to H.dq. Capt Mutch will take over duties of O.M.O Canal Bank vice	

T2134. Wt. W708—776. 500000. 4/15. Sir J. C. & S.

Instructions regarding War Diaries and Intelligence Summaries are contained in F. S. Regs., Part II. and the Staff Manual respectively. Title pages will be prepared in manuscript.

WAR DIARY
or
~~INTELLIGENCE~~ SUMMARY. 133 Fd Amb

(Erase heading not required.)

Army Form C. 2118.

Vol XVI
Page 60.

Place	Date	Hour	Summary of Events and Information	Remarks and references to Appendices
POPERINGHE.				
			Capt Warwick.	
			Slight shelling of Poperinghe - no casualties.	
	19 - 17.		131524 Dr Harrison MT ASC proceeded on 10 days leave -	
			D.A.D.M.S. 31st Div visits 133 Amb and also Essex Farm which will be taken over by that Division at an early date.	
			RE yard shelled by enemy - many casualties - all wounded were removed very speedily by 133 Fd Amb cars - Five dead bodies in mortuary [illegible]	
	20 - 17		15717 Pte Scholes RAMC proceeded on 10 days leave -	
	21 - 17		Warned to be ready to hand over Essex Farm to 1/3 Highland Field Amb and to take over DUHALLOW ADS from 13[illegible] Fd Amb night 22/23rd.	
	21 - 17		132576 Sgt PELL ASC MT proceeded on 10 days leave -	
			Lieut Johnston RAMC to be M.O. for 31 Labour Group and is struck off the strength accordingly -	
			Capt Mansfield RAMC returned to Hosp.	

Instructions regarding War Diaries and Intelligence Summaries are contained in F. S. Regs., Part II. and the Staff Manual respectively. Title pages will be prepared in manuscript.

WAR DIARY
or
INTELLIGENCE SUMMARY.
(Erase heading not required.)

133 Fld Amb.

Army Form C. 2118.

Vol. XVI
Page 5.

Place	Date	Hour	Summary of Events and Information	Remarks and references to Appendices
POPERINGHE	22. 17.		Main dressing station & D.R.S. full - mostly corps troops -	
			Heavy shelling in line - many casualties coming down - mostly leg & abdominal wounds.	
	23-17.		Lt Col Mawford RAMC T. rejoined from 10 days leave in U.K.	
			Capt H.C. [illegible] RAMC 29 DAC attached to unit for (temporary) duty. (ADMS 39 Div)	
			DUHALLOW ADS taken over & ESSEX Farm ADS handed over. Notification forwarded.	
			Much work still to be done to complete DUHALLOW. A.D.S. [signature illegible] Capt	
	25-17.		Capt. Meech, RAMC of this Unit, wounded at DUHALLOW. A.D.S. & evacuated to 46 C.C.S.	
			Two ~~men~~ O.Rs killed & two wounded at the same place & time. These men were attached from 134 Fld A.	
			I received instructions to prepare to move out on 29th inst. & proceed to RED FARM	(A.28 a 5.5)
	26-17.		I visited DUHALLOW A.D.S. with Capt Warwick & arranged with Capt Limbury	(in charge)
			as to constructional arrangements &c.	
	29-17.		This Unit moved out of the CLOISTERS POPERINGHE & took over RED FARM, now called GWENT FARM.	
	30-17.		Capt. DALLIMORE RAMC taken on strength of this Unit from this date.	
			Considerable enemy activity with heavy guns in this district.	

I. S. Mawford. Lt Col RAMC T

T2134. Wt. W708-776. 500000. 4/15. Sir J. C. & S.

Original

War Diary

Volume 17

from

July 1st 1917 to July 31st 1917

of

133 Field Ambulance

Confidential

Vol 17

B.E.F.

SUMMARY OF MEDICAL WAR DIARIES OF 133rd F.A. 39th Div. 18th Corps. 5th ARMY.

To 2nd Army Area from 7th August.

Western Front Operations - July - ~~August~~ 1917.

Officer Commanding - Lt.Col. J.S. Manford.

SUMMARISED UNDER THE FOLLOWING HEADINGS :-

Phase "D" 1. Passchendaele Operations, "July - November 1917."

(a) Operations commencing 1/7/17.

B.E.F.

133rd F.A. 39th Div. 18th Corps. 5th ARMY. Western Front.
July-~~Aug~~. 1917.

Officer Commanding - Lt.Col. J.S. Manford.

PHASE "D" 1. Passchendaele Operations, "July - November 1917."

(a) - Operations commencing 1/7/17.

Headquarters at Red Farm. (Gwent Farm).

July 1st-6th. Ops. Enemy. Continuous shelling.

Ops. R.A.M.C. Constructional work on completion of A.D.S.

Duhallow. Owing to enemy operations, scarcely possible to work in daylight.

13th-14th. Casualties Gas. "Considerable number" of wounded, Gas.

19th. Casualties Gas R.A.M.C. Capt. Mansfield wounded, gas.

21st. Ops. Enemy. Artillery and aircraft activity continuous.

25th. Direct hit on barn used as main ward.

Casualties R.A.M.C. 0 & 1 killed.

0 & 2 wounded.

29th. Moves. Detachment.) Casualties R.A.M.C.) Personnel for A.D.S. and B.D. sent to A.D.S.

0 & 1 killed. 0 & 1 wounded on route.

31st. Operations. Zero. 3.31 a.m. Intense bombardment, all night.

Casualties. 280 wounded through A.D.S. up to noon.

B.E.F.

133rd F.A. 39th Div. 18th Corps. 5th ARMY. Western Front. July-[illegible]. 1917.

Officer Commanding - Lt.Col. J.S. Manford.

PHASE "D" 1. Passchendaele Operations, "July - November 1917."

(a) - Operations commencing 1/7/17.

Headquarters at Red Farm. (Gwent Farm).

July 1st-6th. Ops. Enemy. Continuous shelling.

Ops. R.A.M.C. Constructional work on completion of A.D.S. Duhallow. Owing to enemy operations, scarcely possible to work in daylight.

13th-14th. Casualties Gas. "Considerable number" of wounded, Gas.

19th. Casualties Gas R.A.M.C. Capt. Mansfield wounded, gas.

21st. Ops. Enemy. Artillery and aircraft activity continuous.

25th. Direct hit on barn used as main ward.

Casualties R.A.M.C. 0 & 1 killed.

0 & 2 wounded.

29th. Moves. Detachment.) Casualties R.A.M.C.) Personnel for A.D.S. and B.D. sent to A.D.S.

0 & 1 killed. 0 & 1 wounded on route.

31st. Operations. Zero. 3.31 a.m. Intense bombardment, all night.

Casualties. 280 wounded through A.D.S. up to noon.

Original

Instructions regarding War Diaries and Intelligence Summaries are contained in F. S. Regs., Part II. and the Staff Manual respectively. Title pages will be prepared in manuscript.

WAR DIARY
or
~~INTELLIGENCE SUMMARY.~~
(Erase heading not required.)

133rd Field Ambulance A.28.a 20 65 (Sheet 28)

Army Form C. 2118.

Page I VOL: 17.

Place	Date	Hour	Summary of Events and Information	Remarks and references to Appendices
GWENTFARM	1/7/17		The constructional work ~~of~~ at ADS is being pushed forward. There is much to be done	Fine
	2/7/17		Shelling of this area continues, one HV shell fell within 5 yards of one of the Ward Huts doing absolutely no dammage.	
	5/7/17		All energy is being consentrated on the completion of ADS. Duhellow. It is scarcely possible to work on the superstructure during daylight owing to the observation & shelling of the enemy. The dugouts are being fitted with tressels for stretchers. By this means 18 stretcher cases can be put into each large dug out.	
	6/7/17		Heavy shelling during the day. Gas alarm received about 10.45 pm but nothing developed.	
	8/7/17		Gas goggles were withdrawn from the personnel of the Unit	Heavy Rain
	9/7/17		Full kit inspection & all surplus kit disposed of	
	12/7/17		Intermittent shelling of District continues daily. The enemy generally putting over 5 or 6 shells & then stopping for a few hours. One transport mule killed by a "dud" shell while returning from ADS.	
	13/7/17		Capt Robertson RAMC. of this Unit attached for temporary duty to DHQ	

I. S. Mumford Lt-Col.
O.C. 133 Fd. Amb

T2134. Wt. W708—776. 500000. 4/15. Sir J. C. & S.

Original

Instructions regarding War Diaries and Intelligence Summaries are contained in F. S. Regs., Part II. and the Staff Manual respectively. Title pages will be prepared in manuscript.

WAR DIARY
or
~~INTELLIGENCE SUMMARY.~~
(Erase heading not required.)

Army Form C. 2118.

133rd Field Ambulance
A. 28. a. 20. 65 (Sheet 28)

Page II

VOL. 17.

Place	Date	Hour	Summary of Events and Information	Remarks and references to Appendices
GWENT FARM.	14/7/17		Considerable numbers of gassed cases passed through this unit yesterday & today showing lachrymatory symptoms + lesions on all parts of body similar to those produced by mustard leaves too long applied. (Acute erythema & bullae)	
			I attended a conference at ADMS Office	
	17/7/17		The mobile workshop of No 24 Motor Ambulance Convoy arrived here & was given accommodation in these lines. A repair depot for MAC cars is to be established here.	
	19/7/17		Capt Mansfield RAMC of this Unit evacuated ~~sick~~ to CCS suffering from Gas (Lachrymatory)	
	21/7/17		Enemy artillery & aircraft continue active day & night & intervals.	
			Constructional work at ADS well advanced. A direct hit ~~[illegible]~~ by an enemy 5·9 wh. did not penetrate proving the work that has been ~~[illegible]~~ carried on under considerable difficulty	
	25/7/17		All personnel confined to camp until further notice. Capt Robertson & Capt Warwick proceeded to ADS. to make final arrangements for the prospective advance.	
			An enemy shell burst on barn wh. constitutes main ward, killing one & wounding two	J. S. [illegible] Lt-Col. O.C. 133 Fld. Amb

T2134. Wt. W708–776. 500000. 4/15. Sir J. C. & S.

10f

Original

Instructions regarding War Diaries and Intelligence Summaries are contained in F. S. Regs., Part II. and the Staff Manual respectively. Title pages will be prepared in manuscript.

WAR DIARY or INTELLIGENCE SUMMARY.

(Erase heading not required.)

133rd Field Ambulance. A 28 a 20 65 (Sheet 28)

Army Form C. 2118.

Page III — Vol. 17.

Place	Date	Hour	Summary of Events and Information	Remarks and references to Appendices
GWENT FARM	25/7/17		of my personnel. Fortunately the wards were practically empty. Owing to damage & dirt &c. the reception of patients was stopped for a few hours.	
	26/7/17		Open again for reception of patients this morning.	
	27/7/17		Capt Lembury & Capt Brown proceeded to their posts at ADS.	
			New Officers arriving to complete strength of this Unit. it being four short in Officers	
	29/7/17		Personnel for ADS & Bearer Division sent to ADS. One killed & one wounded on the way.	
			All preparations for the offensive completed.	
	30/7/17		Notified that Z hour is 3·31 am tomorrow.	Thunderstorm
	31/7/17		Intense bombardment all night until Z hour & afterward. News of a successful advance & not a large casualty list. 280 wounded passed through ADS up to mid-day. Everything appears to be working smoothly.	Fine

J. S. [illegible] Lt Col.
O.C. 133 Field Ambulance.

T2134. Wt. W708—776. 500000. 4/15. Sir J. C. & S.

CONFIDENTIAL

Original

War Diary

of

133RD FLD. AMB.

From 1st August 1917

To 31st August 1917

Volume No. XVIII

Sinclair Miller Capt RAMC
O. C. 133RD FLD. AMB.

B.E.F.

SUMMARY OF MEDICAL WAR DIARIES OF 133rd F.A. 39th Div. 18th Corps.

5th ARMY.

To 2nd Army Area from 7th August.

Western Front Operations - ~~July~~ - August 1917.

Officer Commanding - Lt.Col. J.S. Manford.

SUMMARISED UNDER THE FOLLOWING HEADINGS :-

Phase "D" 1. Passchendaele Operations, "July - November 1917."

(a) Operations commencing 1/7/17.

Aug. 1st. Casualties. Wounded came in regularly. At 6 p.m. wounded arrived in very exhausted state.

2nd. Ops. R.A.M.C.) "Conditions appalling."
Evacuation.)
8 bearers to carry 1 L.D.W. (2½ miles carry).

3rd. Bearers very exhausted.

133rd F.A. 39th Div. 18th Corps. 5th ARMY. Western Front July-Aug.1917

Officer Commanding - Lt.Col. J.S. Manford.

To 2nd Army Area from August 7th.

PHASE "D" 1. contd.

(a) Operations commencing 1/7/17.

Headquarters at Red Farm. (Gwent Farm).

Aug. 3rd contd. Assistance. 200 R.S.B's attached, but few were suited to work required of them. Parties detailed for duty would disappear en route.

4th. Bearer question acute. Total Bearers fit for duty 117.

Casualties R.A.M.C.

132nd F.A. 0 & 1 Killed. 0 & 4 wounded.

133rd F.A. 0 & 1 killed. (0 & 7 wounded.
(
(0 & 1 wounded gas.

134th F.A. 0 & 1 killed. (A.S.C. attd.)
0 & 8 wounded.

5th. Capt. Anderson M.O. 16 N.D. wounded.

Casualties. Total wounded avacuated since Zero 2097.

7th. Moves and Transfer. To X.2.6.3.2. 2nd ARMY AREA.

Aug. 1st. Casualties. Wounded came in regularly. At 6 p.m. wounded arrived in very exhausted state.

2nd. Ops. R.A.M.C.) "Conditions appalling."
Evacuation.)

8 bearers to carry 1 L.D.W. (2½ miles carry).

3rd. Bearers very exhausted.

133rd F.A. 39th Div. 18th Corps. 5th ARMY. Western Fron July-Aug.191

Officer Commanding - Lt.Col. J.S. Manford.

To 2nd Army Area from August 7th.

PHASE "D" 1. contd.

(a) Operations commencing 1/7/17.

Headquarters at Red Farm. (Gwent Farm).

Aug. 3rd contd. Assistance. 200 R.S.B's attached, but few were suited to work required of them. Parties detailed for duty would disappear en route.

4th. Bearer question acute. Total Bearers fit for duty 117.

Casualties R.A.M.C.

132nd F.A. 0 & 1 Killed. 0 & 4 wounded.

133rd F.A. 0 & 1 killed. (0 & 7 wounded.
(
(0 & 1 wounded gas.

134th F.A. 0 & 1 killed. (A.S.C. attd.)
0 & 8 wounded.

5th. Capt. Anderson M.O. 16 M.D. wounded.

Casualties. Total wounded evacuated since Zero 2097.

7th. Moves and Transfer. To X.2.6.3.2. 2nd ARMY AREA.

Instructions regarding War Diaries and Intelligence Summaries are contained in F. S. Regs., Part II. and the Staff Manual respectively. Title pages will be prepared in manuscript.

WAR DIARY
or
INTELLIGENCE SUMMARY.
(Erase heading not required.)

133 Fld Amb.

Army Form C. 2118.

Page 1.

Place	Date	Hour	Summary of Events and Information	Remarks and references to Appendices
GWENT FM A 28 a 3.6 Sheet 28.	1/8/17	12 noon	Active operations still in progress. Rain falling. The ADMS 39 Div visited the ADS during the morning. Cases were coming in regularly but the initial rush appears to have	
		2.30pm	ceased. 1 Officer (Lt. PAWLE 1/1 HERTS Reg) and 30 OR reported for duty at the ADS to act as stretcher bearers. The original bearers are very fatigued owing to the long carries and the condition of the ground from the rain.	
		6pm	Wounded cases began to fall off and an attempt was made to rest as many bearers as possible.	
		12 midnight	Rain still falling. Wounded arriving in a very exhausted state. A few shells fell around the ADS during the day but no casualties resulted.	
	2/9/17		Lt Col MANFORD RAMC T. relieved the officer i/c ADS who returned ~~for~~ with 25 OR for 24 hours rest. Bearers were rested as far as possible during the day, but the conditions were appalling, as 8 OR were necessary for each stretcher case and the carry was in many cases a distance of 2½ miles. The road from ADS to DCP at HAMMONDS CORNER became very bad and the horse Ambulances were continually becoming bogged and the large motor ambulances in some distances took as long as two hours on the journey down, thus being ~~[illegible]~~.	

T2134. Wt. W708—776. 500000. 4/15. Sir J. C. & S.

Instructions regarding War Diaries and Intelligence Summaries are contained in F. S. Regs., Part II. and the Staff Manual respectively. Title pages will be prepared in manuscript.

WAR DIARY
or
INTELLIGENCE SUMMARY.
(Erase heading not required.)

133 Fld Amb.

Army Form C. 2118.

Page 2

Place	Date	Hour	Summary of Events and Information	Remarks and references to Appendices
GWENT FRM A28 a 3.6 Sheet 28	2 8/17		partly due to congestion of traffic and partly due to condition of the road. It was found impossible to use the trolley system of evacuation for the following reasons (I) Too many bearer personnel would be used up for pushing these trolleys & they were urgently required at the R.A.P's (II) Evacuation was proceeding by motor + horse ambulances (III) The trolley line was out of repair.	
	3 8/17	8 AM.	Capt G D ROBERTSON relieved Lt Col MANFORD who returned to Hdq of Field Ambulance. Capt L C Ferguson RAMC attached to 133 Fld Amb was posted to 39 Div ASC as MO. Lt STEELE RAMCSR detailed to proceed from the ADS to take over medical charge of 13 Bth Royal Sussex Reg.	
		12 noon	A horse Ambulance badly bogged on DCP road. Telephoned to Hq for spare horses.	
		3.15 pm	The following telephone message from ADMS 39 Div received for transmission to OC Bearers at DCP at HAMMONDS CORNER. "Send to 17 KRRC. 18 attached infantry bearers to act as Reg bearers. Send to 17 N+D. 16 attached infantry bearers to act as Reg bearers. 17 N+D report 16 cases in front line to be removed after dark".	
		4 pm	Lt PAWLE 1/1 Herts and 22 bearers sent down from DCP to ADS for ? hours rest. This party was very fatigued + could not carry on without a rest.	

T2134. Wt. W708—776. 500000. 4/15. Sir J. C. & S.

Instructions regarding War Diaries and Intelligence Summaries are contained in F. S. Regs., Part II. and the Staff Manual respectively. Title pages will be prepared in manuscript.

WAR DIARY
or
INTELLIGENCE SUMMARY.
(Erase heading not required.)

133 Fld Amb

Army Form C. 2118.

Page 3.

Place	Date	Hour	Summary of Events and Information	Remarks and references to Appendices
GWENT F^RM A28a3.6 Sheet 28	3/8/17		Capt ANDERSON RAMC detailed for duty as Medical Officer to 16 N+D.	
			Condition of bearers is becoming worse. They can hardly do any more journeys. The 200 reg attached infantry bearers continue to cause great trouble. Few of them can be found and they are unsuited to the work required of them. Several have rejoined their battalions, others are lost. Often a party will leave the ADS to report to DCP and a certain number will have disappeared en route. Had the party been sent up with a correct proportion of NCO's + Officers who knew the men matters would have been vastly improved	
		5pm	M.O. 17 KRRC reports "no bearers have reached my R.A.P. today". Cases of this description have arisen owing to the fact that certain parties of bearers detailed to report to a certain RAP in compliance ~~from~~ with a request from the M.O. concerned, have been sidetracked by other medical officers who have not notified OC Bearers that this has been done.	
		5.10pm	17 KRRC require 40 stretcher bearers urgently. All available bearers including those in rest sent up to D.C.P.	
		9.45pm	Another party of 50 bearers sent up to DCP. I ~~have~~ ~~are~~ no more bearers at ADS	

Instructions regarding War Diaries and Intelligence Summaries are contained in F. S. Regs., Part II. and the Staff Manual respectively. Title pages will be prepared in manuscript.

WAR DIARY
or
INTELLIGENCE SUMMARY.
(Erase heading not required.)

133 Fld Amb.

Army Form C. 2118.

Page 4

Place	Date	Hour	Summary of Events and Information	Remarks and references to Appendices
GWENT Frm A 28 a 3.6 Sheet 28.		9.45pm	2nd Lt BENNETT. 4/5 BLACK WATCH. one of reg. attached bearers reported sick with synovitis knee & was evacuated to C.M.D.S. This leaves one Reg. attached Infty bearer from the original 200 O.R.	
			Many bearers show signs of trench foot. Unless fresh bearers are sent up it will be nearly impossible to carry on much longer.	
		10.30pm	Telephoned for Capt LIMBERY to return from Hdq for duty as all officers are worn out at the DCP	
	4/8/17	12.45AM	Message from ADMS 39. "10 bearers required at ALBERTA guides waiting at OBLONG Frm send at once".	
			Bearer question has become acute. The Company from 1/4 Ox & Bucks Lt Infty ordered to return to their division. This company which reported as a complete Company with all officers & N.CO's did invaluable work & its return is a great loss.	
		10.30AM	Sent an urgent memo to Hq re bearers to see if fresh bearers could not be sent up. Capt J.H. PORTER RAMC detailed by ADMS 39 Div to take over duties of O/c BEARERS vice Capt WARWICK: RAMC	
		12noon	Requested presence of O.C. Bearers to arrive at some arrangement re bearers.	

Army Form C. 2118.

Instructions regarding War Diaries and Intelligence Summaries are contained in F. S. Regs., Part II. and the Staff Manual respectively. Title pages will be prepared in manuscript.

WAR DIARY
or
INTELLIGENCE SUMMARY.
(Erase heading not required.)

133 Fld Amb. Page 5

Place	Date	Hour	Summary of Events and Information	Remarks and references to Appendices
QWENT F[rm] A28 a 3.6. Sheet 28.				
	4/8/17	12.5pm	Requested that Salvage Coy could remove some of the salvage dump which is growing large and hampering work at ADS	
		12.30pm	Total bearers fit for duty 117.	
			No 92346 PTE BATES. S wounded, evacuated.	
		1 Pm.	Party of 1/1 Ox + Bucks LI attached bearers returned to division –	
		4 pm.	Cases still coming in very slowly – no case yet longer than 20 hours –	
		10.30pm	The following casualties RAMC have occurred since zero hour –	
			132 Fld Amb. Killed – Pt. McCOLLINS wounded Pte's WELFARE, WEBB, HALL, SHRINE.	
			133 Fld Amb Killed – Cpl WINDSOR wounded. Pte's BATES, THOMPSON, BRADWELL, KEPPY, FRY BARRETT, BURRIDGE,	
			gassed – Pte CLIPSON.	
			134 Fld Amb Killed Dr. BELFIELD (M.T. ASC) wounded Pte's LARGE, CHAPMAN, BRADLEY, BOLTON, LEATHERDALE, LEECH, MORRIS, L/Cpl STOKES.	
		4.30am	Orders received to hand over ADS DUHALLOW to 1/2 South MIDLAND Fld amb.	
	5/8/17		Spent most of the day cleaning up and getting most little equipment down to Duhallow from ACP and elsewhere – GS wagons arrived at 3pm –	

T2134. Wt. W708—776. 500000. 4/15. Sir J. C. & S.

Instructions regarding War Diaries and Intelligence Summaries are contained in F. S. Regs., Part II. and the Staff Manual respectively. Title pages will be prepared in manuscript.

WAR DIARY
or
INTELLIGENCE SUMMARY.
(Erase heading not required.)

133 Fed Amb.

Army Form C. 2118.

Page 6.

Place	Date	Hour	Summary of Events and Information	Remarks and references to Appendices
GWENT FARM A28 a.5.6 Sheet 28.	5/8/17	12 am	All tanks left full of water for incoming unit. All salvage has been cleared. Personnell returning in horse ambulances and convoy cars –	
		12.45.	CAPT. ANDERSON RAMC 134 Fed Amb M.O. i/c 16 N+D. wounded and relieved by Capt WARWICK RAMC 133 Fed Amb. Telephoned to ADMS – 39 Div + was informed that Capt CAITHNESS 132 Fed Amb would relieve Capt WARWICK later in the day – The 200 attached infantry remnants reported back to their batt. in the Canal BANK.	
		3pm	All personnel RAMC in except those attached as runners to Battns they have come out with RMO's.	
		6.30pm.	Left the ADS. clear of all 39 Div. and in as clean a state as weather conditions permitted at 6.30 p.m. Total number evacuated since zero 31.7.17 = 2097. lying and sitting cases – From zero hour 31.7.17 to 6 pm 1-8-17 1096 from zero hour to 12 noon 4/8/17 = 1905.	
	6/8/17		Orders to move to the METEREN AREA – Saw 117 Bde and informed that 119 OR + 2 off would entrain at VLAMERTINGHE Capt J.S. PRENTICE RAMC joined for duty and posted to 39 DAC. 39 Div Transferred from 5th to 2nd Army. OC 133 Fed Amb proceeded for the night to 50 CCS with neuritis	

T2134. Wt. W708—776. 500000. 4/15. Sir J. C. & S.

Instructions regarding War Diaries and Intelligence Summaries are contained in F. S. Regs., Part II. and the Staff Manual respectively. Title pages will be prepared in manuscript.

WAR DIARY
or
INTELLIGENCE SUMMARY.
(Erase heading not required.)

Army Form C. 2118.

133 Fd Amb. Page 7.

Place	Date	Hour	Summary of Events and Information	Remarks and references to Appendices
X2b3.2 Sheet 27	7 8/17		Ambulance moved from Quest Farm to Rest area X2b3.2. Advanced party arrived about 12 noon - 3 billets allotted for unit. One very far away & unsuitable. One marked infectious & could not be utilised. The remaining one simply a large field no conveniences as regards a Fd Amb site as it had only be used as an infantry billet heretofore.	
			Entraining party moved from CAESTRE Stn by cars. all in by 4 pm	
			Transport arrived 6.15 pm.	
			OC 133 Fd Amb admitted to 41 CCS (Sick). CAPT G.D ROBERTSON to be in temporary command.	
			Tents all erected before dark and unit ready to take in any patients from 117 Bde units. Weather fine & warm. Water from pump. Good.	
	8 8/17	11 am	Camp being arranged & all necessary structures being erected. ADMS 39 Div visited - fine rain towards night	
	9 8/17		No 65127 St. Sgt SMITH J.A promoted to Q.M. Sgt. and No 72141 A/Sgt BURREN F.W promoted to Sgt. both to take effect from 28-6-17	
			OC 133 Fd Amb evacuated to the BASE. Weather showery. Few sick	

T2134. Wt. W708—776. 500000. 4/15. Sir J. C. & S.

Instructions regarding War Diaries and Intelligence Summaries are contained in F. S. Regs., Part II. and the Staff Manual respectively. Title pages will be prepared in manuscript.

WAR DIARY
or
INTELLIGENCE SUMMARY.
(Erase heading not required.)

Army Form C. 2118.

133 Fld Amb — Page 5.

Place	Date	Hour	Summary of Events and Information	Remarks and references to Appendices
X26 3.2 Sheet 27	10/8/17		Capt L.C. FERGUSON RAMC reported for duty & taken on the strength.	
			15 Reinforcements arrived for duty from the BASE & taken on the strength	good standard physique & ment.
	11/8/17		Capt W BROWN RAMC proceeded to 1/1 HERTS Reg for temp duty as M.O.	
			~~Headquarters~~. Men picking up well with the rest.	
	12/8/17		Lt. BANNERMAN attached to B section + Lt BOYD to C Section for instruction in Fld Amb routine work –	
	13/8/17		One heavy draught of 133 Fld Amb died during the night.	
			39168 St Sgt WILLIAMS O.T granted 10 days leave from 13.8.17 – 23-8-17	
	14/8/17		Fld Amb moved from X26 3.2 to CHIPPEWA CAMP M.D.S. M6 a 8.8. sheet 28.	
			Personnel moved by lorries arriving at 3 pm	
			Transport arrived about 2 pm.	
			Ambulance took over from 140 Fld Amb 41 Div.	
			The Camp is a large one chiefly tents and requires a great deal of attention repair + additions in the way of an adequate packstore, duckboards drains + re-erecting of tents.	
			Ambulance 1 Sgt 2 Cpl 19 OR under strength. 1 Dr ASC H.T.	

Instructions regarding War Diaries and Intelligence Summaries are contained in F. S. Regs., Part II. and the Staff Manual respectively. Title pages will be prepared in manuscript.

WAR DIARY
or
INTELLIGENCE SUMMARY.
(Erase heading not required.)

Army Form C. 2118.

133 Fd Amb. Page 9

Place	Date	Hour	Summary of Events and Information	Remarks and references to Appendices
CHIPPEWA CAMP M6 a C.8 (28)	15/8/17		ADMS 39 Div visited Ambulance & made no adverse remarks. State of camp was pointed out to him.	
			Sick parade about 200 every morning and many wounded. MDS is taking in all cases from 134 Fd Amb as direct admission. Work progressing. Duckboards indented for & wood & lime for constructional purposes also indented for.	
			Weather showery. 1 Off. over establishment. Equip for Off. ward 6 indented for from Red X.	
	16/8/17		Lt BANNERMAN RAMC & 10 OR proceeded to 134 Fd Amb for duty at 9.30 am	
			Capt D.B. SPENCE RAMC reported and taken on the strength from the 16th inst	
			17 OR arrived from Base. * Weather showery.	* good.
			Many wounded still coming in. All arrangements of tents etc altered and a new scheme in working order. Sick parade high.	
	17/8/17		4 N.C.O & 36 OR proceeded to 134 Fd Amb for duty. It is difficult to maintain fatigues in so big a camp with all these men away.	
			2/Lt DAISH RAMC proceeded to 39 Div Reinforcement Camp for duty. This camp is visited daily by a medical officer.	
			DDMS X Corps visited MDS about 11 am & appeared satisfied. Bombs were dropped round the MDS from 10pm – 10.30 pm – no damage to unit.	

T2134. Wt. W708—776. 500000. 4/15. Sir J. C. & S.

Instructions regarding War Diaries and Intelligence Summaries are contained in F. S. Regs., Part II. and the Staff Manual respectively. Title pages will be prepared in manuscript.

WAR DIARY
or
INTELLIGENCE SUMMARY.
(Erase heading not required.)

Army Form C. 2118.

133 Fld Amb — Page 10.

Place	Date	Hour	Summary of Events and Information	Remarks and references to Appendices
CHIPPEWA CAMP				
	18 8/17		1 Driver ASC H.T. reported for duty from 39 Div. Train and taken on the strength.	
			Capt DB SPENCE RAMC proceeded to 6th CHESHIRES for temp duty vice Capt DE BRENT.	
			Pte FRANKS evacuated wounded. Officers ward 6 beds opened.	
	19 8/17		One horse rider evacuated to 50 M.V.S.	
			Pte PATTERSON G evacuated wounded.	
	20 8/17		Capt DB. Spence rejoined unit from 6 Cheshires.	
			Weather fine and warm.	
	21 8/17		Capt DB. Spence ~~ordered~~ to proceed to 13 R.S. Reg but cancelled later	
			Enemy aeroplanes over at night.	
	22 8/17		Cpl ALDRED. S. H. reported for duty from BASE and taken on the strength.	
	23 8/17		Lt W. BOYD RAMC reported to 26 A.F.A. for temp duty. Conference at ADMS 39 Div Office.	
	24 8/17		Work proceeding as usual – All cookhouses whitewashed and duckboards put down and drains dug grease traps erected + gauze put over cookhouse windows where possible. Camp looking much cleaner.	
	25 8/17		A/Cpl HEMMING GA appointed A/L/Sgt. without pay.	
	~~25~~ 8/17		Sandbagging of all tents commenced in accordance with X Corps R.O. 1477.	

T2131. Wt. W708–776. 500000. 4/15. Sir J. C. & S.

Instructions regarding War Diaries and Intelligence Summaries are contained in F. S. Regs., Part II. and the Staff Manual respectively. Title pages will be prepared in manuscript.

WAR DIARY
or
INTELLIGENCE SUMMARY.
(Erase heading not required.)

133 Fd Amb

Army Form C. 2118.

Page 11.

Place	Date	Hour	Summary of Events and Information	Remarks and references to Appendices
CHIPPEWA CAMP. M6a 88	25/8/17		Sgt MASON JJ evacuated sick to No 37 CCS	
	26/8/17		10 OR proceeded to 2nd Army Rest Camp. Lt. BOYD rejoined unit from 26 A.F.A.	
			St Sgt WILLIAMS O.T. rejoined from 10 days leave.	
			Church parade 11 am. Pay parade 5.30 pm. Weather very bad.	
			Capt. G. D ROBERTSON RAMC temp O.C 133 Fd Amb reported sick but not evacuated.	
			Work proceeding. Packstore being rebuilt & sandbagging of tents proceeding.	
			High wind & rain.	
	27/8/17		The following are appointed L/Cpl with pay from 27 inst. 72020 A/Cpl Drinkwater W.J. 65983 A/Cpl Wilson W.A.	
			Capt K.T. LIMBERY & Lt & QM AUDUS proceeded to 39 Div Gas school for course of instruction on 27.8.17.	
			Two marquees blown down by wind during the night.	
			Weather very windy & rain.	
	28/8/17		No 65947 Pte DOWERS A.F. promoted A/Cpl with pay from ~~Aug 11~~ 11-8-17 —	Auth. DGMS 1450/1338/25/8/17
			Capt A.C. MURRAY RAMC is attached to this unit for temp duty from 27.8.17	

Instructions regarding War Diaries and Intelligence Summaries are contained in F. S. Regs., Part II. and the Staff Manual respectively. Title pages will be prepared in manuscript.

WAR DIARY
or
INTELLIGENCE SUMMARY.
(Erase heading not required.)

133 Fld Amb

Army Form C. 2118.

Page 12

Place	Date	Hour	Summary of Events and Information	Remarks and references to Appendices
CHIPPEWA CAMP (28) M6a 88.	29/8/17		Capt D.B. Spence relieved Capt BANNERMAN at the BRASSERIE. Orders received that Capt MILLER RAMC SR 132 Fld Amb will take over temp command of 133 Fld Amb pending return of Col. MANFORD RAMC	Auth. DMS 2nd Army
			[signature] Robertson Capt RAMC O/OC 133 Fld Amb	
	30/8/17		In accordance with instructions from A.D.M.S. 39th Div I have taken over temporary command of this ~~Ambul~~ Field Ambulance pending the return of Lt Col MANFORD R.A.M.C. Capt D.A. ROBERTSON RAMC was admitted sick to hospital today and evacuated to No 11 C.C.S.. No 56301 Pte FRANKS M. rejoined this Unit from C.C.S and is taken on the strength. Thirty P.B. men have arrived from ETAPLES and are being kept under observation pending their departure to join their Units. There were SHOWERS of rain during the day.	
			Sinclair Miller Capt RAMC SR	

T2134. Wt. W708—776. 500000. 4/15. Sir J. C. & S.

Instructions regarding War Diaries and Intelligence Summaries are contained in F. S. Regs., Part II. and the Staff Manual respectively. Title pages will be prepared in manuscript.

WAR DIARY
or
INTELLIGENCE SUMMARY.
(Erase heading not required.)

Army Form C. 2118.

Page 13

Place	Date	Hour	Summary of Events and Information	Remarks and references to Appendices
CHIPPEWA CAMP.	31 8/17		The A.D.M.S. 39th Div. visited the M.D.S. about 11 AM this morning; he suggested the consideration of various changes:- making the Q.M.'s stores more compact, the possibility of changing the Officers' Ward and alterations in the Receiving and DRESSING ROOMS. Capt A.C. MURRAY R.A.M.C. proceeded to the 13th GLOUCESTER battalion to take over MEDICAL Charge of that unit vice Capt BROWN R.A.M.C. who reports to 132 Field Ambulance. The following N.C.O and PRIVATES of this Unit have been awarded the MILITARY MEDAL (D.R.O. 30 8/17). No 65938 Sergt EARL, C. No 44157 Pte MEREDITH, S No 68053 Pte KEPPY V.H. No 63252 Pte MARSTON J.L.I: No 65994 Pte EUSTACE T. There were frequent rain showers throughout the day.	

Sinclair Miller
Capt. R.A.M.C. S.R.
T/O.C. 133 FIELD Amb^ce

T2134. Wt. W708–776. 500000. 4/15. Sir J. C. & S.

II CONFIDENTIAL

140/2438

Vol 19

Sept 1917

5

WAR DIARY OF

133RD FLD. AMB.

from 1st Sept. 1917
to 30th Sept 1917.

VOLUME 19.

Volume 19.

Instructions regarding War Diaries and Intelligence Summaries are contained in F. S. Regs., Part II. and the Staff Manual respectively. Title pages will be prepared in manuscript.

WAR DIARY
or
INTELLIGENCE SUMMARY.
(Erase heading not required.)

Army Form C. 2118.

Page 1

Place	Date	Hour	Summary of Events and Information	Remarks and references to Appendices
CHIPPEWA CAMP. M 6 A 8 8. Sheet 28	1 9/17		The weather continues unsettled and stormy: work of concentration of Q.M.'s depart[ments] departments commenced; the "Supply" + "Clothing" departments have been arranged in same hut thus freeing one hut as billet for the personel. Collection of bricks for the Horselines is being carried out, three G.S. wagon loads of bricks being obtained from VOORMEZEELE today. An instructional conference was held here today on The PREPARATIONS for and the Duties of a MEDICAL Officer during "Active Operations". There were present Major ROYERS Capt SINCLAIR MILLER (PRESIDING), Capt COOKE, Capts DE BRENT, BROWN W 1/1st Herts, BROWN W. 13th GLOUCESTERS, CAITHNESS, DENNIS, WILLIS-BUND BADD, MURRAY, WARWICK, LIMBREY, FERGUSON and Lieuts BANNERMAN and BOYD. An interesting and instructive discussion took place.	
			Sinclair Miller Capt RAMC SR O.C. 133 Field Amb.	
	2 9/17		The weather still showery: work of sand-bagging the tents and marquees continued also collection of brick for horse lines. Capt. BOYD W. proceeded to the 17th Battn K.R.R.C. for temporary duty as M.O. with that unit. Ten (10) O.R. "P B" men have been taken on this	

T2134. Wt. W708–776. 590000. 4/15. Sir J. C. & S.

Instructions regarding War Diaries and Intelligence Summaries are contained in F. S. Regs., Part II. and the Staff Manual respectively. Title pages will be prepared in manuscript.

WAR DIARY
or
INTELLIGENCE SUMMARY.
(Erase heading not required.)

Army Form C. 2118.

Page 2

Place	Date	Hour	Summary of Events and Information	Remarks and references to Appendices
Chippewa Camp. M6 A 8.8. Sheet 28	2 9/17		this Unit to replace ten (10) Category "A" men of the A.S.C. attached. The following N.C.O and men have been evacuated to the base sick and are accordingly struck of the Strength:- No. 72083 Sergt MASON J.J. (26/8/17) No 95048 Pte PREGNALL H. (29 8/17). No 63282 Pte MARSTON J.W.I (29 8/17). Numerous bombs were dropped in the neighbourhood of the M.D.S. during the night (2/3rd). No ~~damage~~ injuries were sustained by personel or patients.	
	3 9/17		Climatic conditions: good. Lieut BANNERMAN R.A.M.C inspected The SALVAGE Dump 39th Div + reported on the SANITARY Condition of it; he made various suggestions for improvement in sanitation of same. The construction of an ablution bench commenced; also the flooring of the horse standings with brick begun. The Sand bagging of the tents completed. Throughout the night bombs were dropped at intervals in the vicinity of M.D.S. No damage sustained	

T2134. Wt. W708—776. 500000. 4/15. Sir J. C. & S.

Instructions regarding War Diaries and Intelligence Summaries are contained in F. S. Regs., Part II. and the Staff Manual respectively. Title pages will be prepared in manuscript.

WAR DIARY
or
INTELLIGENCE SUMMARY.
(Erase heading not required.)

Army Form C. 2118.

Page 3

Place	Date	Hour	Summary of Events and Information	Remarks and references to Appendices
Chippewa Camp M6 A. 8.8. Sheet 28	4 9/17		Weather conditions perfect. Work continued on patients ablution shed: also on bricking the horselines. Material for horse lines obtained from VOORMEZEELE. Heavy bombing of the neighbourhood between 12.0C midnight + 3.30 A.M. Several casualties amongst the Artillery	
	5 9/17		The day bright and very warm: commenced protecting the huts of personel with wire revetments + soil packed between [sketch] wire mesh / soil. Work continues on the horse lines. Patients ablution shed completed. Work on pack store well in hand. Personel had bath + clean clothing. Night was quiet.	
	6 9/17		A heavy rain storm early in the morning; bright sunshine throughout the rest of the day. One N C O + 19 O.R.s proceeded to 225 Coy R.E. to do constructional this morning. Work of collecting brick and flooring horse-standings continued with; also protection of huts from bomb splinters. Capt WARWICK H.F. proceeded on leave today. Capt TRIMBREY K.T. and Lieut ANDRIS C.W. completed their "Gas course" today. No. 88907 Pte. SULLIVAN A.J. and	

T2134. Wt. W708—776. 500000. 4/15. Sir J. C. & S.

Instructions regarding War Diaries and Intelligence Summaries are contained in F. S. Regs., Part II. and the Staff Manual respectively. Title pages will be prepared in manuscript.

WAR DIARY
or
INTELLIGENCE SUMMARY.
(Erase heading not required.)

Army Form C. 2118.

Page 4

Place	Date	Hour	Summary of Events and Information	Remarks and references to Appendices
CHIPPEWA CAMP. A.8.8. M6 Sheet 28	6 9/17		and N° 72007 Pte. WHITELEY J.C. ~~to~~ were transferred to N°. 2 C.C.S. today for duty and struck off the strength. The night was quiet.	
	7 9/17		Climatic conditions good. Work of collection of brick &c. continued with. The revettment of personnels huts continued. Erection of water tank for ablution bench of patients. N°. 9233 Pte FINCH G. J. + N°. 38968 Pte Thompson R.G. reported for duty from N°. 2 C.C.S. + are taken on the strength. Lieut ANDERSON reported for duty today from the 12th Battn SUSSEX Regt	
	8 9/17		Weather continues very good: work on horse lines continued; the re laying of trench boards commenced in the M.D.S. Revetting of huts for personnel continued. The A.D.M.S. 39th Division held an investiture for and presented with the ribbon of the Military Medal the following N.C.O's and men Staff Sergt. SEARLE (134 F.A.), Sergt. CRADDOCK 134 F.A., Sergt. EARL 133 F.A. Sergt. LOAKES 132 F.A., Pte EUSTACE (133 F.A) + Pte MEREDITH 133 F.A. The night was quiet. MEDICAL Arrangements for ~~Aptive~~ Active Operations received.	

T2134. Wt. W708–776. 500000. 4/15. Sir J. C. & S.

Instructions regarding War Diaries and Intelligence Summaries are contained in F. S. Regs., Part II. and the Staff Manual respectively. Title pages will be prepared in manuscript.

WAR DIARY
or
INTELLIGENCE SUMMARY.
(Erase heading not required.)

Army Form C. 2118.

Page 5

Place	Date	Hour	Summary of Events and Information	Remarks and references to Appendices
Chippewa Camp M6a 8.8 Sheet 28			The A.D.M.S 39th Div inspected the M.D.S. after the investiture and spoke appreciatingly of the progress of work at the M.D.S since his last visit. He suggested that the horse lines should be completely cemented with brick rubble sand + cement.	
	9/9/17		Climatic conditions continue perfect. Conference at A.D.M.S.' office in the morning and an instructional conference for the junior officers was held here in the afternoon. Subject:– The arrangements (Medical) for the coming operations. Thirty A.S.C. Batmen proceeded to A.S.C. H.T. Base Le HAVRE this morning — ten from each of the three Field Ambces of the Div — No 6932 Sgt STEWART H.W.M. reported for duty today and is taken on the strength of the unit. Work on horse lines, trench boards + revetting huts continued. Night quiet.	
	10/9/17		Climatic conditions perfect. Capt SPENCE D.B. + Lieut BOYD W. proceeded to ~~Eng~~ ENGLAND today and have been struck off the strength of the	

T2134. Wt. W708–776. 500000. 4/15. Sir J. C. & S.

Instructions regarding War Diaries and Intelligence Summaries are contained in F. S. Regs., Part II. and the Staff Manual respectively. Title pages will be prepared in manuscript.

WAR DIARY
or
INTELLIGENCE SUMMARY.
(Erase heading not required.)

Army Form C. 2118.

Page 6.

Place	Date	Hour	Summary of Events and Information	Remarks and references to Appendices
Chippewa Camp M6 a 88			the strength of the unit. The usual work continued and arrangements for the coming "Operations" commenced. Capt. LIMBREY K.T. & 2 N.C.O'S + 2 O.R'S proceeded to 134 F.A today to do a reconnaisance of the forward area. The night was quiet.	
	11 9/17		Climatic condition good. Work on horselines continued: also preparations for the coming operations. An inspection of Box Respirators + P.H. Helmets was held and Mr. Audus gave a lecture on "Gas Shells" to the unit.	
	12 9/17		Weather continues good. ANNEXE to "Receiving ~~[illegible]~~ ROOM" completed. Other preparations being continued with. The Horse Amb^{ce} wagon detached with 117th brigade has returned. Ten O.R'S proceeded to 134 F.A. as a working party at D.C.P. ZWARTELEEN. Capt LIMBREY K.T + party returned from making reconnaisance of the forward area. The night was quiet.	
	13 9/17		Weather continues dry but somewhat like rain. D.D.M.S. X Corps	

T2134. Wt. W708—776. 500000. 4/15. Sir J. C. & S.

Instructions regarding War Diaries and Intelligence Summaries are contained in F. S. Regs., Part II. and the Staff Manual respectively. Title pages will be prepared in manuscript.

WAR DIARY
or
INTELLIGENCE SUMMARY.
(Erase heading not required.)

Army Form C. 2118.

Page 7

Place	Date	Hour	Summary of Events and Information	Remarks and references to Appendices
Chippewa Camp M6a88.			visited C. M. D. S. today and was quite satisfied with the progress of the preparations for the coming "operations". He laid stress upon all arrangements being made for the rapid despatch of patients to the C.C.S. The area around the C. M. D. S. was shelled during the night. No damage was sustained	
	14 9/17		There was rain during the night. Capt Kirby a/Adjt. C.R.E. 39th Div. visited the C. M. D. S this morning to report on the advisibility of making a section of WOOD road for M. A. C. cars for evacuation. He was of the opinion that it was necessary + highly desirable. Preparations continued. Shelter store for stretchers + blankets completed. Capt. Robinson G. D. RAMC evacuated "sick" has been struck off the strength of the unit from 31 8/17 Lieut Anderson C.W. RAMC. proceeded to England to report to the War Office + is struck off the strength 15 9/17 Nine O.R.s (reinforcements) reported for duty + are taken on the strength.	

T2134. Wt. W708—776. 500000. 4/15. Sir J. C. & S.

Instructions regarding War Diaries and Intelligence Summaries are contained in F. S. Regs., Part II. and the Staff Manual respectively. Title pages will be prepared in manuscript.

WAR DIARY
or
INTELLIGENCE SUMMARY.
(Erase heading not required.)

Army Form C. 2118.

Place	Date	Hour	Summary of Events and Information	Remarks and references to Appendices
CHIPPEWA CAMP - M 6 a 88.	15 9/17		Climatic conditions good. The A.D.M.S 39th Div. visited the C. M. D.S this morning and suggested methods of improving the Standings of the Horselines. The C. E. Xth Corps also visited the C.M.D.S. reference the roadway for M.A.C. cars. Work on Horselines + preparations for Active Operations are being pushed on with. The following extract from D.M.S. Second Army was forwarded for information from A.D.M.S 39th Div. "Captain SINCLAIR MILLER, M.C., R.A.M.C (S.R.) 132 FIELD Amb^ce is appointed to command 133 Fd Amb^ce vice Captain (acting Lieut-Col.) MANFORD R.A.M.C to Base sick"	
	16 9/17		Climatic conditions good. Work of equipping C.M.D.S. continued with, also work on horse lines. In the diarrhoea admissions there is a big decrease - there being only 9 admissions today. Night was quiet.	
	17 9/17		Climatic conditions continue good. Roadway for M.A.C Amb^ce cars commenced. Work on Horselines + on wards continued. The D.A.D.M.S	

Instructions regarding War Diaries and Intelligence Summaries are contained in F. S. Regs., Part II. and the Staff Manual respectively. Title pages will be prepared in manuscript.

WAR DIARY
or
INTELLIGENCE SUMMARY.
(Erase heading not required.)

Army Form C. 2118.

Page 9

Place	Date	Hour	Summary of Events and Information	Remarks and references to Appendices
Chippewa Camp. M 6 a 5.8.	17/9/17	Contd	visited the C.M.D.S. this afternoon & was satisfied with progress. Two Stoves were obtained to complete the formation of the Drying Room.	
	18/9/17		Climatic conditions continue good: work on roadway for M.A.C. Ambce cars continued: also work on the Horse lines. The D.D.M.S. X visited the R.M.D.S. this morning and expressed his satisfaction with the arrangements for the coming operations. Later in the day the D.M.S. II Army paid a visit and was completely satisfied. The following equipment was issued to 134 F.A. today. Blankets 1000, STRETCHERS 200, Thomas Splints complete with suspension bars 50 wheeled Stretchers 20 & other expendable stores.	
	19/9/17		Climatic conditions continue good: Capt K.T. AMBREY R.A.M.C. as bearer officer 2 Sergts and 72 O.R's reported to O.C. 134 F.A. this morning for duty in the forward area during the coming operations. Roadway for M.A.C Ambce cars completed. Also the C.M.D.S. is completely ready to receive seriously	

T2134. Wt. W708–776. 500000. 4/15. Sir J. C. & S.

Instructions regarding War Diaries and Intelligence Summaries are contained in F. S. Regs., Part II. and the Staff Manual respectively. Title pages will be prepared in manuscript.

WAR DIARY
or
INTELLIGENCE SUMMARY.
(Erase heading not required.)

Army Form C. 2118.

Place	Date	Hour	Summary of Events and Information	Remarks and references to Appendices
Chippewa Camp M6a 88	19/7/17	Contd	Seriously wounded cases. Capt FERGUSON L.C. RAMC reported for duty to OC 134 FIELD Amb. Mr. STaggers M.C. U.S.A. and Capt. Bogg RAMC of the 33rd Division reported here for temporary duty: also Capt SLOAN of 39th Div. D.A.C. reported for temporary duty. About 250 wounded passed through this Station today.	
	20/7/17		Weather: Rain during the night but the day was bright & there was a good drying wind. Active operations began this morning. About 8.30 AM the first cases after zero hour arrived and ~~[illegible]~~ about 11 AM. the ~~[illegible]~~ rate of admissions reached its maximum point but at no time was there any congestion. About 770 cases passed through the C.M.D.S for lying wounded during the ~~day~~ first 24 hours of Active Operations. The D.D.M.S. visited the C.M.D.S. during day and expressed his complete satisfaction of the working out of the scheme of evacuation & receiving at C.M.D.S. The neighbourhood was shelled during the night. No damage was done to this unit. Capt DUNCAN RAMC of X Corps School reported for temporary duty at C.M.D.S. today	

T2134. Wt. W708—776. 500000. 4/15. Sir J. C. & S.

Instructions regarding War Diaries and Intelligence Summaries are contained in F. S. Regs., Part II. and the Staff Manual respectively. Title pages will be prepared in manuscript.

WAR DIARY
or
INTELLIGENCE SUMMARY.
(Erase heading not required.)

Army Form C. 2118.

Place	Date	Hour	Summary of Events and Information	Remarks and references to Appendices
Chippewa Camp. M6 a 88	21/9/17		Climatic conditions good: A steady stream of wounded continued to pass through the C. M. D. S. throughout the night. The D. D. M. S. visited the C. M. D. S. this morning. In the afternoon the D. M. S. II Army inspected this Dressing Station and directed that his thanks should be conveyed to the officers, N. C. O's and men here for the excellency of the work done and the untiring efforts displayed by them during the Operations of the 20th. The night was quiet	
	22/9/17		Climatic conditions continue good: During the past 48 hours over 1000 cases (Seriously wounded) passed through this station. Throughout the operations the evacuations from the C. M. D. S. ran very consistently with the admissions and at no time were there above 40 Stretcher cases in the C. M. D. S. Capt Warwick H. F. rejoined the unit after 14 days' leave of absence. The A. D. M. S. visited the C. M. D. S. this morning and expressed his satisfaction in the carrying out of the work ~~[illegible] [illegible] [illegible]~~ of admission & evacuation of wounded at the C. M. D. S. during the recent operations	

Instructions regarding War Diaries and Intelligence Summaries are contained in F. S. Regs., Part II. and the Staff Manual respectively. Title pages will be prepared in manuscript.

WAR DIARY
or
INTELLIGENCE SUMMARY.
(Erase heading not required.)

Army Form C. 2118.

Page 12

Place	Date	Hour	Summary of Events and Information	Remarks and references to Appendices
Chippewa Camp M 6 a 8.8.	23/9/17		Weather conditions perfect. Work on the Standings of Horse Lines continued. Capt. K T. LIMBREY returned from the FORWARD AREA for one night only. One Horse Amb^ce wagon was returned from 134 F. A. today	
	24/9/17		Climatic conditions good: visibility low. Work on horselines continued. Sergt. WELCH P. G reported for duty from 69th F.A. vice Q. M. S. Smith J.A. who is to proceed to that unit. Capt. GRASSWELLER H. reported for duty and is taken on the strength of the unit from today. One Sunbeam car + driver reported for duty from the Base. A large number of "gassed" cases passed through the C. M. D. S. during the evening and last night.	
	25/9/17		Climatic conditions perfect. Capt. Boag + Mr. Staggers of 33rd Div. (and attached here for temporary duty) reported to A. D. M. S. 33rd Div. in the forenoon. Capt FERGUSON L. C. returned from the FORWARD AREA for duty at the C. M. D. S. Work on horse lines + on the painting of the limbered wagons continued. All preparations for Active Operations completed.	

Instructions regarding War Diaries and Intelligence Summaries are contained in F. S. Regs., Part II. and the Staff Manual respectively. Title pages will be prepared in manuscript.

WAR DIARY
or
INTELLIGENCE SUMMARY.
(Erase heading not required.)

Army Form C. 2118.

Place	Date	Hour	Summary of Events and Information	Remarks and references to Appendices
Chippewa Camp M6 a 88	26/9/17		Climatic conditions perfect. Active operations began at dawn this morning. The first batch of wounded after zero hour reached the C.M.D.S. about 8 30 A.M. The number of wounded admitted throughout was small compared with the operations of the 20th. During the morning the D.D.M.S. X Corps visited the C.M.D.S. Everything was satisfactory. The A.D.M.S. 39th Div made a visit in the afternoon. Capt FERGUSON L.C + Capt CRASSWELLER H proceeded to report to O.C 134 FIELD Amb for temporary duty. Capt Caithness reported from 132 FIELD AMB for temporary duty at C.M.D.S. Colonel Gordon-Watson C.M.G Consulting Surgeon II Army visited the C.M.D.S. in the evening. The night was quiet.	
	27/9/17		A light shower of rain during the night. Weather good but visibility low. The O.C 134 F.A. reports that Capt LIMBREY K.T was killed in action yesterday by a shell. Capt Ferguson L.C rejoined this unit from temporary duty with 134 F.A. Capt CAITHNESS reported to 132 Field Amb for duty. The A.D.M.S visited the C.M.D.S. during the afternoon.	

Instructions regarding War Diaries and Intelligence Summaries are contained in F. S. Regs., Part II. and the Staff Manual respectively. Title pages will be prepared in manuscript.

WAR DIARY
or
INTELLIGENCE SUMMARY.
(Erase heading not required.)

Army Form C. 2118.

Place	Date	Hour	Summary of Events and Information	Remarks and references to Appendices
CHIPPEWA Camp M 6 a 88	28.9/17		Climatic conditions perfect. Capt Warwick H. F. & two bearer sub-divisions returned from FORWARD AREA today. Capt CRASSWELLER H. reported for duty as R.M.O. to the 11th ROYAL SUSSEX Regt and is struck off the strength.	
	29/9/17		Climatic conditions good. The body of Capt. LIMLEEY was interred at GODERSWELTE today with that of Capt FIELD, 136 F.A. The 22nd F.A. arrived here today under instructions from their A.D.M.S. to take over this site; the Amb^ce parked here for the night pending further instructions. Bombs were dropped in the neighbourhood during the night.	
	30/9/17		Climatic conditions perfect. Capt FERGUSON L.C. proceeded on 10 days leave to ENGLAND today. The 22nd F.A. took over the FIELD Amb^ce site at CHIPPEWA CAMP M 6 a 88. at 12 O'c noon today. All preparations are completed for the Amb^ce to move out to new site at M 21 b 3.2 (Sheet 28) tomorrow morning. Sinclair Miller. Capt (acting Lt. Col.) R.A.M.C. S.R	

T2134. Wt. W708—776. 500000. 4/15. Sir J. C. & S.

Original

Contd Original

Vol 20

War Diary

of

133rd Field Ambulance

From:- October 1st 1917

To- October 31st 1917

(Volume 20)

4

S

Volume XX

Instructions regarding War Diaries and Intelligence Summaries are contained in F. S. Regs., Part II. and the Staff Manual respectively. Title pages will be prepared in manuscript.

WAR DIARY
or
~~INTELLIGENCE SUMMARY.~~
(Erase heading not required.)

Army Form C. 2118.

Page 1.

Place	Date	Hour	Summary of Events and Information	Remarks and references to Appendices
M21 b 4.2. SHEET 28.	1.X.17		The Weather continues good: the FIELD Amb^ce moved from CHIPPEWA Camp M6 a 88 at 7.30 A.M. this morning to present site M21 b 4.2. The day was spent in putting up Canvas + revetting the tents. The D.D.M.S. IX Corps visited the camp in the afternoon. Bombs were dropped in the vicinity during the night. Capt. JOHNSTONE J. G. and Capt Young J. reported for duty yesterday evening (30.IX.17) and are taken on the strength of the unit from this date.	
	2.X.17		Weather conditions good. Sand bagging of tents continued. Erection of cook house for officers' mess completed. Also shelter for Quarter Master's Stores.	
	3.X.17		Slight shower of rain during the night. Day dry. Sand bagging of tents completed. Also drainage of camp commenced. A lecture on the evacuation of wounded from the FRONT line to C.C.S.'s given to the junior officers. Erection of a Recreation Shelter for the personnel commenced.	

T2134. Wt. W708—776. 500000. 4/15. Sir J. C. & S.

Volume XX

Instructions regarding War Diaries and Intelligence Summaries are contained in F. S. Regs., Part II. and the Staff Manual respectively. Title pages will be prepared in manuscript.

WAR DIARY
or
~~INTELLIGENCE SUMMARY.~~
(Erase heading not required.)

Army Form C. 2118.

Place	Date	Hour	Summary of Events and Information	Remarks and references to Appendices
M21 b 4 2 Sheet 28	4 10 17		Weather continues cold & Showery. Capt WARWICK H.F. and Capt Young J. proceeded to 58th FIELD Amb for temporary duty with Unit during Active Operations. Heavy Showers of rain fell throughout the day.	
	5 10 17		Weather conditions unfavourable. Capt Johnston G J took over temporarily duties as M.O. to IX Corps Hdqrs today. Capt WARWICK H.F & Capt Young J. rejoined this Unit from temporary duty with 58th F.A. A concert for the personnel of the Unit was given by "The Twolis" of the Division in the evening	
	6 10 17		Weather continues Showery. A.D.M.S visited the FIELD Amb site and Horse-lines this morning. Recreation SHELTER for personnel completed. Capt STOKES H.K having been posted to this Unit is taken on the strength from today.	
	7 10 17		Weather still broken. Capt Young J. proceeded for temporary duty as M.O. to the 27th Labour Group. Work of laying TRENCH BOARDS in camp completed so far as supply allowed.	

T2134. Wt. W708–776. 500000. 4/15. Sir J. C. & S.

Volume XX

Instructions regarding War Diaries and Intelligence Summaries are contained in F. S. Regs., Part II. and the Staff Manual respectively. Title pages will be prepared in manuscript.

WAR DIARY
or
~~INTELLIGENCE~~ SUMMARY.
(Erase heading not required.)

Army Form C. 2118.

Place	Date	Hour	Summary of Events and Information	Remarks and references to Appendices
M.21 b 4 2 Sheet 28	8/10/17		Weather continues poor. Training of ~~Sections~~ under Sectional commanders carried out in the morning: inter-section football matches in afternoon	
	9/10/17		Weather conditions improved. Drilling of sections continued.	
	10/10/17		Weather very bad. Capt WARWICK H.F. and an advance party proceeded to HAEGDOORNE Camp (S 9 a 5.8. Sheet 28) to learn the routine of the work there. Lieut BONNERMAN C.H. proceeded to ENGLAND on leave today.	
	11/10/17		Weather conditions fair. 20 O.R's proceeded to HAEGDOORNE Camp to reinforce Capt. WARWICK's party. Preparations to move from M21 b 4 2 completed	
S 9 a 5 8 Sheet 28	12/10/17		Weather continues poor. Headquarters of this Unit moved from M21 b 4 2 to S 9 a 5 8 at 9 A.M. this morning. The Dysentery Camp at HAEGDOORNE Camp S 9 a. 58. has been taken over by this Unit at 6 P.M. ~~today~~ from 50th	

Volume XX

Instructions regarding War Diaries and Intelligence Summaries are contained in F. S. Regs., Part II. and the Staff Manual respectively. Title pages will be prepared in manuscript.

WAR DIARY
or
~~INTELLIGENCE SUMMARY.~~
(Erase heading not required.)

Army Form C. 2118.

Page 4

Place	Date	Hour	Summary of Events and Information	Remarks and references to Appendices
Sq. a 5. 8.	12/10/17	Contd-	FIELD Amb^ce^. A working party of one Sergt. and 24 O.R.'s reported to O/c IX Corps Hutting for temporary duty. ~~The~~ A D M S. 39th. Division visited ~~the~~ this Camp in the evening. Capt FERGUSON returned from leave in ENGLAND today.	
	13/10/17		Weather conditions continue unfavourable. Erection of Shelter for Q. M. Stores completed. Relaying and repairing of Trench Boards commenced. Seven reinforcements reported for duty today and are taken on the strength of this Unit.	
	~~14/10/17~~			
	14/10/17		Weather conditions fair. Capt FERGUSON L. C. and one bearer Sub. division proceeded to report to O.C. 132 F.A. at VORMEZEELE at 12 Oc noon today. One Sunbeam Ambulance car reported to O.C. 132 F.A for temporary duty. The fitting up a Pack Store for the DYSENTERY Camp commenced; also repair of patients' kitchen.	
	15			

T2134. Wt. W708—776. 500000. 4/15. Sir J. C. & S.

Volume XV

Instructions regarding War Diaries and Intelligence Summaries are contained in F. S. Regs., Part II. and the Staff Manual respectively. Title pages will be prepared in manuscript.

WAR DIARY
or
~~INTELLIGENCE~~ SUMMARY.

(Erase heading not required.)

Army Form C. 2118.

Page 5.

Place	Date	Hour	Summary of Events and Information	Remarks and references to Appendices
Sq a 5.8.	15 10/17		Weather conditions continue fair. Work on kitchen and pack store continued. Sergt HERBERT F.H. reported to A.D.M.S 39th Div. for duty and is struck off the strength of this unit. Sergt MILLS M.G. reported for duty and is taken on the strength. A DOUGLAS MOTOR CYCLE was stolen from the Cab Stand at this camp on the night of the 14/15th between the hours of 10 P.M. & 6 A.M.	
	16 10/17		Weather conditions continue favourable. Patients' kitchen completed; also the racks in the pack store. The refitting of the officers' ward completed.	
	17 10/17		Weather conditions good. Erection of a canvas screen in front of the Officers' WARD. A coal dump enclosed by ~~with~~ wire entanglement with door way completed. Completing of Dining Room for "Light Diet" patients.	
	18 10/17		Weather continues favourable. Erection of blanket shelter commenced.	

T2134. Wt. W708—776. 500000. 4/15. Sir J. C. & S.

Instructions regarding War Diaries and Intelligence Summaries are contained in F. S. Regs., Part II. and the Staff Manual respectively. Title pages will be prepared in manuscript.

Volume XX

WAR DIARY
or
INTELLIGENCE SUMMARY.
(Erase heading not required.)

Army Form C. 2118.

Page 6.

Place	Date	Hour	Summary of Events and Information	Remarks and references to Appendices
S9 a 58.	19 10/17		Weather continues good. A court of Enquiry was convened at this Camp to investigate the loss of the Douglas Motor Cycle on the night of the 14/15th. Work on blanket store continued.	
	20 X/17		Weather continues very favourable. Capt FERGUSON L. C. rejoined the unit from temporary duty with 132 F. A. Blanket store completed. Erection of tents at N 7 a 2.0. (Sheet 28) commenced.	
	21 X/17		Weather continues good. D. D. M. S. IX Corps visited the DYSENTERY Camp here this morning and expressed his satisfaction of the routine work going on. The pitching, the drainage + camouflaging the tents at N 7 a 2 0 completed. One Sunbeam car returned from 132 F. A. damaged by shell fire.	
	22 X/17		Weather has turned showery again. Work of relaying trench boards in Dysentery Camp commenced. Capt. Young J. returned from temporary duty with 27th Labour Group. Capt Johnstone J. G. proceeded to the	

T2134. Wt. W708—776. 500000. 4/15. Sir J. C. & S.

14th

Volume XX

Instructions regarding War Diaries and Intelligence Summaries are contained in F. S. Regs., Part II. and the Staff Manual respectively. Title pages will be prepared in manuscript.

WAR DIARY
or
~~INTELLIGENCE SUMMARY.~~
(Erase heading not required.)

Army Form C. 2118.

Page 17.

Place	Date	Hour	Summary of Events and Information	Remarks and references to Appendices
39a 6.8.	22 X/17	Contd	the 1/1st HERTS battalion for duty and is struck off the strength of the Unit. Lieut BANNERMAN C. H. returned from leave in ENGLAND today.	
	23 X/17		Weather continues bad. Work on relaying TRENCH BOARDS continued. Fixing up stoves in patients' wards commenced.	
	24 X/17		Weather continues poor. Capt FERGUSON L. C. admitted to hospital sick ~~and~~ sent to D. R. S. Bearer sub-division from 132 F. A. rejoined this Unit today. One tent-subdivision reported to 11 C.C.S. for temporary duty.	
	25 X/17		Weather continues unfavourable. Three marquees were blown down during the night. Relaying of Trench Boards continued. Extension to Officers Mess Kitchen completed.	
	26 X/17		Weather still unsettled. A further inquiry into the loss of the Douglas	

Volume XX

Instructions regarding War Diaries and Intelligence Summaries are contained in F. S. Regs., Part II. and the Staff Manual respectively. Title pages will be prepared in manuscript.

WAR DIARY
or
INTELLIGENCE SUMMARY.
(Erase heading not required.)

Army Form C. 2118.

Page 8.

Place	Date	Hour	Summary of Events and Information	Remarks and references to Appendices
Sq a 5.8.	26 X/17		Contd. Motor Cycle was held at 4 P.M.	
	27 X/17.		Weather conditions favourable. 25 bearers proceeded by lorry to report to O/c A.D.S. LARCH WOOD at 6 A.M. The D.D.M.S. IX Corps visited the DYSENTERY CAMP, HAEGDOORNE in the morning and expressed his complete satisfaction with the Camp and the route work. Relaying of Trench boards completed	
	28 X/17		WEAther bright and frosty. The bearer party attached to 7th Div. for temporary duty in the FORWARD Area rejoined the Unit. The erection of night urinal stands for the wards completed.	
	29 X/17		Weather unfavourable. One bearer subdivision reported to O.C. 132 F.A. for temporary duty in the FORWARD Area. Six Clerks reported for temporary duty at Central Bureau, GODERSWELDE. The tent subdivision attached to 11 C.C.S. for temporary duty rejoined Unit.	

Volume XX

Instructions regarding War Diaries and Intelligence Summaries are contained in F. S. Regs., Part II. and the Staff Manual respectively. Title pages will be prepared in manuscript.

WAR DIARY
or
~~INTELLIGENCE SUMMARY.~~
(Erase heading not required.)

Army Form C. 2118.

Place	Date	Hour	Summary of Events and Information	Remarks and references to Appendices
Sq. a. 5.8	29 X/17	Contd.	Capt STOKES H. K. was evacuated "GASSED" and is struck off the strength. Lieut BANNERMAN C. H. reported to O.C. 132 FIELD Ambce for temporary duty. The erection of storage hut for meat commenced; also the building of ~~[illegible]~~ "FIELD OVEN T.C." in the personnel's kitchen.	
	30 X/17		Weather continues very unfavourable. The Advance party sent to the Entraining Centre at DICKEBUSCH rejoined the Unit. Work on meat store and personnel's cook house continued.	
	31 X/17		Weather conditions favourable. Capt. Young J. proceeded to report to O.C. 132 FIELD Ambce for duty and is struck off the strength. Lieut BOYER G. H. M.O. R.C. U.S.A. reported for duty and is taken on the strength of the Unit. The wards are completed with CANADIAN Stoves as far as supply allows. The cookhouse of personnel completed. Also storage hut for meat. Drainage of the Camp improved.	

Sinclair Miller
LT COL.
O. C. 133rd FLD. AMB.

T2131. Wt. W708—776. 500000. 4/15. Sir J. C. & S.

CONFIDENTIAL

WAR DIARY

Vol 21

VOLUME XXI.

NOVEMBER 1st 1917

TO

NOVEMBER 30th 1917.

133rd Field Ambulance.

R.A.M.C.

4

S

Signed.

H.F. Warwick

a/ O. C. 133rd FLD. AMB.

Volume XXI

Instructions regarding War Diaries and Intelligence Summaries are contained in F. S. Regs., Part II. and the Staff Manual respectively. Title pages will be prepared in manuscript.

WAR DIARY
or
~~INTELLIGENCE SUMMARY.~~
(Erase heading not required.)

Army Form C. 2118.

Page I

Place	Date	Hour	Summary of Events and Information	Remarks and references to Appendices
HAEGDOORNE Dysentery Camp Sq a 5.8.	1/XI/17		Weather conditions fair. The Horse Transport lines were moved from M15 c4.8 (Sheet 28) to CHIPPEWA FIELD Amb^ce Site M6 a 8.8. (Sheet 28)	
	2/11/17		Weather continues foggy. The Dysentery Camp HAEGDOORNE Sq a5.8. was handed over to 50th Field Amb^ce and the FIELD Amb^ce Site at CHIPPEWA (M6 a 8.8) was taken over from the 21st FIELD Amb^ce. Capt FERGUSON L. C. rejoined the unit from D. R. S. Headquarters moved from HAEGDOORNE to CHIPPEWA at 2 P.M.	
CHIPPEWA. M6. a. 8.8	3/11/17		Weather conditions poor. Thirty days leave has been granted me and I have handed over command of the Unit in my absence to Capt WARWICK H. F. Sinclair Miller Lt. Col. R.A.M.C. S.R.	
			CAPT DE BRENT. H. J. reported to this unit for duty & is taken on the strength from 3/11/17.	

D. D. & L., London, E.C.
(A5001) Wt. W1271/M2031 750,000 5/17 Sch. 52 Forms C2118/14

Instructions regarding War Diaries and Intelligence Summaries are contained in F. S. Regs., Part II. and the Staff Manual respectively. Title pages will be prepared in manuscript.

WAR DIARY
or
INTELLIGENCE SUMMARY.
(Erase heading not required.)

Army Form C. 2118.

Page. 2

Place	Date	Hour	Summary of Events and Information	Remarks and references to Appendices
CHIPPEWA MEAES	4/11/17		Weather conditions improved. Bright & clear.	
"	5/11/17		Weather fine. CAPT FERGUSON L.C. detailed for temporary duty with 6th Cheshires vice Capt HARMAN who was suffering from gas poisoning. Numerous cases of patients suffering from gas poisoning were admitted.	
"	6/11/17		Weather dull & foggy. Number of patients admitted much above normal.	
"	7/11/17		Weather foggy. CAPT MACMILLAN. F.W. RAMC. posted to this unit & taken on strength from 7/11/17. On the same date he was temporarily attached to 132 F.A. for duty. Twelve O.R's proceeded to 132 F. Ambulance in relief of a similar number. Five regimental Stretcher bearers were attached to this unit from 16th R.B. for a course of instruction.	
"	8/11/17		Weather wet. CAPT. PILE C.R. RAMC posted to this unit & taken on the strength from 8/11/17. Twelve O.R's proceeded to 132 F.A. in relief of a similar number	

D. D. & L., London, E.C. (A8001) Wt. W1771/M2031 750,000 5/17 Sch. 52 Forms C2118/14

Instructions regarding War Diaries and Intelligence Summaries are contained in F. S. Regs., Part II. and the Staff Manual respectively. Title pages will be prepared in manuscript.

WAR DIARY
or
INTELLIGENCE SUMMARY.
(Erase heading not required.)

Army Form C. 2118.

Page 3.

Place	Date	Hour	Summary of Events and Information	Remarks and references to Appendices
CHIPPEWA. M6A88	9/11/17		acting A.D.M.S 39th DW visited the unit & inspected fifty patients suffering from gas poisoning. He also presided at a medical board held here. One NCO & 8 OR's proceeded to 132 F.A. in relief of a similar number.	
"	10/11/17		Weather very wet. G.O.C 39th Division accompanied by ADMS visited & inspected the camp. LIEUT. BANNERMAN. C.H. R.A.M.C. rejoined the unit from 132 Field Ambulance.	
"	11/11/17		Weather cloudy & showery with occasional bright intervals. One N.C.O & 20 men from this unit proceeded to 132 F. Ambulance for temporary duty under instructions from A.D.M.S. CAPT L C FERGUSON rejoined at headquarters	
"	12/11/17		Weather fine during the day, wet at night. LIEUT BANNERMAN C.H. was detailed to go to VOORMEZEELE to inspect sick.	

D. D. & L., London, E.C.
(A8091) Wt. W1771/M2031 750,000 5/17 Sch. 52 Forms C2118/14

Instructions regarding War Diaries and Intelligence Summaries are contained in F. S. Regs., Part II. and the Staff Manual respectively. Title pages will be prepared in manuscript.

WAR DIARY
or
INTELLIGENCE SUMMARY.
(Erase heading not required.)

Army Form C. 2118.

Page 4

Place	Date	Hour	Summary of Events and Information	Remarks and references to Appendices
CHIPPEWA	13/11/17		Weather showery. CAPT PILE C.D. proceeded to 132 F.A. for temporary duty	
"	14/11/17		Weather bright & fine. Holding party of one officer and ten O.R's proceeded to "THE SCHOOLS" WESTOUTRE in relief of the 13th Field Ambulance. A.D.M.S visited the Ambulance and inspected several men who had been reported as unfit for general service	
LA CLYTTE N.7.c.	15/11/17		Weather fine. Headquarters of the Ambulance moved from CHIPPEWA to LA CLYTTE & opened for the reception of sick. Transport lines at CHIPPEWA were retained & a holding party consisting of two NCO's & five men were left a CHIPPEWA to look after area & B.R.C. stores.	

D. D. & L., London, E.C. (A8001) Wt. W1771/M2031 750,000 5/17 Sch. 52 Forms C2118/14

Instructions regarding War Diaries and Intelligence Summaries are contained in F. S. Regs., Part II. and the Staff Manual respectively. Title pages will be prepared in manuscript.

WAR DIARY
or
INTELLIGENCE SUMMARY.
(Erase heading not required.)

Army Form C. 2118.

Page. 5

Place	Date	Hour	Summary of Events and Information	Remarks and references to Appendices
LA CLYTTE N 7 C	16/11/17		Weather fine. DDMS IXth CORPS visited & inspected the Ambulance.	
"	17/11/17		Weather fine. Twelve OR's proceeded to 132 Field Ambulance for duty. ADMS visited the Ambulance.	
"	18/11/17		Weather dull but no rain fell. Number of sick admissions for the past few days somewhat higher than the average.	
"	19/11/17		Weather dull. No rain. CAPT FERGUSON L.C. proceeded to England	

Instructions regarding War Diaries and Intelligence Summaries are contained in F. S. Regs., Part II. and the Staff Manual respectively. Title pages will be prepared in manuscript.

WAR DIARY
or
INTELLIGENCE SUMMARY.
(Erase heading not required.)

Army Form C. 2118.

Page 6

Place	Date	Hour	Summary of Events and Information	Remarks and references to Appendices
LA CLYTTE	19/11/17		on termination of Contract & is struck off the strength of this unit. LIEUT AUDUS of this unit proceeded on 14 days leave.	
HOSPICE WESTOUTRE	20/11/17		The headquarters of the Ambulance moved from LA CLYTTE to THE HOSPICE WESTOUTRE taking over from 2nd New ZEALAND F.A. at 2pm. CAPT DR BRENT A.J. remaining with one section of the Ambulance at LA CLYTTE. Holding parties were also left at CHIPPEWA & THE SCHOOLS, WESTOUTRE. Weather fine & Sunny. PTE BALCOMBE G.W. (M72098) died of wounds received in action on 19/11/17.	
"	21/11/17		Weather dull & misty. LIEUT. BOYER MORC USA proceeded on temporary duty to 132 F.A. CAPT. MACMILLAN F.W. RAMC of this unit, but temporarily attached to 132 F.A. was admitted sick to this Field Ambulance	
"	22/11/17		Weather dull & foggy.	

D. D. & L., London, E.C. (A7001) Wt. W1771/M2031 750,000 5/17 Sch. 52 Forms C2118/14

Army Form C. 2118.

Instructions regarding War Diaries and Intelligence Summaries are contained in F. S. Regs., Part II. and the Staff Manual respectively. Title pages will be prepared in manuscript.

WAR DIARY
or
INTELLIGENCE SUMMARY.
(Erase heading not required.)

Page 7

Place	Date	Hour	Summary of Events and Information	Remarks and references to Appendices
THE. HOSPICE WESTOUTRE	23/11/17		Weather dull & showery. ADMS visited and inspected the Ambulance.	
"	24/11/17		Weather fine, very windy. Twenty OR's reinforcements reported from the Base & were inspected & medically examined. Five OR's rejoined this unit from temporary duty with 132 F.A. No 93945. Sgt MITCHELSON P.J. promoted to a/S/Sgt from 19.9.17. Authority DGMS 1450/1705. a O.C. of this unit proceeded to OUDERZEELE & inspected site of field Ambulance there	
"	25/11/17		One NCO & five OR's proceeded to OUDERZEELE as an advance party. An advance party from 98 F.A. arrived at THE HOSPICE. Advance parties from 98 F.A. took over from this unit at CHIPPEWA THE SCHOOLS & LA CLYTTE & our personnel from these places returned to headquarters at THE HOSPICE. Weather bright, cold, with occasional showers of hail.	

D. D. & L., London, E.C. (A^8001) Wt. W1771/M2031 750,000 5/17 Sch. 52 Forms C2118/14.

Instructions regarding War Diaries and Intelligence Summaries are contained in F. S. Regs., Part II. and the Staff Manual respectively. Title pages will be prepared in manuscript.

WAR DIARY
or
INTELLIGENCE SUMMARY.
(Erase heading not required.)

Army Form C. 2118.

Place	Date	Hour	Summary of Events and Information	Remarks and references to Appendices
OUDERZEELE J.14 A.1.1.	26/11/17		After handing over the Ambulance site, stores etc at THE HOSPICE, WESTOUTRE to 98 Field Ambulance the unit moved to OUDERZEELE, taking over the Hospital site at that place from 96 Field Ambulance. The Ambulance left WESTOUTRE at 10 am and arrived OUDERZEELE at 4pm The length of the march was about 13 miles, & both men & horses arrived at the latter place fresh & in good condition The ambulance opened on arrival for the reception of sick. Weather Sunny & Cold.	
"	27/11/17		Weather Cold & Showery. LIEUT BOYER MORC. USA & remainder of stretcher bearers on temporary duty with 132 F.A. rejoined this unit.	
"	28/11/17		Weather Fine, Mild. CAPT. PILE C.D. RAMC proceeded on duty to the 1st Cambs & is struck off the strength of this unit from this date.	

Instructions regarding War Diaries and Intelligence Summaries are contained in F. S. Regs., Part II. and the Staff Manual respectively. Title pages will be prepared in manuscript.

WAR DIARY
or
INTELLIGENCE SUMMARY.
(Erase heading not required.)

Army Form C. 2118.

Page 9[4]

Place	Date	Hour	Summary of Events and Information	Remarks and references to Appendices
OUDERZEELE	29/11/17		Weather bright & sunny. A.D.M.S visited the Field Ambulance and inspected the Hospital & billets.	
"	30/11/17		Weather bright & sunny. CAPT. MACMILLAN F.W. RAMC proceeded on fourteen days leave.	

H. F. Warwick Capt. RAMC.
a. O.C. 133 Field Ambulance

D. D. & L., London, E.C.
(A7o3) Wt. ...1 71/M2031 750,000 5/17 Sch. 52 Forms C2.../14

Original

Confidential

War Diary

of

133rd Field Ambulance

From :- December 1st 1917
To :- December 31st 1917

—

(Volume 22)

—

140/2618.

4

5

Dec. 1917

VOL. 22.

Instructions regarding War Diaries and Intelligence Summaries are contained in F. S. Regs., Part II. and the Staff Manual respectively. Title pages will be prepared in manuscript.

WAR DIARY
or
~~INTELLIGENCE SUMMARY.~~
(Erase heading not required.)

Army Form C. 2118.

Page. 1.

Place	Date	Hour	Summary of Events and Information	Remarks and references to Appendices
OODERZEELE. J14 a 11 Sheet 27	1/12/17		Weather dull and very cold. 1st LIEUT. BOYER G. H. U.S.A. MORC. proceeded for temporary duty with 13th Gloster Regt. CAPT. MACMILLAN .7 W. RAMC. proceeded on 14 days leave from 1.12.17 to 15.12.17.	
"	2.12/17		Weather cold, generally fine but sleet at intervals	
"	3.12/17		Weather cold. frost. Nothing of importance to report.	
"	4/12/17		Weather cold & frosty Nothing of importance to report	
"	5/12/17		Weather bright & sunny.	
			H F Warwick Capt RAMC	

D. D. & L., London, E.C.
A^00) Wt. 1 71/M2031 750,000 5/17 Sch. 52 Forms C2118/14

Vol. 22.

WAR DIARY
or
INTELLIGENCE SUMMARY.
(Erase heading not required.)

Instructions regarding War Diaries and Intelligence Summaries are contained in F. S. Regs., Part II. and the Staff Manual respectively. Title pages will be prepared in manuscript.

Army Form C. 2118.

Page. 2.

Place	Date	Hour	Summary of Events and Information	Remarks and references to Appendices
OUDEZEELE J. 14 a 11 Sheet 27	6/12/17		Weather conditions excellent. Lt Col. SINCLAIR MILLER, and Lieut C. W. AUDUS rejoined the Unit from leave expiring 4/12/17. The former took over charge of the Unit. Sinclair Miller Lt Col. RAMC.	
	7/12/17		Weather continues favourable. Capt WARWICK H.F. and one N.C.O. proceeded as billeting party to the LUMBRES AREA.	
	8/12/17		Weather conditions mild, some rain. The Horse Transport of the Unit joined the 117th Brigade transport for the LUMBRES AREA, Mr. BANNERMAN being in charge. An advance Party from the 99th F.A. took over the FIELD Amb^ce site at OUDEZEELE. (J 14 a 11 Sheet 27).	
	9/12/17		Weather conditions poor. Rain from time to time throughout the day. The personnel of the Unit to VIEIL MOUTIER entraining at ABEELE and detraining at LOTTINGHEN (Pas de Calais). Headquarters closed at	

D. D. & L., London, E.C. (A7900.) Wt. W1771/M2031 750,000 5/17 Sch. 52 Forms C2118/14

Instructions regarding War Diaries and Intelligence Summaries are contained in F. S. Regs., Part II. and the Staff Manual respectively. Title pages will be prepared in manuscript.

Vol. 22.

WAR DIARY
or
INTELLIGENCE SUMMARY.
(Erase heading not required.)

Army Form C. 2118.

Page 3.

Place	Date	Hour	Summary of Events and Information	Remarks and references to Appendices
			OUDEZEELE at 7 AM. and opened at VIEIL MOULIER (Pas de CALAIS) at noon. I made an inspection of X Corps Officers Rest Station at Le VAL RESTANT with a view to taking the place over	
VIEIL Moulier (Pas de Calais)	10/12/17		Weather conditions fine. The Horse transport arrived about 4.30 A.M. Capt. WARWICK H.F. and a party proceeded to take over X Corps Rest Station at Le Val RESTANT, Bois de THIEMEBRONNE.	
	11/12/17		Weather conditions good. Hospital for the sick of the 117th Brigade was opened up in large barn. Arrangements completed for getting all horses and mules under cover.	
	12/12/17		Weather continues fine. The A.D.M.S. 39th Div. visited the Ambulance today & found the condition of things satisfactory	
	13/12/17		Weather dull & misty. Route march for all available personnel of the Ambulance	

D. D. & L., London, E.C. (A8001) Wt. W1-71/M2031 750,000 5/17 Sch. 52 Forms C2118/14

Vol. 22.

WAR DIARY
or
INTELLIGENCE SUMMARY.
(Erase heading not required.)

Army Form C. 2118.

Instructions regarding War Diaries and Intelligence Summaries are contained in F. S. Regs., Part II. and the Staff Manual respectively. Title pages will be prepared in manuscript.

Page 4.

Place	Date	Hour	Summary of Events and Information	Remarks and references to Appendices
VIEIL MOULIER Pas de Calais	14/12/17		Weather dull; showers throughout the day. Squad and company drill in the morning; games in the afternoon. Lieut BOYER G. H. rejoined Unit.	
	15/12/17		Weather conditions excellent. D.A.D.M.S. 39th Division visited FIELD Ambulance site. Squad + company drill in the morning. Games in the afternoon.	
	16/12/17		Weather continues good. Message received at 3.30 A.M. for all available medical Aid to be sent to DESVRES to deal with collision of troop train. The O.C. unit + ~~Lieut~~ BOYER with ~~nursing orderlies~~ orderlies + all available cars attended. Football match + Tug of War in Divnal Competition contested today.	
	17/12/17		Weather bright frosty with snow at night. Squad drill + route march in morning for personnel	
	18/12/17		Weather continues clear + frosty.	

D. D. & L., London, E.C. (A7001) Wt. W1771/M2031 750,000 5/17 Sch. 52 Forms C2118/14

Instructions regarding War Diaries and Intelligence Summaries are contained in F. S. Regs., Part II. and the Staff Manual respectively. Title pages will be prepared in manuscript.

VOL. 22

WAR DIARY
or
INTELLIGENCE SUMMARY.
(Erase heading not required.)

Army Form C. 2118.

Page 5.

Place	Date	Hour	Summary of Events and Information	Remarks and references to Appendices
VIEIL MOUTIER Pas de CALAIS	19/12/17		Weather continues bright and frosty. Conference at the A.D.M.S.'s office of O.C.'s FIELD Amb[ce]. Special stress was laid on the training of officers and especially of officers of the U.S. Army. The personnel of the Unit bathed.	
	20/12/17		Weather bright & frosty. O.C.'s parade at 8.30 Am. Company and Squad drill under Capt. McMILLAN and Lieut BOYER. Kit inspection. Route march. Lieut BANNERMAN C.H. proceeded for duty today to the 75th Labour Group and is struck off the strength of this Unit. Instructional conference for the junior officers	
	21/12/17		Weather clear and frosty. Lieut D. J. VALENTINE R.A.M.C. S.R. reported for duty and is taken on the strength of the Unit from today.	
	22/12/17		Weather continues bright & frosty. Squad and company drill and recreational training continued. Capt: McMILLAN F.W. proceeded for temporary duty to 13th ROYAL SUSSEX Reg[t]. Lieut G. H. BOYER M.O.R.C. U.S.A. proceeded for temporary duty to 12th ROYAL SUSSEX Batt[n].	
	23/12/17		Weather continues clear and frosty. Capt WARWICK H.F. proceeded on 14 days leave to ENGLAND. Instructional conference. Subject TRENCH Foot. Its Prevention & treatment.	

D. D. & L., London, E.C. (A7001) Wt. W1771/M2031 750,000 5/17 Sch. 52 Forms C2118/14

Army Form C. 2118.

WAR DIARY
or
INTELLIGENCE SUMMARY.

(*Erase heading not required.*)

Instructions regarding War Diaries and Intelligence Summaries are contained in F. S. Regs., Part II. and the Staff Manual respectively. Title pages will be prepared in manuscript.

Vol. 22.

Page 6

Place	Date	Hour	Summary of Events and Information	Remarks and references to Appendices
VIELL MOUTIER (Pas de Calais)	24/12/17		Weather continues clear + frosty. Lieut FARRELL M.O.R.C. U.S.A. reported for duty and is taken on the strength of the Unit from today	
	25/12/17		Weather: Slight thaw has set in. Snow in evening. Transport packed preparatory to moving off.	
	26/12/17		Weather: Heavy fall of snow. Transport proceeded to FORWARD AREA. Under charge of Capt. H. De BRENT and Lieut VALENTINE. D.J. A. Small advance party proceeded on Aml^ce car to FORWARD Area	
	27/12/17		Weather: Snow and frost continued.	
	28/12/17		Weather: Frosty. Personnel moved to 134 F.A. site at Alfringues for the night.	
	29/12/17		Weather: A slight thaw set in. Personnel entrained at WIZERNES and detrained at St. JEAN and proceeded to FIELD Aml^ce site at Duhallow. Capt. De BRENT and small party proceeded to A.D.S. at St. JULIEN	
Duhallow	30/12/17		Weather: Thaw continues. Bearers of this Unit proceeded to the FORWARD posts in charge of Lieut VALENTINE D.J.	

D. D. & L., London, E.C. (A8001) Wt. W1771/M2031 750,000 5/17 Sch. 52 Forms C2118/14

Army Form C. 2118.

Instructions regarding War Diaries and Intelligence Summaries are contained in F. S. Regs., Part II. and the Staff Manual respectively. Title pages will be prepared in manuscript.

WAR DIARY
or
INTELLIGENCE SUMMARY.

(Erase heading not required.)

Vol. 22.

Page 7.

Place	Date	Hour	Summary of Events and Information	Remarks and references to Appendices
Duhallow	31/12/17		Weather has become frosty again. The relief of the bearers of the 92nd F.A. completed today: also the taking over of the FIELD Ambulance site at Duhallow. As all the personnel are under canvas a strong appeal has been sent to A.D.M.S. 39th Div. to endeavour to obtain NISSEN Huts for this site.	

Sinclair Miller
LT COL.
O. C. 133RD FLD. AMB.

D. D. & L., London, E.C.
(A8001) Wt. W1771/M2031 750,000 5/17 Sch. 52 Forms C2118/14

Confidential

Vol 23

Original

War Diary

of

133rd Field Ambulance

R. A. M. C.

From :- 1st January 1918
To :- 31st January 1918.

Volume XXIII

5

Jan. 1918

Army Form C. 2118.

WAR DIARY
or
INTELLIGENCE SUMMARY.
(Erase heading not required.)

Instructions regarding War Diaries and Intelligence Summaries are contained in F. S. Regs., Part II. and the Staff Manual respectively. Title pages will be prepared in manuscript.

Vol 23

Page 1.

Place	Date	Hour	Summary of Events and Information	Remarks and references to Appendices
Duhallow I.6.c5 Sheet 28.	1/1/18		Weather continues frosty. Visited A.D.S. at St. JULIEN and all the FORWARD Posts including the R.A.P.s. The C.R.E. 39th Div. visited A.D.S. St. JULIEN and considered present accommodation there very small. The A.D.M.S. 39th Div. visited Amb.ce site at Duhallow; also A.D.S. St. JULIEN. He agreed that extensions to the A.D.S. highly desirable. 2 N.C.O's + 68 O.R's reported for temporary duty from 132 F.A. Also a bearer party of 80 from 134 F.A. for work in the FORWARD Area.	
	2/1/18		Thaw has set in. Relief of the bearers in the FORWARD Post. Cleaning up of Hdqrs and A.D.S. St. JULIEN continued.	
	3/1/18		Weather cold + frosty. Working on the improvement of the A.D.S. St. JULIEN	
	4/1/18		Weather dry and cold. Inspected proposed FIELD Amb.ce site at SEIGE Billets suitable but G.O.C. 116th Brigade desires to occupy them. The matter is in abeyance for the moment.	
	5/1/18		Weather fair. A slight thaw. The bearers of 132 F.A proceeded to forward area to relieve those of 134 F.A. ~~Lieut.~~ C A FARREL M.O.R.C. U.S.A. proceeded	

Instructions regarding War Diaries and Intelligence Summaries are contained in F. S. Regs., Part II. and the Staff Manual respectively. Title pages will be prepared in manuscript.

WAR DIARY
or
INTELLIGENCE SUMMARY.
(*Erase heading not required.*)

Army Form C. 2118.

Vol. 23. Page 2

Place	Date	Hour	Summary of Events and Information	Remarks and references to Appendices
DUHALLOW I 1 b. 8 8 Sheet 28.	5/1/18		to A.D.S. St-JULIEN for duty. Lieut G. H. BOYER M.O.R.C. U.S.A. rejoined this Unit from temporary duty with 12th ROYAL SUSSEX Battn. FORWARD Bearers relieved	
	6/1/18		Weather continues frosty. A.D.M.S. inspected transport at GWALIA Farm and considered the condition satisfactory. Work continued at A.D.S. St. JULIEN.	
	7/1/18		Thaw has set in. This Unit moved from DUHALLOW to new site at SIEGE Camp (B. 27 a 5.6 Sheet 28)	
SIEGE Camp B 27 a 5.6 Sheet 28	8/1/18		Weather has turned frosty. Transport moved from GWALIA FARM to SIEGE Camp. Forward bearers (132 F.A.) relieved by bearers of 133 F.A. this morning. Working party of 1 N.C.O. and 20 OR's attached to R.E's temporarily for the building of an R.A.P. right battn.	
	9/1/18		Fall of snow. Capt H. F. WARWICK M.C. R.A.M.C. rejoined the Unit from leave to ENGLAND. A.D.M.S. 39th Div visited the Fd. Ambce site and made several suggestions for improvements. Work at A.D.S. progressing favourably	
	10/1/18		Weather. Thaw has set in. The D.A.D.M.S. 39th Div. visited the Fd. Ambce Site and together we proceeded to the FORWARD Area visiting St. JULIEN A.D.S. and	

D. D. & L., London, E.C. (A8001) Wt. W1-71/M2031 750,000 5/17 Sch. 52 Forms C2118/14

Instructions regarding War Diaries and Intelligence Summaries are contained in F. S. Regs., Part II. and the Staff Manual respectively. Title pages will be prepared in manuscript.

Vol. 23

WAR DIARY
or
INTELLIGENCE SUMMARY.
(*Erase heading not required.*)

Army Form C. 2118.

Page 3

Place	Date	Hour	Summary of Events and Information	Remarks and references to Appendices
SIEGE CAMP. B27 a 5.8. Sheet 28	10/1/18	Contd –	Some of the FORWARD Relay Posts.	
	11/1/18		Weather dull with rain. Relief of the bearers in the FORWARD Area. Laying of TRENCH BOARDS in SIEGE Camp.	
	12/1/18		Weather dull, thaw continues. Major-General E. FEETHAM C.B. C.M.G. Commanding 39th Div. visited the FIELD Ambce site and inspected the transport. Lieut M CLINTON M.O. R.C. U.S.A. reported for duty and is taken on the strength of the Unit from today.	
	13/1/18		Weather has become cold: frost during the night and fall of snow in the morning. Capt McMILLAN F.W. proceeded to CASTLE CREAGH A.D.S. St JULIEN in relief of Lieut FARREL. Capt H.E. WARWICK proceeded to take over temporary duty of M.O. to 16th NOTTS + DERBY Regt. Lieut VALENTINE proceeded to take over temporary duty of M.O. to 11th Royal SUSSEX Battn.	
	14/1/18		Weather dull, but dry. Lecture by Lieut C.O. ANDUS to the N.C.O's of the Unit	

D. D. & L., London, E.C. (A7091) Wt. W1771/M2031 750,000 5/17 Sch. 52 Forms C2118/14

Instructions regarding War Diaries and Intelligence Summaries are contained in F. S. Regs., Part II. and the Staff Manual respectively. Title pages will be prepared in manuscript.

WAR DIARY
or
~~INTELLIGENCE SUMMARY.~~
(Erase heading not required.)

Army Form C. 2118.

Vol 23.

Page 4

Place	Date	Hour	Summary of Events and Information	Remarks and references to Appendices
SIEGE CAMP B27.a.5.8.	15/1/18		Weather conditions poor: heavy rain and gales. The A.D.M.S. 39th Div visited the FIELD Amb^ce site. I made an inspection of A.D.S ST. JULIEN and forward posts. Conditions ~~[illegible]~~ found satisfactory. Personnel of Unit bathed.	
	16/1/18		Weather continues stormy with showers. Lieut C.A. FARREL M.O.R.C. U.S.A. has been detailed for temporary duty with 1/1st HERTS.	
	17/1/18		Weather wet and dull. Conference held for Junior Officers. Subject:- "The Duties of Regt Medical Officer". Relief of bearers in FORWARD Area	
	18/1/18		Weather dry. Lecture on "The Water Cart" to Junior Officers. Classification of the personnel of No 2, 3 + 4 Companies of the Div^al TRAIN. Work at the A.D.S ST. JULIEN. Also on the right R.A.P. O.C. 106 F.A. visited the HdQrs. of this Unit. Mutual arrangements were made for the forthcoming relief	
	19/1/18		Weather mild and dry. Classification of personnel of Divl train continued.	

T2134. Wt. W708—776. 500000. 4/15. Sir J. C. & S.

Instructions regarding War Diaries and Intelligence Summaries are contained in F. S. Regs., Part II. and the Staff Manual respectively. Title pages will be prepared in manuscript.

WAR DIARY
or
INTELLIGENCE SUMMARY.
(Erase heading not required.)

Army Form C. 2118.

Vol. 23

Page 5

Place	Date	Hour	Summary of Events and Information	Remarks and references to Appendices
SIEGE Camp B27 a 5.8. Sheet 28	20/1/18		Weather continues dry. Attached bearers of 132 FIELD Amb^ce returned to their Unit today. Advance party proceeded to new Site at School Camp.	
	21/1/18		Weather continues mild and dry. TRANSPORT wagons loaded. Personnel from forward area relieved by the 106th F.A. and rejoined Hdqrs.	
	22/1/18		Wether conditions: Showers in the morning. The Unit moved from SIEGE camp at 9 A.M. and Hdqrs. were established at School Camp at 12 noon.	
School Camp L.3.a.8.4. Sheet 27.	23/1/18		Weather conditions dry with Sunshine. Detachment of A.S.C. under Lieut CLINTON proceeded to PROVEN for instruction in the details of Entraining.	
	24/1/18		Weather continues good. Conference for the ~~young~~ junior officers on the mechanism of a Divisional "move." The whole Unit bathed.	

T2134. Wt. W708—776. 500000. 4/15. Sir J. C. & S.

Instructions regarding War Diaries and Intelligence Summaries are contained in F. S. Regs., Part II. and the Staff Manual respectively. Title pages will be prepared in manuscript.

WAR DIARY
or
~~INTELLIGENCE SUMMARY.~~
(Erase heading not required.)

Army Form C. 2118.

Vol 23

Page 6

Place	Date	Hour	Summary of Events and Information	Remarks and references to Appendices
School Camp L.3.a.6.4 Sheet 27	25/1/18		Weather conditions perfect. Squad + Section drill in the morning. Games in the afternoon. Lieut BOYER proceeded with advance part to New Area.	
	26/1/18		Weather conditions continue good. The Unit moved from School Camp to entrain at PROVEN. The transport moved off at 8.45 P.M. and personnel at 10 P.M. ~~to~~	
	27/1/18		Weather continues fine. Entrainment completed at 0.20 A.M. The Unit reached detraining station MERICOURT L'ABBE at 12.30 P.M. and its destination SAILLY-LE-SEC at 3 P.M.	
SAILLY LE SEC (AMIENS Map)	28/1/18		Weather fine: sunshine. Improvement of billets + the provision of latrines commenced. The wagons of the transport cleaned.	
	29/1/18		Weather fine + warm. A.D.M.S. visited FIELD Amb^y site. Lieut BOYER with advance party proceeded to New Area. Wagons packed.	

T2134. Wt. W708—776. 500000. 4/15. Sir J. C. & S.

Instructions regarding War Diaries and Intelligence Summaries are contained in F. S. Regs., Part II. and the Staff Manual respectively. Title pages will be prepared in manuscript.

WAR DIARY
or
~~INTELLIGENCE~~ SUMMARY.
(Erase heading not required.)

Army Form C. 2118.

Vol. 23

Page 7.

Place	Date	Hour	Summary of Events and Information	Remarks and references to Appendices
SAILLY Le Sec (Near Amiens)	30/1/18		Weather continues good: white frost during the night. Personnel under Capt De BRENT moved off at 4.30 A.M. & transport under Mr. CLINTON at 7. A.M. Headquarters moved by Motor Amb^ce cars leaving SAILLY Le Sec at 9 AM. and reaching HAUT ALLAINE (near PERONNE) at 11 A.M. Lieut FARRELL proceeded to take over temporary medical Charge of the 14th Hants Reg^t.	
	31/1/18		Weather misty. Heavy frost during the night. Capt H. De BRENT, ~~Lieut~~ BOYER & Lieut ANDUS proceeded to NURLU to take over the D.R.S. there from the 9th F.A. (South African). Some of the personnel of the unit accompanied them. Capt H. F. WARWICK M.C. and Lieut D. J. VALENTINE rejoined the unit from temporary duty.	

Sinclair Miller
LT. COL.
O. C. 133RD FLD. AMB.

T2134. Wt. W708—776. 500000. 4/15. Sir J. C. & S.

133rd Field Ambulance R.A.M.C.

133rd Fd Amb
JL 24
140/2784

WAR DIARY.

Month ending
Feb. 28th 1918.

VOLUME 24

4
Feb. 1918

Original Copy.

Sinclair Miller LT COL.
O. C. 133rd FLD. AMB.

Instructions regarding War Diaries and Intelligence Summaries are contained in F. S. Regs., Part II. and the Staff Manual respectively. Title pages will be prepared in manuscript.

WAR DIARY
or
~~INTELLIGENCE~~ SUMMARY.

(Erase heading not required.)

Army Form C. 2118.

Vol 24 Page 1.

Place	Date	Hour	Summary of Events and Information	Remarks and references to Appendices
Haut ALLAINE	1/2/18		Weather continues frosty. The D.R.S. at NURLU (D4 b53 Sheet 63) was taken over by advance party from 1st S.A.F.A. (9th Div) at 8 A.M. The Unit moved from Haut ALLAINE at 8.30 AM and arrived at NURLU at noon. Headquarters Established at NURLU at same hour. A.D.M.S. visited D.R.S. site.	
NURLU. D4. b53. Sheet 63.	2/2/18		Weather conditions still severe. Heavy frost during the night. Roofing of the Horse Standings completed. Erection of Shelters for officers commenced. Bomb proof revetting around hutments continued.	
	3/2/18		Weather continues cold. Work on Officers' Shelters continued. Also revetment of horse lines. Lieut. D.J. VALENTINE proceeded to 17th K.R.R.C. for duty and is struck off the strength of this Unit from today.	
	4/2/18		Weather: clear and sunshine. Constructional work continued on horse lines, cook house and officers quarters.	

T2134. Wt. W708—776. 500000. 4/15. Sir J. C. & S.

Instructions regarding War Diaries and Intelligence Summaries are contained in F. S. Regs., Part II. and the Staff Manual respectively. Title pages will be prepared in manuscript.

WAR DIARY
or
INTELLIGENCE SUMMARY.
(*Erase heading not required.*)

Army Form C. 2118.

Vol 24. Page 2

Place	Date	Hour	Summary of Events and Information	Remarks and references to Appendices
NARLU D4 b 53 Sheet 63	5/2/18		Weather dull but dry. Erection of bath house commenced with FRENCH spray bath. The A.D.M.S. 39th Div. visited the D.R.S. site and made several suggestions from improvement which were duly noted.	
	6/2/18		Weather poor: Showers throughout the day. Work on bath house continued. Completion of FIELD oven in the Cook house. Revetting of Patients' Huts continued.	
	~~7/2/18~~ 7/2/18		~~Weat~~ Weather continues dull. A bearer party of 30 O.R's proceeded for duty to 134 F.A. Improvements on Horse Lines & revetment continued.	
	8/2/18		Weather dull ~~and~~ with drizzling rain. The G.O.C. 39th Div. visited the D.R.S. site and was satisfied with the condition of things. Work on camp continued.	
	9/2/18		Weather brighter. Capt H.J. DE BREAT M.C. proceeded on 14 days leave to ENGLAND.	

T2131. Wt. W708—776. 500000. 4/15. Sir J. C. & S.

Instructions regarding War Diaries and Intelligence Summaries are contained in F. S. Regs., Part II. and the Staff Manual respectively. Title pages will be prepared in manuscript.

Vol. 24

WAR DIARY
or
~~INTELLIGENCE SUMMARY.~~
(Erase heading not required.)

Army Form C. 2118.

Page 3.

Place	Date	Hour	Summary of Events and Information	Remarks and references to Appendices
NURLU D4 b 5.3. Sheet 63	10/2/18		Weather conditions good. Lieut J. B. CLINTON M.O.R.C. U.S.A. proceeded for temporary duty to 1st CAMLS Regt in relief of Capt PILE proceeding on leave. Lieut D. J. VALENTINE rejoined this Unit from 17th K.R.R. and is taken on the strength from today.	
	11/2/18		Weather conditions excellent. Bath house for patients brought into use from today. Revettment of huts continued.	
	12/2/18		Weather misty. Hut revettment continued. The lowering of the beds in the Hospital wards commenced. Also erection of NISSEN Hut for ORDERLY ROOM.	
	13/2/18		Weather conditions poor: showers throughout the morning. Work on the various ~~parts~~ parts of the Camp continued	
	14/2/18		Weather dull and damp. Conference at A.D.M.S.' Office on Defence Scheme	

Army Form C. 2118.

WAR DIARY
or
~~INTELLIGENCE SUMMARY.~~
(Erase heading not required.)

Instructions regarding War Diaries and Intelligence Summaries are contained in F. S. Regs., Part II. and the Staff Manual respectively. Title pages will be prepared in manuscript.

Vol. 24

Page 4.

Place	Date	Hour	Summary of Events and Information	Remarks and references to Appendices
NURLU D4 b 5 3 Sheet 62B	15/2/18		Weather conditions good. Sunshine. Work on the D.R.S. continued. Capt F.W. McMILLAN R.A.M.C. proceeded to ~~the~~ report to O.C. LUCKNOW Casualty Clearing Station for duty and is struck off the strength of this Unit from today. Lieut C.A. FARRELL M.O. R.C. U.S.A. rejoined this Unit from temporary duty with the 1/1st Camb.s Regt.	
	16/2/18		Weather clear and frosty. Work on camp continued. Hostile aircraft active early in the night.	
	17/2/18		Weather conditions continue good. D.M.S. Fifth Army visited the Divisional Rest Station and commented favourably on the amount of work for the improvement of the camp and the protection of the patients that had been carried out. The Consulting Physician Fifth Army also visited the Amb^ce site. Hostile aeroplanes active during the night	
	18/2/18		Weather clear & frosty. A.D.M.S. 39th Div visited the camp and was well satisfied with the improvements.	

T2134. Wt. W708—776. 500000. 4/15. Sir J. C. & S.

Instructions regarding War Diaries and Intelligence Summaries are contained in F. S. Regs., Part II. and the Staff Manual respectively. Title pages will be prepared in manuscript.

WAR DIARY
or
~~INTELLIGENCE SUMMARY.~~
(Erase heading not required.)

Army Form C. 2118.

Vol. 24 | Page 5

Place	Date	Hour	Summary of Events and Information	Remarks and references to Appendices
NURLU D4 b5 3 Sheet 62c	19/2/18		Weather conditions remain good. Frost continues. Work on the revettment of huts continued. Also on latrines, incinerator & grease traps. The night was quiet.	
	20/2/18		Weather continues good. General work on camp continued. New coal shed erected.	
	21/2/18		Weather clear & frosty. Work on Camp improvement continued	
	22/2/18		Weather showery. Lieut G H. BOYER M.O.R.C. U.S.A. proceeded on temporary duty as M.O. i/c 4/5th Black Watch Battn. The a/A.D.M.S 39th Div. visited and inspected the Divisional Rest Station and expressed his satisfaction with the state of things. ~~[illegible]~~ The Corps Commander and D.D.M.S. VII Corps visited the D.R.S. They suggested increased amusements for the patients. This is being carried out as far as possible.	
	23/2/18		Weather dull. 39th Divl "TIVOLIES" gave concert for patients & personnel.	

Instructions regarding War Diaries and Intelligence Summaries are contained in F. S. Regs., Part II. and the Staff Manual respectively. Title pages will be prepared in manuscript.

WAR DIARY
or
~~INTELLIGENCE SUMMARY.~~
(Erase heading not required.)

Vol 24.

Army Form C. 2118.

Page 6

Place	Date	Hour	Summary of Events and Information	Remarks and references to Appendices
NURLU D4 b 53 Sheet 63.	24/2/18		Weather dull and showery. Lieut. VALENTINE proceeded to the Fifth ARMY School of Instruction to attend a course. Football match with No 1 section D.A.C. Patients were present.	
	25/2/18		Weather Showery. Box Respirator inspection and drill. Work on camp continued in the afternoon.	
	26/2/18		Weather dull, Showers at times. Work on camp continued.	
	27/2/18		Weather conditions improved. Advance party from 28th F.A. arrived for the D.R.S. Advance party proceeded to new Field Ambce Site at BRAY. Capt. H. DE BRENT rejoined the Unit from leave in ENGLAND.	
	28/2/18		Weather conditions cold with sleet showers. The FIELD AMBce moved from NURLU at 9 A.M. The move was cancelled en route and headquarters were again established at NURLU.	

Sinclair Miller.
LT COL.
O. C. 133RD FLD. AMB.

T2134. Wt. W708—776. 500000. 4/15. Sir J. C. & S.

133rd Field Ambulance R.A.M.C.

Vol 25

Original

140/2849.

WAR DIARY.

March 1918

VOLUME 25.

MARCH 1918.

7

Sinclair Miller LT COL.
O. C. 133RD FLD. AMB.

Army Form C. 2118.

Instructions regarding War Diaries and Intelligence Summaries are contained in F. S. Regs., Part II. and the Staff Manual respectively. Title pages will be prepared in manuscript.

Vol. 25

WAR DIARY
or
~~INTELLIGENCE SUMMARY.~~
(Erase heading not required.)

Page 1

Place	Date	Hour	Summary of Events and Information	Remarks and references to Appendices
Nurlu D4 b 5 3 Sheet 63 b.	1/3/18		Weather misty: snow showers throughout the day. A bearer party of 1 N.C.O and 22 O.R's proceeded for duty to 134 F.A. for FORWARD Area.	
	2/3/18		Weather frosty: snow showers.	
	3/3/18		Weather conditions severe. Snow showers throughout the day. Work on Camp improvement continued	
	4/3/18		Weather milder: heavy mist in afternoon. Lieut C.A FARRELL M.R.C and 5 O.R's proceeded to PERONNE to ~~[illegible]~~ attend a lecture on "ECONOMY." Lieut J. B CLINTON M.R.C. proceeded on 48 hours leave to AMIENS.	
	5/3/18		Weather conditions poor. Leave of Absence from the 7th inst has been granted me and I have handed over Charge of the Unit to Major H.F. WARWICK MC in my absence. Sinclair Miller Lt. Col. R.A.M.C. 133rd Field Ambulance.	

T2134. Wt. W708-776. 500000. 4/15. Sir J. C. & S.

Instructions regarding War Diaries and Intelligence Summaries are contained in F. S. Regs., Part II. and the Staff Manual respectively. Title pages will be prepared in manuscript.

WAR DIARY
or
INTELLIGENCE SUMMARY.
(Erase heading not required.)

Army Form C. 2118.

Vol 25

Page 2.

Place	Date	Hour	Summary of Events and Information	Remarks and references to Appendices
NURLU 64B53 Sheet 63B	6/3/18		Weather fine dry & clear. LIEUT VALENTINE D.J. RAMC rejoined unit from course of instruction at fifth army school. Lt CLINTON MORC rejoined from two days leave at Amiens A high tea & concert was held in the evening to celebrate the completion of two years service with the E.F.	
"	7/3/18		Weather fine & dry. COL NIXON, consulting physician fifth army visited & inspected the Ambulance in the afternoon, & a/ADMS 39th Div. visited the ambulance in the forenoon.	
"	8/3/18		Weather clear & fine. Nothing of special interest to report	
"	9/3/18		Weather clear & fine CAPT. H. J. De BRENT M.C. RAMC proceeded on a course of four lectures, lasting one day on the subject "Chemistry of German Gases. Place VIIth Corps Gas School, Peronne. CAPT. SKELTON AVC inspected horses & mules of this unit	

T2131. Wt. W708—776. 500000. 4/15. Sir J. C. & S.

Instructions regarding War Diaries and Intelligence Summaries are contained in F. S. Regs., Part II. and the Staff Manual respectively. Title pages will be prepared in manuscript.

Army Form C. 2118.

WAR DIARY
or
~~INTELLIGENCE SUMMARY.~~
(Erase heading not required.)

Vol. 25

Page 3.

Place	Date	Hour	Summary of Events and Information	Remarks and references to Appendices
NURLU. ~~MOISLANS~~	10/3/18		Weather fine & clear	
MOISLANS C17B80 Sheet 62C	11/3/18		Ambulance moved from DRS NURLU to MOISLANS relieving 28th Field Ambulance at the later place. LT. CLINTON J.D. MORC proceeded to 11th Sussex Rgt for six days temporary duty. Twenty two other ranks returned to H.Q.s from temporary duty with 134 F.A. Weather warm & sunny	
"	12/3/18		Weather very hot & sunny. ADMS visited & inspected the camp during the afternoon	
"	13/3/18		Weather clear & hot.	
"	14/3/18		Weather fine & sunny. LT BOYER G.H. MORC. rejoined unit after temporary duty with 4/5 Black Watch	

T2134. Wt. W708–776. 500000. 4/15. Sir J. C. & S.

Instructions regarding War Diaries and Intelligence Summaries are contained in F. S. Regs., Part II. and the Staff Manual respectively. Title pages will be prepared in manuscript.

WAR DIARY
or
INTELLIGENCE SUMMARY.
(Erase heading not required.)

Army Form C. 2118.

Vol. 25

Page 4

Place	Date	Hour	Summary of Events and Information	Remarks and references to Appendices
MOISLANS	15/3/18		Weather clear & fine. Hostile aircraft warning given at 8.50 pm. All lights were extinguished	
	16/3/18		Weather fine & sunny. Nothing of importance to relate	
	17/3/18		Weather warm & bright. Corps Foden Lorry arrived at this Scabies station & was immediately got to work on scabies clothing. D.D.M.S. VIIth Corps visited & inspected the Camp. Two H.D. horses arrived to complete deficiencies	
	18/3/18		Weather clear & warm. Brigadier-General G.A.S. CAPE CMG Commanding 39th Div killed in action & his body was brought to this F.A.	
	19/3/18		Weather wet. LIEUT CLINTON J.B. M.O.R.C. rejoined unit after temporary duty with 11th Sussex Regt	

T2134. Wt. W708—776. 500000. 4/15. Sir J. C. & S.

Instructions regarding War Diaries and Intelligence Summaries are contained in F. S. Regs., Part II. and the Staff Manual respectively. Title pages will be prepared in manuscript.

WAR DIARY
or
INTELLIGENCE SUMMARY.
(Erase heading not required.)

Army Form C. 2118.

Vol. 25

Page 5

Place	Date	Hour	Summary of Events and Information	Remarks and references to Appendices
MOISLAINS	20/3/18		Weather wet in the morning, fine later. Body of late Brigadier-General C A S CAPE CMG removed for burial at PERONNE. A/O.C. & two O.R's of this unit attended the funeral	
	21/3/18		Weather conditions very misty. Heavy firing along a wide front. Only a few cases of wounded admitted	
	22/3/18		Weather continues dry & misty. The Corps Rest Station at MOISLAINS opened as a Main Dressing Station. About one thousand wounded cases passed through. FIELD Amb^ce^ bombed. Only a few ~~cases~~ of casualties. F^d^ Amb^ce^ moved from MOISLAINS to COMBLES at 11.30 P.M.	
COMBLES.	23/3/18		Weather conditions continue good. F^d^ Amb^ce^ moved from COMBLES to FLAUCOURT at 1.30 P.M. and from there to CAPPY.	
CAPPY	24/3/18		Weather continues good. F^d^ Amb^ce^ established a dressing station in the Corps Rest Station site at CAPPY. About 200 wounded passed through. A.D.M.S. 39th Div. established their Headquarters at same site.	

T2134. Wt. W708—776. 500000. 4/15. Sir J. C. & S.

Instructions regarding War Diaries and Intelligence Summaries are contained in F. S. Regs., Part II. and the Staff Manual respectively. Title pages will be prepared in manuscript.

WAR DIARY
or
INTELLIGENCE SUMMARY.
(Erase heading not required.)

Army Form C. 2118.

Vol 25

Page 6.

Place	Date	Hour	Summary of Events and Information	Remarks and references to Appendices
CAPPY	25/3/18		Weather bright + sunny. Slight frost. Lieut Col. SINCLAIR MILLER rejoined the Unit from leave in ENGLAND and took over command of the Ambulance from this date. FIELD Amb^ce site at CAPPY handed over to O.C. 132 FIELD Amb^ce at midnight 25/26.3.18. FIELD Amb^ce moved to CHIGNOLLES.	
CHIGNOLLES	26/3/18		Weather continues good. Lieut J. D. VALENTINE R.A.M.C. reported for duty to O.C. 11th Royal SUSSEX Batt^n. FIELD Amb^ce moved to HAMEL.	
HAMEL.	27/3/18		Weather continues good. FIELD Amb^ce moved from HAMEL to WARFUSÉE-ABANCOURT and then to CACHY.	
CACHY	28/3/18		Weather good. FIELD Amb^ce moved to HANGARD and hence to BOIS de BOVES. Unit billetted in a LODGE.	
BOIS de BOVES nr. AMIENS	29/3/18		Heavy rain during the night and during the morning. Afternoon dry. Lieut D. G. K. GARRETT and Lieut S. BARDAL reported for duty + are taken on the strength of the Unit.	

T2131. Wt. W708—776. 500000. 4/15. Sir J. C. & S.

Instructions regarding War Diaries and Intelligence Summaries are contained in F. S. Regs., Part II. and the Staff Manual respectively. Title pages will be prepared in manuscript.

WAR DIARY
or
INTELLIGENCE SUMMARY.
(Erase heading not required.)

Army Form C. 2118.

Vol. 25

Page 7.

Place	Date	Hour	Summary of Events and Information	Remarks and references to Appendices
Bois de Boves nr. Amiens	30/3/18		Weather continues showery. Unit moved to Petit Cagny near St Fuscien. Personnel rejoined from 134 F.A. from doing bearer work in the FORWARD area	
Petit Cagny	31/3/18		Weather conditions good. Unit moved to BOVELLES (S. W. of AMIENS) Major H. F. WARWICK M.C. rejoined the Unit from duty with 134 F. A.	

Sinclair Miller
LT. COL.
O. C. 133rd FLD. AMB.

T2134. Wt. W708—776. 500000. 4/15. Sir J. C. & S.

133rd Field Ambulance R.A.M.C.

Original 26

WAR DIARY.

Month ending April 30th 1918.

Volume 26.

Sinclair Miller LT COL.
O. C. 133RD FLD. AMB.

Instructions regarding War Diaries and Intelligence Summaries are contained in F. S. Regs., Part II. and the Staff Manual respectively. Title pages will be prepared in manuscript.

WAR DIARY or ~~INTELLIGENCE SUMMARY.~~

(Erase heading not required.)

Army Form C. 2118.

Vol. 26.

Page 1

Place	Date	Hour	Summary of Events and Information	Remarks and references to Appendices
BOVELLES	1/4/18		Weather continues good: Funeral of Major Genl. Feetham at Guignemicourt. Lieut J. B. ~~Clinto~~ CLINTON proceeded to 1/1st Camb. for duty as Medical Officer.	
~~Bo~~	2/4/18		Weather conditions good. Unit moved to AVELESQUES en route for the OISEMENT area.	
AVELESQUES	3/4/18		Weather good Unit moved to FRESNE-TILLOLOY near OISEMENT.	
FRESNE-TILLOLOY	4/4/18		Weather continues good. Hospital established. The Major General ~~[illegible]~~ commanding the 39th Division visited the Ambulance. Lieut FARREL proceeded to No. Base hospital for duty	
	5/4/18		Weather continues good. Inspection of the Unit. Box respirator drill Lecture on Correspondence to Junior officers	
	6/4/18		Weather dull. Drill in the morning. Route march in afternoon.	
	7/4/18		Weather conditions fair. Unit moved to HOCQUELUS.	

T2131. Wt. W708—776. 500000. 4/15. Sir J. C. & S.

Instructions regarding War Diaries and Intelligence Summaries are contained in F. S. Regs., Part II. and the Staff Manual respectively. Title pages will be prepared in manuscript.

WAR DIARY
or
~~INTELLIGENCE~~ SUMMARY.
(Erase heading not required.)

Army Form C. 2118.

Vol 26

Page 2

Place	Date	Hour	Summary of Events and Information	Remarks and references to Appendices
HOCQUELUS	8/4/18		Weather good. Drill for personnel in the morning. ~~[illegible]~~	
	9/4/18		Weather fair. Unit entrained at WOINCOURT, detrained at St. OMER to proceed to MOULLE	
MOULLE	10/4/18		Weather continues good. The morning was spent in cleaning transport vehicles.	
	11/4/18		Weather continues dry. The Unit entrained at St. OMER to proceed with 39th Div. Composite BRIGADE to 22nd Corps and detrained at VLAMERINGHE. The Unit moved in "battle order", the major portion of the transport being left at MONECOVE (near MOULLE) under Lieut & Qm. Cw. AUDUS. Headquarters were established at SCOTTISH LINES 28/G.23b. central. On reporting personally to Hdqrs. of Composite Bde, orders were received that Bde. was attached to 21st Div. Reported to A.D.M.S. 21st Div. and through him to D.D.M.S. 22nd CORPS.	28/G.23b cent.

T2134. Wt. W708–776. 500000. 4/15. Sir J. C. & S.

Army Form C. 2118.

Instructions regarding War Diaries and Intelligence Summaries are contained in F. S. Regs., Part II. and the Staff Manual respectively. Title pages will be prepared in manuscript.

WAR DIARY
or
~~INTELLIGENCE~~ SUMMARY.
(Erase heading not required.)

Vol. 26

Place	Date	Hour	Summary of Events and Information	Remarks and references to Appendices
Scottish Lines 28/G23.b cent	12th		Weather continues good. Unit moved to MANCHESTER Camp 28/N.2.b.5.8. There was considerable hostile shelling during the night and one shell fell in the middle of the camp. No casualties. Also enemy bombing planes overhead.	
MANCHESTER Camp 28/N2b.5.8.	13th		Weather dry but dull. Unit bathed in the morning by 21st Div. baths with clean clothing. Instruction given to the junior officers on methods of evacuation from FORWARD AREA. Lieut S. BARDAL proceeded to 63/F.A for temporary duty. Hostile shelling throughout the night.	
	14th		Weather very dull. Unit moved to La CLYTE Camp M6 d 4.8. Lieuts. EGAN, MORALES R.C. U.S.A. + Lieut SHAW R.A.M.C. reported for temporary duty from 132 F.A. The night was quiet.	
La CLYTE Camp 28/M6 d 4.8.	15th		Weather wet + cold. The Unit moved to WARATAH Camp G.15 c 3.8. Sheet 28. 16 O.R's proceeded to the FORWARD area to be attached to battns of Composite Bde. Lieut S. BARDAL rejoined Unit from 63rd F.A.	

T2134. Wt. W708—776. 500000. 4/15. Sir J. C. & S.

Instructions regarding War Diaries and Intelligence Summaries are contained in F. S. Regs., Part II. and the Staff Manual respectively. Title pages will be prepared in manuscript.

WAR DIARY
or
~~INTELLIGENCE~~ SUMMARY.
(Erase heading not required.)

Army Form C. 2118.

Vol. 26

Page 4

Place	Date	Hour	Summary of Events and Information	Remarks and references to Appendices
WARATAH Camp 28/G15 C 3.8.	16th		Weather conditions poor. Rain & sleet. Lieut G.H. BOYER M.O.R.C. & 40 O.R.s proceeded to 64th F.A. as bearer officer to the Composite Bde. Hostile artillery activity in the neighbourhood. No 2 & No 3 Composite Battns are temporarily loaned to 9th Div. Medical arrangements satisfactory.	
	17th		Weather very cold; sleet showers. Visited Lieut BOYER in FORWARD Area & also 9th Divl area where the two battns of Composite Bde are situated.	
	18th		Weather cold & rainy: situation report from Lieut BOYER normal. Hostile shelling of neighbourhood.	
	19th		Snow fell during the day. Hostile shelling in vicinity of the camp. No casualties.	
	20th		Weather dry but dull. Major H.J. DE BRENT, Lieuts BARDAL, EGAN with a bearer party &c. proceeded to take over the Collecting Post at	

Instructions regarding War Diaries and Intelligence Summaries are contained in F. S. Regs., Part II. and the Staff Manual respectively. Title pages will be prepared in manuscript.

WAR DIARY
or
~~INTELLIGENCE SUMMARY.~~
(Erase heading not required.)

Army Form C. 2118.

Vol. 26

Page 5

Place	Date	Hour	Summary of Events and Information	Remarks and references to Appendices
WARATAH Camp 28/G15C38	20th cont'd –		VORMEZEELE and Spoil Bank and to function the 21st Bde (30th Div) now attached to 21st Div. This Bde has relieved a Bde of the 9th Div. The Medical relief reported completed and satisfactory at 11 A.M. The Bde front extends from 28/I 21 c.0.5 – 28/O 3 d 5.3. This Unit is also functioning the 39th Div'l Composite Bde holding a reserve line from 28/I 27 a central to O 1 c central. In the afternoon I visited VOORMEZEELE and Spoil Bank and found the condition of the posts satisfactory	
	21/4/18		Weather conditions good. Lieut G.A. BOYER rejoined Hdqrs. Situation of Forward Areas quiet.	
	22/4/18		Weather conditions continue good Visited the FORWARD Area and LARCH Wood posts. Conditions satisfactory. Situation quiet. Lieut GARRET proceeded to FORWARD Area.	
	23/4/18		Weather fine and dry. Hostile Shelling in the neighbourhood of the camp. No casualties to personnel.	

Instructions regarding War Diaries and Intelligence Summaries are contained in F. S. Regs., Part II. and the Staff Manual respectively. Title pages will be prepared in manuscript.

Army Form C. 2118.

WAR DIARY
or
~~INTELLIGENCE SUMMARY.~~
(Erase heading not required.)

Vol. 26.

Page 6

Place	Date	Hour	Summary of Events and Information	Remarks and references to Appendices
WARATAH Camp 28/G 15 c 38	24/4/18		Weather continues fine. Lieut G. H. BOYER proceeded to see morning sick at Scottish Camp 28/ G. 23. b central. Visited Forward Area & found situation satisfactory	
	25/4/18		Weather foggy. Heavy shelling all around during the night of 24/25th. An Emergency dressing opened at 10 A.M. and about 300 wounded passed through it during the day. Heavy fighting reported around KEMMEL and KEMMEL Hill. Withdrawal of Lieuts EGAN & GARRETT from Spoil Bank to VOORMEZEELE.	
	26/4/18		Weather continues foggy. Visited the Forward Area with O.C. 64 F.A. Spoil BANK captured by enemy about 9.30 A.M. All wounded & personnel cleared. VOORMEZEELE evacuated & WOODCOTE HOUSE ~~opened~~ 28/ I 20. c. opened up as Main Collecting Post. Cases being brought back by SWAN Chateau 28/H. 19. c. 6.8. to BELGIAN BATTERY CORNER 28/G 24 a 6.8. by bearers & thence by car to TRINITY A.D.S. 28/H 14 c. central. Larch wood & Rutledge	

WAR DIARY
or
INTELLIGENCE SUMMARY.
(Erase heading not required.)

1st 2/c [illegible]

Place	Date	Hour	Summary of Events and Information	Remarks and references to Appendices
Waratah Camp	[illegible]		Post 28/I.6.5.8 continues to function.	
	[illegible]		Weather continues hazy. On the night 26/27th line withdrawn to one just East of YPRES. O/C WOODCOTE HOUSE – Major H DE BRENT M.C. – and all personnel attached of F.A. from RUTLEDGE POST 28/I.6.5.8 & LARCH WOOD rejoined HdQrs. Evacuation from forward area is now being done by 64/F.A. (21st Div). The S.S.P. has been fully opened up as a dressing station and functioned by this Unit.	
	[illegible]		Weather fog but gradually lifting. Front Bearer S.H. & one bearer subdivision provided to VIJVERHOEK to function the right sector of 9th Div Front; later in the day a second bearer subdivision proceeded to forward area. Transport horses and personnel less one tent subdivision and two bearer subdivisions moved to REMY SIDING 27/L.22.d.2.8. Heavy shelling throughout the night. Major WARWICK H.F. M.C. with one tent subdivision continues to function WARATAH Camp as a walking wounded station.	

Instructions regarding War Diaries and Intelligence Summaries are contained in F. S. Regs., Part II. and the Staff Manual respectively. Title pages will be prepared in manuscript.

WAR DIARY
or
~~INTELLIGENCE SUMMARY.~~
(*Erase heading not required.*)

Army Form C. 2118.

Vol. 26.

Page 8

Place	Date	Hour	Summary of Events and Information	Remarks and references to Appendices
REMY SIDING 27/I 23d28	29 4/18		Weather conditions continue good. Great artillery activity along the whole front. TRANSPORT lines moved to 28/K11 a 5.4. Over 100 cases passed through the Walking Wounded Station at WARATAH Camp. The night was quiet.	
	30 4/18		Weather dull and threatening. Visited W.W. Station and Transport lines. Congratulatory message received from the Major General commanding the 21st Divn to the 39th Composite Bde: "Well done the 39th Division. You have done splendid work under the most adverse circumstances and I am sure you will continue to do so whenever your services are required. I fully realize what you have been through and cannot express my admiration for the behaviour of all ranks". Sgd. David J M Campbell Major Genl 21st Div.	

Sinclair Miller
LT COL.
O. C. 132nd FLD. AMB.

T2134. Wt. W708—776. 500000. 4/15. Sir J. C. & S.

Original

War Diary

of

133rd Field Ambulance

Volume 27.

From :- 1st May 1918

To :- 31st May 1918.

Instructions regarding War Diaries and Intelligence Summaries are contained in F. S. Regs., Part II. and the Staff Manual respectively. Title pages will be prepared in manuscript.

Vol. 27.

WAR DIARY
or
~~INTELLIGENCE~~ SUMMARY.
(Erase heading not required.)

Page 1.

Army Form C. 2118.

Place	Date	Hour	Summary of Events and Information	Remarks and references to Appendices
REMY SIDING 27/I 23 d 2 8	1/5/18		Weather continues excellent. Visited ~~[illegible]~~ 39th Composite Bde. The battalions of Composite Brigade reorganising. Sector quiet.	
	2 5/18		Weather continues good. Transport rejoined Hdqrs. at REMY Siding. Lieut BOYER + bearers returned from FORWARD AREA.	
	3 5/18.		Weather conditions perfect. Parade and inspection of personnel.	
	4 5/18		Weather good.	
	5 5/18		Weather dull and showery. The Unit moved from REMY Siding, the personnel by train, the transport by road to AUTINGUES	
AUTINGUES Pas de CALAIS	6 5/18		Weather warm and dry. A.D.M.S. 39th Div. visited and inspected the Ambulance and congratulated all on the good work done in the FORWARD AREA.	

T2134. Wt. W708—776. 500000. 4/15. Sir J. C. & S.

Instructions regarding War Diaries and Intelligence Summaries are contained in F. S. Regs., Part II. and the Staff Manual respectively. Title pages will be prepared in manuscript.

Vol. 27

WAR DIARY
or
INTELLIGENCE SUMMARY.
(Erase heading not required.)

Army Form C. 2118.

Place	Date	Hour	Summary of Events and Information	Remarks and references to Appendices
ANTINQUES Pas de Calais	7 5/18		Weather showery but warm. Hospital established at the Chateau at ANTINQUES.	
	8 5/18		Weather conditions good. Lieut. T. W. Shaw proceeded for duty as M.O. i/c 1/1st HERTS Regt and is struck off strength of the Unit. Capt. J. C. JOHNSTONE joined the Unit and is taken on the strength. Lieut MORALES attached for temporary duty from 132 F.A. is taken on the strength of the Unit.	
	9 5/18		Weather fine and warm. The Major GENl Commanding the 39th DIV. visited the Ambulance	
	10 5/18		Weather dull and cold. Inspection of personnel. Drill. A small D.R.S. established.	
	11 5/18		Weather misty. Section drill and route march.	
	12 5/18		Weather conditions improved. Capt J. G. JOHNSTONE & Lieut BOYER proceeded to 134 and 132 F.A. to conduct surplus personnel to ROUEN.	

Instructions regarding War Diaries and Intelligence Summaries are contained in F. S. Regs., Part II. and the Staff Manual respectively. Title pages will be prepared in manuscript.

Vol 27

WAR DIARY
or
~~INTELLIGENCE SUMMARY.~~
(Erase heading not required.)

Army Form C. 2118.

Page 3

Place	Date	Hour	Summary of Events and Information	Remarks and references to Appendices
AUTINGUES Pas de Calais	13/5/18		Weather Showery. The Divisional Surgeon, 77th Div. A.E.F. with D.A.D.M.S. 39th Div. visited the FIELD Amb.ce site. Unit bathed.	
	14/5/18		Weather improved. Capt. S. J. L. LINDEMAN awarded the M.C. for bravery in the FIELD. Drill and route march for personnel.	
	15/5/18		Weather dry. Bright sunshine in the afternoon. Lieuts. D. G. K. GARREL, & Lieut. S. BARDAL R.A.M.C. and Lieut M. G. MORALES M.O.R.C. proceeded to report for duty to A.D.M.S. 37th Division.	
	16/5/18		Weather conditions good. Drill and route march for personnel.	
	17/5/18		Weather conditions perfect. Bright sunshine. Sergt. WISHART, Pte COUSINS + CONNOR awarded the Military Medal for bravery in the FIELD.	
	18/5/18		Weather continues good. Drill and route march for personnel.	

T2134. Wt. W708–776. 500000. 4/15. Sir J. C. & S.

Instructions regarding War Diaries and Intelligence Summaries are contained in F. S. Regs., Part II. and the Staff Manual respectively. Title pages will be prepared in manuscript.

WAR DIARY
or
~~INTELLIGENCE~~ SUMMARY.
(*Erase heading not required.*)

Army Form C. 2118.

Vol. 27

Page 4

Place	Date	Hour	Summary of Events and Information	Remarks and references to Appendices
Autingues. Pas de Calais	19/5/18		Weather conditions perfect. FIELD Ambulance Sports held today. Prizes presented by A.D.M.S. 39th Div	
	20/5/18		Weather conditions excellent. Surplus personnel to training cadre proceeded to the base under Capt. J. G. JOHNSTONE. 308 American FIELD ~~Ambulance~~ moved in.	
	21/5/18		Weather Good.	
	22/5/18		Weather Good. Instruction of American FIELD Ambulance	
	23/5/18		Weather fine and dry. Lieut G. H. BOYER proceeded to 1/6th CHESHIRES for duty. Instructional lectures &c. arranged	
	24/5/18		Weather. Heavy rains throughout the day	
	25/5/18		Weather bright & warm. Major H. F. WARWICK M.C. proceeded to report for duty to DDMS II Corps	

T2134. Wt. W708–776. 500000. 4/15. Sir J. C. & S.

Instructions regarding War Diaries and Intelligence Summaries are contained in F. S. Regs., Part II. and the Staff Manual respectively. Title pages will be prepared in manuscript.

WAR DIARY
or
~~INTELLIGENCE~~ SUMMARY.
(Erase heading not required.)

Army Form C. 2118.

Vol. 27

Page 5.

Place	Date	Hour	Summary of Events and Information	Remarks and references to Appendices
Autingues Pas de Calais	25 5/18	Cont^d	and Major S. J. LINDEMAN to A.D.M.S. 6th Division	
–	26 5/18		Weather continues good. Capt J. G. Johnstone rejoined Unit.	
	27 5/18		Weather bright and warm. Capt. J. G. Johnstone proceeded to report for duty to A.D.M.S. 6th Div. Instruction in FIELD Work to the 308 AMERICAN FIELD Amb^e.	
	28 5/18		Weather conditions perfect. A.D.M.S. 39th visited the Ambulance site.	
	29 5/18		Weather continues good. Instruction in FIELD work continued.	
	30 5/18		Weather conditions good. The G.O.C. 77th AMERICAN Division inspected the FIELD Ambulance site	
	31 5/18		Weather perfect. Field operations carried out. Sinclair Miller LT. COL. O. C. 133rd FLD. AMB.	

T2134. Wt. W708–776. 500000. 4/15. Sir J. C. & S.

Original

Confidential

War Diary

of

133rd Field Ambulance

Volume 28.

From :- June 1st 1918
To :- June 30th 1918

140/3076.

7

June 1918.

Instructions regarding War Diaries and Intelligence Summaries are contained in F. S. Regs., Part II, and the Staff Manual respectively. Title pages will be prepared in manuscript.

WAR DIARY
or
~~INTELLIGENCE SUMMARY.~~
(Erase heading not required.)

Army Form C. 2118.

Vol. 28

Page 1.

Place	Date	Hour	Summary of Events and Information	Remarks and references to Appendices
Autingues Pas de Calais	1/6/18		Weather conditions Excellent. Field work for the American Unit.	
	2/6/18		Weather Good.	
	3/6/18		Weather continues fine. Lecture of to American Unit on GAS DEFENSE	
	4/6/18		Weather conditions good. Lecture to Officers on MAP READING	
	5/6/18		Weather Excellent. Instruction to American Unit in loading transport.	
	6/6/18		Weather Excellent. The 308 AMERICAN FIELD Ambulance moved from this area at 12 noon today. Hospital established in FIELD Ambulance site.	
	7/6/18		Weather conditions perfect.	
	8/6/18		Weather continues Good. A. S. C. personnel and P. B. men of this unit	

T2134. Wt. W708—776. 500000. 4/15. Sir J. C. & S.

Instructions regarding War Diaries and Intelligence Summaries are contained in F. S. Regs., Part II. and the Staff Manual respectively. Title pages will be prepared in manuscript.

WAR DIARY
or
~~INTELLIGENCE~~ SUMMARY.
(Erase heading not required.)

Army Form C. 2118.

Vol. 28

Page 2.

Place	Date	Hour	Summary of Events and Information	Remarks and references to Appendices
Autingues. Pas de Calais	8/6/18		proceeded to join No. 4 Coy. 39th Divisional Train today. Two officers and 10 O.R.s of the 30th AMERICAN Division reported for duty. Conference of FIELD Ambulance commanders by A.D.M.S. 39th Div.	
	~~9/6/18~~		~~Weather showery.~~	
	9/6/18		Weather showery.	
	10/6/18		Weather showery. Accommodation (hospital) for Scabies patients arranged.	
	11/6/18		Weather dry but cloudy. The D.A.D.M.S. visited the Field Amb.e site.	
	12/6/18		Weather good.	
	13/6/18		Weather continues dry. A.A. & Q.M.G. visited the Field Amb.ce site to arrange for additional improvements of the site.	
	14/6/18		Weather continues good. Instructions from A.H.Q. to retain patients only 24 hours at most.	

T2131. Wt. W708—776. 500000. 4/15. Sir J. C. & S.

Instructions regarding War Diaries and Intelligence Summaries are contained in F. S. Regs., Part II. and the Staff Manual respectively. Title pages will be prepared in manuscript.

Vol. 28

WAR DIARY
or
~~INTELLIGENCE SUMMARY.~~
(Erase heading not required.)

Page 3

Army Form C. 2118.

Place	Date	Hour	Summary of Events and Information	Remarks and references to Appendices
Autingues	14/6/18		Weather excellent. The two American M.O's & 10 O.R's proceeded to LICQUES for duty.	
	16/6/18		Weather continues good. Reconnaissance of Field Amb^y site at AFFRINGUES.	
	17/6/18		Weather perfect.	
	18/6/18	– 21st.	Weather continues good.	
	22nd		Weather good. Presentation of ribbons of recently awarded medals by A.D.M.S. 39th Div. to the following. Lt. Col. S. MILLER: D.S.O. Sergt-Major HERBERT: M.S.M. Sergt PEEL: D.C.M.	
	~~23rd~~		~~Weather cooler~~	
	23rd	–	Weather continues good.	
	24th –		Weather Excellent.	

T2134. Wt. W708–776. 500000. 4/15. Sir J. C. & S.

Instructions regarding War Diaries and Intelligence Summaries are contained in F. S. Regs., Part II. and the Staff Manual respectively. Title pages will be prepared in manuscript.

WAR DIARY
or
~~INTELLIGENCE SUMMARY.~~
(Erase heading not required.)

Army Form C. 2118.

Vol. 28

Page 4

Place	Date	Hour	Summary of Events and Information	Remarks and references to Appendices
AUTINQUES	25th –		Weather good. FIELD day for the 30th – American Division Sanitary Train.	
	26th –		Weather good. The Unit proceeded to ~~Abb~~ ABBEVILLE to re-equip. Reported to A.D.M.S. ABBEVILLE AREA.	
ABBEVILLE	27th –		Weather excellent. Surplus personnel from ROUEN reported	
–	28th –		Weather continues good.	
–	29th		Weather continues good. A.S.C. H.T. personnel rejoined Unit.	
–	30th		Weather good. Refitting complete. Transport proceeded by road to AUTIQQUES under Lieut & Qm. COWTAN. D.C.M. Sinclair Miller LT. COL. O. C. 133RD FLD. AMB.	

T2134. Wt. W708–776. 500000. 4/15. Sir J. C. & S.

Original

War Diary

of

133rd Field Ambulance

From:- 1st July 1918

To:- 31st July 1918

(Volume 29)

Instructions regarding War Diaries and Intelligence Summaries are contained in F. S. Regs., Part II. and the Staff Manual respectively. Title pages will be prepared in manuscript.

Army Form C. 2118.

WAR DIARY
or
~~INTELLIGENCE SUMMARY.~~
(Erase heading not required.)

Vol. 29.

Page 1

Place	Date	Hour	Summary of Events and Information	Remarks and references to Appendices
ABBEVILLE	1/7/18		Weather continues good. Unit less horse transport entrained at ABBEVILLE for AUTINGUES via AUDRUICQ.	
Autingues	2/7/18		Weather excellent. Unit arrived at AUTINGUES at 4 P.M.	
	3/7/18		Weather dry and warm. Capt H F WARWICK M.C. reported for duty and is taken on the strength of the Unit from this date. Hospital established	
	4/7/18		Weather continues good. Drill and route march for personnel.	
	5/7/18		Weather fine and dry. Orders received to hold the Unit in readiness to move to 2nd CORPS. Capt. C.F Knight R.A.M.C. posted for duty.	
	6/7/18		Weather continues good. Move postponed until 7th inst. Lieut D.G.K. GARRETT reported for duty and is taken on the strength of the Unit from today.	

T2134. Wt. W708—776. 500000. 4/15. Sir J. C. & S.

Instructions regarding War Diaries and Intelligence Summaries are contained in F. S. Regs., Part II. and the Staff Manual respectively. Title pages will be prepared in manuscript.

WAR DIARY
or
~~INTELLIGENCE~~ SUMMARY.
(Erase heading not required.)

Army Form C. 2118.

Vol. 29.

Page 2

Place	Date	Hour	Summary of Events and Information	Remarks and references to Appendices
Autingues	7/7/18		Weather excellent. Unit left AUTINGUES at 8.30 A.M. for the PROVEN Area to be attached to the 30th AMERICAN Division. Staging area ~~Volkeringhove~~ for the night VOLKERINCKHOVE.	
PROVEN.	8/7/18		Weather continues good. Headquarters established at BALLANCE Camp 27/E6. d. 4.2. at 4 30 P.M.	
BALLANCE Camp 27/E6.d.4.2	9/7/18		Weather warm. Rain in the evening. Hospital established. The Divisional Surgeon, 30th AMERICAN DIVISION visited the Amb. site.	
	10/7/18		Weather SHOWERY.	
	11/7/18		HEAVY rain fell during the day. Collection of AMERICAN sick commenced [illegible]	
	12/7/18		Weather continues Showery. Lieut ANDUS C.W. granted 14 days leave [illegible] 13 - 27th inst.	

T2134. Wt. W708—776. 500000. 4/15. Sir J. C. & S.

Army Form C. 2118.

WAR DIARY
or
~~INTELLIGENCE SUMMARY.~~
(Erase heading not required.)

Instructions regarding War Diaries and Intelligence Summaries are contained in F. S. Regs., Part II. and the Staff Manual respectively. Title pages will be prepared in manuscript.

Vol. 29

Page 3

Place	Date	Hour	Summary of Events and Information	Remarks and references to Appendices
BALLANCE Camp 27/E 6. d. 4.2		13/7/18	Weather continues good. Lieut S BARDAL reported for duty and is taken on the Strength of the Unit. Capt Durham, Dental Surgeon 30th Am. Div. attached for temporary duty. D.D.M.S. Corps visited the Camp.	
		14/7/18	Weather Showery. Divisional Surgeon visited FIELD Ambce site. Condition Satisfactory	
		15/7/18	Weather dull; heavy showers throughout the day. Under instructions from D. S. 30th American Division Major WARWICK with Lieut BARDAL and party proceeded to BOLLEZEELE to take over the CORPS Rest Station	
		16/7/18	Weather continues showery: Locality bombed last night. Several casualties amongst American troops.	
		17/7/18	Weather fine and dry. Headquarters of Unit moved to II Corps Rest Station at BOLLEZEELE. Capt Knight + Lieut GARRETT with bearers remaining at BALLANCE CAMP. D.D.M.S II Corps visited the Rest Station	

T2134. Wt. W708—776. 500000. 4/15. Sir J. C. & S.

Army Form C. 2118.

Instructions regarding War Diaries and Intelligence Summaries are contained in F. S. Regs., Part II. and the Staff Manual respectively. Title pages will be prepared in manuscript.

WAR DIARY
or
INTELLIGENCE SUMMARY.
(Erase heading not required.)

Vol 29. Page 4.

Place	Date	Hour	Summary of Events and Information	Remarks and references to Appendices
BOLLEZEELE 27/A22 d7.6	18/7/18		Weather continues good.	
	19/7/18		Weather good. Constructional work in C.R.S commenced.	
	20/7/18		Weather Showery.	
	21/7/18		Weather improved.	
	22/7/18		Weather good. D.D.M.S. II Corps visited site of FIELD Amb^y	
	23/7/18		Weather continues good. Work on improvement of C.R.S. continued. Concert for the patients. O.C. proceeded to 18 C.C.S for Xray of ankle.	
	24/7/18 25/7/18		Weather Showery	
	26/7/18		Weather continues broken. D.D.M.S. II Corps visited and inspected the Corps Rest Station. Various improvements suggested.	
	27/7/18 28/7/18		Weather Showery.	
	29/7/18		Weather fine. Lieut C.W. ANDUS returned from 14 days leave of Absence in England. CRICKET Match in afternoon.	

A5834 Wt. W4973/M687 750,000 8/16 D. D. & L. Ltd. Forms/C.2118/13.

Army Form C. 2118.

Instructions regarding War Diaries and Intelligence Summaries are contained in F. S. Regs., Part II. and the Staff Manual respectively. Title pages will be prepared in manuscript.

WAR DIARY
or
INTELLIGENCE SUMMARY.
(Erase heading not required.)

Vol. 29.

Page 5

Place	Date	Hour	Summary of Events and Information	Remarks and references to Appendices
BOLLEZEELE. 27/A22 d 7.6	30/7/18		Weather excellent. D.D.M.S. visited camp. O.C. rejoined unit from 18 C.C.S.	
	31/7/18		Weather continues perfect. D.M.S. 2nd Army and D.D.M.S. II Corps visited the Corps Rest Station. Condition satisfactory. Cricket match in the afternoon against A.O.D. 39th Div.	

Sinclair Miller Lt. Col.
O.C. 133rd FLD. AMB.

A5834 Wt. W4973/M687 750,000 8/16 D. D. & L. Ltd. Forms/C.2118/13.

Original

Confidential

140/3200.

War Diary

of

133rd Field Ambulance

From:- 1st August 1918

To:- 31st August 1918

Volume 30

14

Aug/1918

Army Form C. 2118.

WAR DIARY
or
~~INTELLIGENCE SUMMARY~~.
(Erase heading not required.)

Instructions regarding War Diaries and Intelligence Summaries are contained in F. S. Regs., Part II. and the Staff Manual respectively. Title pages will be prepared in manuscript.

Vol. 30 Page 1.

Place	Date	Hour	Summary of Events and Information	Remarks and references to Appendices
BOLLEZEELE 27/A22d76	1/8/18		Weather conditions good. Band of East SURREY Regt present during the evening	
	2/8/18 – 5/8/18		Weather Showery.	
	6/8/18		Weather continues showery. D.D.M.S. II Corps visited the Ambulance Site.	
	7/8/18 to 9/8/18		Weather conditions good.	
	10/8/18		Weather excellent. D.D.M.S II Corps visited the Corps Rest Station. Condition satisfactory. Cricket match in afternoon	
	11/8/18		Weather continues good. Church Service in the morning	
	12/8/18		Weather excellent. D.A.D.M.S. 39th Div. visited Amb. site.	
	13/8/18		Weather conditions good.	
	14/8/18 – 15/8/18		Weather good.	
	16/8/18		Weather good. Advanced party from 103 F.A. arrived to take over C.R.S. BOLLEZEELE	

A5834 Wt. W4973/M687 750,000 8/16 D. D. & L. Ltd. Forms/C.2118/13.

Army Form C. 2118.

Instructions regarding War Diaries and Intelligence Summaries are contained in F. S. Regs., Part II. and the Staff Manual respectively. Title pages will be prepared in manuscript.

WAR DIARY
or
~~INTELLIGENCE SUMMARY.~~
(Erase heading not required.)

Vol 30 Page 2

Place	Date	Hour	Summary of Events and Information	Remarks and references to Appendices
BOLLEZEELE 27/A22 d76	17/8/18		Weather excellent. Unit moved to BOWLBY Camp, PROVEN and took over Main Dressing Station there from 99th F.A.	
PROVEN. 27/E6.a42	18/8/18		Weather Showery. Instruction of American FIELD Ambce attached to Unit	
	19/8/18 } 20/8/18 }		Weather dull.	
	21/8/18		Weather fine. Unit moved to ZERMEZEELE Area 27/I.4.b.8.7.	
ZERMEZEELE Area 27/I.4.b.8.7	22/8/18		Weather good	
	23/8/18		Weather good. Unit moved to ARNEKE and took over XIX Corps Rest Station from 2/1st East Lanc. FIELD Ambce.	
ARNEKE. 27/H.24.a8.5	24/8/18		Weather good in the forenoon: rain in the evening.	
	25/8/18		Weather showery: D.D.M.S. XIX visited the C.R.S.: also the Divisional Surgeon 27th Div. Condition satisfactory	
	26/8/18 } 27/8/18 } 28/8/18 }		Weather showery.	

A5834 Wt. W4973/M687 750,000 8/16 D. D. & L. Ltd. Forms/C.2118/13.

Army Form C. 2118.

Instructions regarding War Diaries and Intelligence Summaries are contained in F. S. Regs., Part II. and the Staff Manual respectively. Title pages will be prepared in manuscript.

Vol. 30.

WAR DIARY
or
INTELLIGENCE SUMMARY.
(Erase heading not required.)

Page 3

Place	Date	Hour	Summary of Events and Information	Remarks and references to Appendices
ARNEKE 27/H.24.a.95	29/8/18		Weather Showery	
	30/8/18		Weather conditions poor. Advanced party under charge of Capt. C. F. KNIGHT proceeded to II Army Advanced DYSENTERY Hillhoek to take over that site.	
	31/8/18		Weather conditions improved. Unit moved from XIX Corps Rest Station at ARNEKE to A. A. Dysentery Centre at HILLHOEK 27/L 20.p.8.8. Headquarters established at HILLHOEK at 12 O'c noon. D.D.M.S. XIX Corps visited the FIELD Amb^ce site in the afternoon.	

Sinclair Miller, Lt. Col.
O. C. 132nd Fld. Amb.

A5834 Wt. W4973/M687 750,000 8/16 D. D. & L. Ltd. Forms/C.2118/13.

Original

War Diary

of

133rd Field Ambulance

R.A.M.C.

From 1st Sept 1917

To 30th Sept 1917

Volume 31

Confidential

Vol 31

140/3259

7 Sept 1918

Army Form C. 2118.

Instructions regarding War Diaries and Intelligence Summaries are contained in F. S. Regs., Part II. and the Staff Manual respectively. Title pages will be prepared in manuscript.

WAR DIARY
or
INTELLIGENCE SUMMARY.
(Erase heading not required.)

Vol 31 Page I

Place	Date	Hour	Summary of Events and Information	Remarks and references to Appendices
HILLHOEK 27/L20 b58	1/9/18 – 2/9/18		Weather good.	
	3/9/18		Weather conditions good. D.D.M.S. XIX Corps visited Field Amb^ce site. An advance party from 138 F.A. reported to take over the Advanced Dressing Centre	
	4/9/18		Weather showery. Unit moved from HILLHOEK to entrain at HEIDBEKE Siding (PROVEN) for Third Army area	
	5/9/18		Unit on train.	
BEAUVAL	6/9/18		Weather conditions good. Unit detrained at CANDAS and marched to BEAUVAL (near DOULLENS). Headquarters established at BEAUVAL at 6 A.M.	
	7/9/18		Weather showery.	
ORVILLE	8/9/18		Weather showery. Unit moved to ORVILLE (DOULLENS)	
	9/9/18		Weather continues broken.	

A5834 Wt. W4973/M687 750,000 8/16 D. D. & L. Ltd. Forms/C.2118/13

Instructions regarding War Diaries and Intelligence Summaries are contained in F. S. Regs., Part II. and the Staff Manual respectively. Title pages will be prepared in manuscript.

WAR DIARY
or
~~INTELLIGENCE SUMMARY.~~
(Erase heading not required.)

Army Form C. 2118.

Page II

Place	Date	Hour	Summary of Events and Information	Remarks and references to Appendices
ORVILLE	10/9/18		Weather stormy. The Corps Surgeon II Am. Corps + Divisional Surgeon 27th Am. Division visited FIELD Amb^ce^ site.	
	11/9/18 to 15/9/18		Weather conditions fair. Unit employed in training and route marches. Nothing of importance to report.	
	16/9/18		Weather good. Unit bathed.	
	17/9/18		Weather showery. Route march	
	18/9/18		Weather good. A bearer party and all motor transport reported to O.C. Sanitary Train 27th Am Division to take part in manoeuvres.	
	19/9/18		Weather conditions fair	
	20/9/18		Weather showery.	

A5834 Wt. W4973/M687 750,000 8/16 D. D. & L. Ltd. Forms/C.2118/13.

Instructions regarding War Diaries and Intelligence Summaries are contained in F. S. Regs., Part II. and the Staff Manual respectively. Title pages will be prepared in manuscript.

WAR DIARY
or
INTELLIGENCE SUMMARY.
(*Erase heading not required.*)

Army Form C. 2118.

PAGE 3.

Place	Date	Hour	Summary of Events and Information	Remarks and references to Appendices
ORVILLE	21/9/18		LIEUT-COL MILLER proceeded to United Kingdom on 14 days leave. Weather wet	
	22/9/18		Weather stormy. Orders received from 27th Amer Divn for unit to be ready to move. Transport departed at 4 pm	
DRIENCOURT (62c/ J.3.d.9.1)	23/9/18		Unit moved from ORVILLE entraining 7.40 a.m at DOULLENS, detraining at TINCOURT. Unit marched to DRIENCOURT (Sheet 62C. J3d91). Headquarters established	
	24/9/18		Weather fine. One officer & 41 O.R's left at 2pm to report to MAJOR CRANSTON at LONGAVESNES	
	25/9/18		Weather stormy. Three ambulance cars proceeded for duty to A.D.S ST. EMILIE & later on two additional cars proceeded to the same place	
	26/9/18		Weather fine, cloudy later rain during the night. Hospital site taken over from 105 FIELD HOSPITAL & established as a Divisional Sick Collecting Station	
	27/9/18		Weather cloudy cooler. MAJOR KNIGHT & 71 OR's returned to H.Q's	
	28/9/18		Weather very cloudy dull cold. Hospital evacuated & transport loaded in readiness to move at short notice	
	29/9/18		Weather fine & clear. Heavy rain at night. MAJOR WARWICK & three other officers proceeded with 108 O.R's to RONSOY for purpose of evacuating line in view of imminent coming operations arriving at RONSOY at ZERO -1. Six nursing orderlies proceeded for duty to M.D.S. VILLERS FAUCON & six nursing orderlies to ~~C.C.S.~~ Sick Collecting Post	

A5834 Wt. W4973/M687 750,000 8/16 D. D. & L. Ltd. Forms/C.2118/13.

Instructions regarding War Diaries and Intelligence Summaries are contained in F. S. Regs., Part II. and the Staff Manual respectively. Title pages will be prepared in manuscript.

WAR DIARY
or
INTELLIGENCE SUMMARY.
(Erase heading not required.)

Army Form C. 2118.

Page 4.

Place	Date	Hour	Summary of Events and Information	Remarks and references to Appendices
			LONGAVESNES. Transport remained at DRIENCOURT awaiting further orders	
	30/9/18		Weather cold & stormy LIEUT. D. G. R. GARRETT RAMC killed in action.	
			H. F. Warwick Major RAMC O.C. 133 Field Ambulance	

A5834 Wt. W4973/M687 750,000 8/16 D. D. & L. Ltd. Forms/C.2118/13

Confidential

996/11

D.A.G., 3rd Echelon
B.E.F., France.

---

1. Forwarded.

C. C. Collins

C. C. Collins,
Colonel, Medical Corps, USA.

Office of Corps Surgeon,
Headquarters II Corps, Am.E.F.
7th November, 1918.

Original

Oct 1918

War Diary
for
October 1918

VOLUME 32.

133rd Fd Amb

Instructions regarding War Diaries and Intelligence Summaries are contained in F. S. Regs., Part II. and the Staff Manual respectively. Title pages will be prepared in manuscript.

WAR DIARY
or
INTELLIGENCE SUMMARY.
(Erase heading not required.)

Army Form C. 2118.

Volume 32. Page 1.

Place	Date	Hour	Summary of Events and Information	Remarks and references to Appendices
DRIENCOURT. 62c J.3.d.9.1.	1/10/18		Weather Clear. Cold. Personnel returned to DRIENCOURT as Division was brought out of the line	
"	2/10/18		Weather fine. Cold rain at night. Unit moved from DRIENCOURT to COURCELLES 62C J32.C.	
COURCELLES 62C J32.C	3/10/18		Billeting party 1 Officer 1 NCO & 2 OR's proceeded to SUZANNE.	
"	4/10/18		Weather fine, Cold. Billeting party recalled from SUZANNE.	
"	5/10/18		Weather Showery	
"	6/10/18		Weather fine	
"	7/10/18		Weather Showery	
TEMPLEUX-LE-GERARD	8/10/18		Under instructions from Division Surgeon unit moved to vicinity of TEMPLEUX-LE-GERARD & staged there for the night. Weather fine	
WIANCOURT	9/10/18		Unit moved to WIANCOURT & parked there for the night. Weather fine	
PREMONT	10/10/18		Weather fine. Unit moved to PREMONT & went under Canvas	

D. D. & L., London, E.C. (A8001) Wt. W1271/M2031 750,000 5/17 Sch. 52 Forms C2118/14

Instructions regarding War Diaries and Intelligence Summaries are contained in F. S. Regs., Part II. and the Staff Manual respectively. Title pages will be prepared in manuscript.

WAR DIARY
or
INTELLIGENCE SUMMARY.
(Erase heading not required.)

Army Form C. 2118.

Volume 32 Page 2.

Place	Date	Hour	Summary of Events and Information	Remarks and references to Appendices
PREMONT	11/10/18		Weather dull, misty, rain later. Village shelled intermittently.	
"	12/10/18		Weather showery. Motor Ambulances proceeded to A.D.S BUSIGNY for duty	
"	13/10/18		Misty, some rain. All bearers of B & C Sections under Major C.F. KNIGHT RAMC moved to vicinity of BUSIGNY & were held in reserve.	
"	14/10/18		Weather fine warm. Nothing of importance to relate	
"	15/10/18		Weather wet	
BUSIGNY	16/10/18		Weather wet. Unit (less transport) moved to BUSIGNY & remained in readiness to proceed & open A.D.S at a place to be selected later	
ESTCAUFORT Q31 c 9.5 Sheet 57B.	17/10/18		A.D.S opened at 8.a.m at ESTCAUFORT. Casualties began to arrive immediately. About 750 casualties dressed & sent to M.D.S BUSIGNY.	
"	18/10/18		Weather fine. Casualties still coming in in large numbers. Transport moved to BUSIGNY (V22. a1.5). On way up a bomb accidentally exploded wounding two men & three horses. One horse died & two were evacuated.	
"	19/10/18.		Transport moved to Chateau ESTCAUFORT. A.D.S closed at this place & Motor ambulances	

Instructions regarding War Diaries and Intelligence Summaries are contained in F. S. Regs., Part II. and the Staff Manual respectively. Title pages will be prepared in manuscript.

WAR DIARY
or
INTELLIGENCE SUMMARY.
(Erase heading not required.)

Army Form C. 2118.

Volume 32. Page 3.

Place	Date	Hour	Summary of Events and Information	Remarks and references to Appendices
ESTCAUFORT	19/10/18		proceeded on duty to new A.D.S ST. SOUPLET. Casualties sustained by unit during period of active operations, four O.R's wounded & sixteen O.R's gassed	
ESTCAUFORT	20/10/18		Weather wet. Nothing of importance to relate	
BRANCOURT	21/10/18		Weather wet & roads in a bad condition. Unit moved to BRANCOURT & remained parked for the night	
BELLICOURT	22/10/18		Weather wet. Unit moved to BELLICOURT & stayed there for the night	
MARQUAIX	23/10/18		Fine & Sunny. Unit moved to MARQUAIX & remained there for the night prior to entraining at ROISEL. Cars moved to new destination at CORBIE.	
CORBIE	24/10/18		Unit proceeded to ROISEL station & entrained at 3 p.m. arriving CORBIE at midnight, where personnel were accomodated in billets. Weather cold & dry	
"	25/10/18		Transport having moved by road arrived at CORBIE. Weather dull & misty	
"	26/10/18		Weather showery. Lieut-Col. Sinclair Miller rejoined unit from leave to U.K. & took over command	

H F Warwick Major RAMC.

D. D. & L., London, E.C. (A7091) Wt. W1771/M2031 750,000 5/17 Sch. 52 Forms C2118/14

Instructions regarding War Diaries and Intelligence Summaries are contained in F. S. Regs., Part II. and the Staff Manual respectively. Title pages will be prepared in manuscript.

WAR DIARY
or
INTELLIGENCE SUMMARY.
(Erase heading not required.)

Army Form C. 2118.

Volume 32 Page 4.

Place	Date	Hour	Summary of Events and Information	Remarks and references to Appendices
CORBIE.	27/10/18		Weather showery. Sergt Major of the Unit – Sergt Major HERBERT – evacuated sick.	
–	28/10/18		Weather good. Route march for unit.	
–	29/10/18		Weather continues favourable.	
–	30/10/18		Weather showery. Unit bathed.	
–	31/10/18		Weather continues showery.	

Sinclair Miller LT COL R.A.M.C.
O.C. 133RD FLD. AMB.

T2134. Wt. W708–776. 500000. 4/15. Sir J. C. & S.

133rd Field Ambulance R.A.M.C.

Original.

WAR DIARY.

Nov 1918

5

VOLUME 33.

Month ending.

Nov. 30th 1918.

14/2/71

Vol. 33

30th
2/724

Instructions regarding War Diaries and Intelligence Summaries are contained in F. S. Regs., Part II. and the Staff Manual respectively. Title pages will be prepared in manuscript.

WAR DIARY
or
INTELLIGENCE SUMMARY.
(Erase heading not required.)

Army Form C. 2118.

Volume 33. Page 1.

Place	Date	Hour	Summary of Events and Information	Remarks and references to Appendices
Corbie	1/11/18 to 3/11/18		Weather conditions excellent. Drill for unit.	
	4/11/18		Weather continues good. One tent subdivision proceeded to 41 Stationary Hospital for temporary duty	
	5/11/18 6/11/18		Weather showery.	
	7/11/18		Weather conditions poor. Inspection of Horse TRANSPORT by O.C. of the 27th American ~~Divisional~~ Transport. Report good.	
	7/11/18 to 10/11/18		Weather good Route marches + drill.	
	11/11/18		Weather excellent News of the signing of the armistice received	
	12/11/18 to 15/11/18		Weather excellent. Games + Route marches.	

T2134. Wt. W708–776. 500000. 4/15. Sir J. C. & S.

Army Form C. 2118.

Instructions regarding War Diaries and Intelligence Summaries are contained in F. S. Regs., Part II. and the Staff Manual respectively. Title pages will be prepared in manuscript.

WAR DIARY
or
Vol. ~~Page~~ 33 INTELLIGENCE SUMMARY.

(Erase heading not required.)

Page 3

Place	Date	Hour	Summary of Events and Information	Remarks and references to Appendices
ABBEVILLE	29/11/18		Weather showery. Nothing of importance to note	
	30/11/18		Weather conditions improved Route march for Unit.	

Sinclair Miller.
O. C. 133rd FLD. AMB.

D. D. & L., London, E.C.
(A8001) Wt. W1771/M2031 750,000 5/17 Sch. 52 Forms C2118/14

133rd Field Ambulance R.A.M.C.

WAR DIARY

for

December

1st to 12th 1918.

Instructions regarding War Diaries and Intelligence Summaries are contained in F. S. Regs., Part II. and the Staff Manual respectively. Title pages will be prepared in manuscript.

WAR DIARY
or
INTELLIGENCE SUMMARY.
(Erase heading not required.)

Army Form C. 2118.

Volume 34

Place	Date	Hour	Summary of Events and Information	Remarks and references to Appendices
ABBEVILLE	1/12/18		Weather wet & Cold.	
"	2/12/18		Weather wet & cold. M.T. A.S.C. personnel proceeded together with cars to Reserve Vehicle Park WISSANT.	
"	3/12/18		Nothing of importance to Note	
"	4/12/18		Ditto	
"	5/12/18		Lieut-Col Sinclair Miller DSO. M.C. RAMC S.R. proceeded to England in order to report to the War Office & is struck off the strength of the unit from this date. Major H.F. WARWICK. M.C. RAMC T.C. took over command of the unit	
"	6/12/18		Nothing to report	
"	7/12/18		Ditto.	
"	8/12/18		Equipment of unit handed in to No 8 Ordnance Depot to-day	
"	9/12/18		Major KNIGHT. C.F. DSO. RAMC reported to War Office on termination of contract & is struck off the strength of the unit from this date. Unit moved to ETAPLES	
"	10/12/18		Unit was handed over to RAMC school of instruction BEF	
"	11/12/18		Imprest account closed & receipt forwarded to Command paymaster Base	
"	12/12/18		Receipts & remaining records sent to A.G. Base	

H.F. Warwick Major RAMC
O.C. [illegible] Field Ambulance

D. D. & L., London, E.C. (A7001) Wt. W1771/M2031 750,000 5/17 Sch. 52 Forms/C2118/14

www.ingramcontent.com/pod-product-compliance
Lightning Source LLC
Chambersburg PA
CBHW080841010526
44114CB00017B/2346

9781474519106